DUBAI, THE CITY AS CORPORATION

DUBAI
THE CITY AS CORPORATION

Ahmed Kanna

University of Minnesota Press
Minneapolis · London

A version of chapter 2 will appear as "Urbanist Ideology and the Production of Space in the UAE: An Anthropological Critique," in *Global Downtowns*, ed. Marina Peterson and Gary McDonogh (Philadelphia: University of Pennsylvania Press, forthcoming). A version of chapter 4 appeared previously as "Flexible Citizenship in Dubai: Neoliberal Subjectivity in the Emerging 'City-Corporation,'" *Cultural Anthropology* 25, no. 1 (February 2010).

All photographs are reproduced courtesy of the author unless otherwise credited.

Every effort was made to obtain permission to reproduce material in this book. If any proper acknowledgment has not been included here, we encourage copyright holders to notify the publisher.

Published by the University of Minnesota Press
111 Third Avenue South, Suite 290
Minneapolis, MN 55401-2520
http://www.upress.umn.edu

Library of Congress Cataloging-in-Publication Data
Kanna, Ahmed.
Dubai, the city as corporation / Ahmed Kanna.
p.   cm.
Includes bibliographical references and index.
ISBN 978-0-8166-5630-1 (hc : alk. paper)
ISBN 978-0-8166-5631-8 (pb : alk. paper)
1. Cities and towns—United Arab Emirates—Dubai. 2. Cities and towns—Growth. 3. Cities and towns—Social aspects—United Arab Emirates—Dubai. 4. Rural development—United Arab Emirates—Dubai.
I. Title.
HT147.5.K36 2011
307.76095357—dc22

2010032642

Printed in the United States of America on acid-free paper

The University of Minnesota is an equal-opportunity educator and employer.

18 17 16 15 14 13 12 11   10 9 8 7 6 5 4 3 2 1

For Ines

CONTENTS

PREFACE

With this book, I try to bring a perspective informed by recent developments in cultural anthropology, the field in which I was trained, and Middle East history, a field in which I was not, onto the analysis of the ways Dubai has urbanized over the past decade. Although history is a field I frequently draw on in my research and in which I have abiding intellectual and teaching interests, this book is not meant to be a serious contribution to the historical literature on Dubai, the United Arab Emirates (UAE), or the Arab Gulf. The book is meant to be a contribution to the analysis of cultural and urban processes and the political factors that set the conditions in which these processes can occur. Although I have been hesitant to do so, I have found it necessary to proffer claims, in a prefatory manner, based on the acquaintance I attempted to make with certain relevant, primary and secondary historical materials treating the history of Dubai, the UAE, and other Gulf states, along with that of the wider Indian Ocean and Middle Eastern arenas. The (somewhat) historical section of the book, primarily chapter 1, is meant to establish the context for the conditions of cultural and urban process analyzed in the subsequent chapters. It is meant to be neither a contribution to the historical scholarship on Dubai nor an exhaustive, detailed review of the historical literature on Dubai or the UAE.

What chapter 1, along with the rest of the book, does offer is a new interpretation of Dubai urbanism during the past decade. We are now familiar with stories and images of Dubai's emergence, and more recently of its hard times. Like much of the scholarship on the UAE, these stories tend to take the perspective of the so-called winners and prominent institutions—the ruling dynasty, Western expatriates, etc. Work of a more critical persuasion tends to be produced by activists, such as Human Rights Watch. As valuable as this activist work is, it is not analytical social science. Like Anh Nga Longva working on Kuwait and Robert Vitalis on Saudi Arabia, I have attempted to bring the insights of social science to the demystification of social and state power as well as to the clichéd images of the city and culture in a Gulf society. Also new, I believe, are the ways in which I interpret Dubai's urban spaces and built environment as connected to and mediating sociopolitical realities. In my usage, space is a polysemous term, referring to multiple phenomena, such as the representations of institutional actors (e.g., states and architectural and real estate firms); the spatial logics and territorializing discourses of the term "culture" in the usages of everyday Dubayyans; the types of governance enacted by powerful actors, such as, again, states along with parastatal corporations; and the appropriation and remaking of that governance by everyday actors. All of these connotations of space point in the direction of a kind of exercise of power that Michel Foucault has termed "disciplinary," internal and productive of subjectivity and individual identity rather than external and constraining of individuals (Mitchell 2006, 178). To my knowledge, no one has yet looked at a specific society of the Arab Gulf in this way.

Some of my interlocutors, to say nothing of Dubai officialdom, will perhaps take issue with a few of my claims, such as the existence and character of political contestation of definitions of modernity and urbanity in modern Dubai. In discussing a manuscript of one of the following chapters with me, a colleague based in the UAE made a comment that suggested that the book might cause misunderstandings. The colleague, an expatriate residing in Dubai, wondered why, if my critiques of the politics of the ruling Maktoum dynasty were true, did

> hundred[s of] thousands of people from across the globe—Arabs of all nationalities, Iranians, Indians, Pakistanis, and [Filipinos]; Americans; British; and scores of other European and Asian migrants labor so hard . . . to extend their stay and work in Dubai if the regime did not create relatively favorable living and work conditions particularly in reference to their own home conditions.

Of course, my colleague has a point. Conditions in Dubai, even in the aftermath of the 2008 financial crisis, are favorable relative to many other parts of the Middle East, South Asia, and even North America and the British Commonwealth. For many expatriates, Dubai is a refuge, a place to improve life circumstances or to further economic survival. Emiratis are justifiably proud of their society's openness (in a fashion) to some foreigners. More distressingly, my colleague may be implying (and some Emiratis might agree with him) that this text is merely a Western-produced litany of Emirati failings or sociopolitical "pathologies," as the eminent UAE scholar Christopher Davidson has recently put it (2005). I very much hope that my critique of politics and processes of cultural representation in Dubai is taken to be a social scientific, and not a polemical or normative, critique. The United States of the "Global War on Terror," Guantánamo, and Bagram, and the hegemony of imperial self-regard, militarized foreign policy, and know-nothing politicians hardly constitute a strong foundation from which to criticize other societies. None of the subsequent material is meant to imply that I, as a U.S. social scientist, possess some privileged access to the truth of Emirati society or that any of my inferences are more than provisional. But, in response to my colleague, as the aforementioned and ongoing financial crisis has so vividly demonstrated, not every foreigner benefits equally from migration to Dubai. Many, as I show in this book, don't seem to benefit at all, something connected to structural inequalities resulting from Dubai governance. In turn, the kind of city (spatially, culturally, nationally, architecturally) imagined by elites and other relatively well-situated actors is connected to the political economic system. Focusing only on the favorable aspects of the ruling dynasties or privileging the viewpoints of the already privileged would be intellectually irresponsible.

It is especially important for me to avoid the kind of misunderstanding my colleague seems to have, because I want to distance myself from Western biases, in particular U.S. policies vis à vis the Arab world. My colleague's point about the UAE's and Dubai's "achievements" (in quotation marks not to denigrate these achievements but to point to the ways in which societies are anthropomorphized by such terminology, an act of homogenization that I critique in this book) is easy to forget when we are so often bombarded with stereotypes about the lack of modernity and democracy in the Arab world. In writing this book, however, I attempted to take seriously one of Edward Said's lessons in *Orientalism* (1978) that a way to move beyond these stereotypes is not by simply trusting the official judgments made by Arab regimes about themselves but rather through a close attention to the historical processes and (in my case) social processes and diversity of particular Arab societies, as well as to their interconnections with other parts of the world (not least an imperial and hegemonic West led by the United States).

Thus, while possessing a kind of truth that it is important not to forget, such assertions about Dubai's "achievements" do not move the analysis of social and cultural process very far. We end up with stories about forward-looking big men and the societies to which they gave the gift of modernity. These are beautiful stories, but reality does not work this way. States do not simply turn up in history, like Athena from the head of Zeus, and they do not maintain their power simply because their legitimacy is transparent to their citizenry. They must defeat other positions, other voices, other interpretations of progress, and they must continue to remake their domination through (among other things) everyday processes of hegemony. To point this out in the context of Dubai is not to denigrate what the Maktoum dynasty has done or to foist Western stereotypes on it. It is to view Dubai, its state, and its ruling class as products of history and social contestation.

In this book I assume that processes of state domination, urban spatial conception and representation, and the cultural arena of discourse (claims about identity and attitudes of different communities both nationals and expatriates to one another), are interconnected. In this, an anthropological perspective is ideally situated to follow the workings of the hegemonic family-state project of presenting Dubai as a synthesis between reified cultural values and neoliberal discourses of consumerist individualism.

Somehow, and contrary to what might appear to be a monolithic orientalism in which the Arab world is homogeneously backward and anti-modern, in the early twenty-first century certain parts of the Arab Gulf have come to represent a kind of modernity that is palatable to many in the West. The most well known example of those who celebrate this kind of modernity is Thomas Friedman of the *New York Times,* for whom Dubai became a rhetorical weapon with which to attack that part of the Arab world not as sympathetic to Washington's policies during the "Global War on Terror." Dubai became, in Friedman's narrative, an enclave of Arab progress and dignity in a much larger benighted Arab neighborhood. Dubai was about the free market, efficiency, and, crucially, pro-Western values, while the larger part of the rest of the Arab region was a backwater of hulking socialist states, religious extremism, and on and on. How did the Gulf, in particular Dubai, where under British colonialism most of the people who were not colonial intermediaries were regarded with deep suspicion, become transformed into a symbol of pro- Western modernity? Cooperating with U.S. empire helps, whatever part of the world is being discussed. But there were also local factors. This is captured by the phrase "city-corporation" (*al-madīna al-sharika*), coined by the Dubai political scientist

Abdul Khaleq Abdulla (2006). One of the genuine talents of the Dubai rulers Rashid bin Said Al Maktoum and his son, the current ruler, Muhammad bin Rashid Al Maktoum, along with that of important merchants, such as Majid Al Futtaim, has been an adaptability to the economic and ideological currents of the global economy. At the same time that they were building increasingly larger holding corporations and expanding their portfolio with investments in new global markets, these urban leaders were fashioning a glittering, seductive image of their city as a consumer, resort utopia. How this took place was both a political and a cultural process. These processes, and how they shaped Emirati and South Asian identity in Dubai during the first decade of this century, a decade in which Dubai became Dubai, the fashionable global city, are the subjects of this book.

NOTE ON TRANSLITERATION

Transliterations of Modern Standard Arabic and Emirati dialect are based on the system employed by the International Journal of Middle East Studies. The symbols ʿ and ʾ represent, respectively, the glottals ʿayn and hamza. Proper nouns recognized in English, such as Beirut or Al Maktoum, remain in conventional English transliterations.

DUBAI CONTEXTS AND CONTESTATIONS

> We live in a wonderland. . . . I didn't come to Dubai for anything
> "real." . . . I've already lived in real places.
>
> —White-collar expatriate in Dubai

> You should tell your readers that we're not just Bedouins with more
> money than we know what to do with. We have social problems. We
> have poverty.
>
> —Raghad, management-level employee of Majid Al Futtaim
> Corporation

Today it still seems acceptable to represent the Arab Gulf, in ways no
longer so acceptable in the case of other postcolonies, ahistorically
and apolitically, as a region somehow exempt from the structural
constraints of empire and capital.[1] In spite of the efforts and successes
of postcolonial theory in connecting the practices of cultural representation, capitalism, and empire (Ahmad 1992; Ahmad 2006; Said 1978) and
the labors of some brilliant recent (and not so recent) scholars of the Gulf
(Abdulla 1984; Al Rasheed 2005; Fuccaro 2009; Halliday; Longva; Vitalis), it still seems natural and obvious to write about the region as *traditional,* a unique part of the Middle East, as supposedly governed by popular dynasties whose legitimacy rests on the pillars of cultural authenticity,
tribal or Arabian desert democracy, and a sophisticated if intuitive grasp
of modern capitalism. Like some caricature of the colonial gaze demolished by Edward Said, Western representations of the Gulf have tended to
excise history in any but a superficial, teleological, even hagiographical,
sense.[2] In turn, the object of this gaze becomes a monolith, impervious to

Figure 1. Return of the repressed: an ad for Jumeirah Hotels and Resorts that appeared in the New York Times in 2007 depicting Asians at the service of Europeans. Tacitly approved by the family-state and other corporate elites, this image of Dubai stands in opposition to enduring nationalist critiques of Western domination of the Gulf. Source: Jumeirah Hotels and Resorts.

the workings and dialectics of economic, social, and political process. Not coincidentally, perhaps, in a region governed by dynasties that have been generally hostile to anticolonial (or indeed most other kinds of) modernizing reforms, the Gulf becomes a repository of tradition, timeless if not mysterious. Thirty years after orientalism was demystified (Said 1978), the Gulf seems a recalcitrant holdout. It remains a throwback to an "Orient" that is no longer possible elsewhere.

British and, in the case of Saudi Arabia, American officials and oilmen often imposed not entirely ingenuous notions of tradition and modernity on their Gulf colonies and neocolonies. On the one side were visionary, modernizing, and moderate rulers, on the other tribal, primitive, and irrational populations. "Good Muslims" and "bad Muslims" is a dichotomy, according to Mahmood Mamdani, of great utility in the workings of empire. In a postcolonial and U.S.-dominated, post–cold war world where colonial nostalgia (Rosaldo) has become deeply problematic for the resistances and counterhegemonies arising out of the former colonies, the Gulf (in particular, certain of its privileged enclaves, such as Dubai and Qatar) seems to offer a guiltless counternarrative—the traditional societies whose visionary rulers, with the help of well-meaning Westerners, fashioned impressive modernization projects, developed the desert, and gave their peoples the gift of progress.[3]

Yet to the old story of an orientalist gaze and its culturalization of the histories and politics of empire, there is a new twist. In going to the Gulf (and especially to Dubai) in recent years, orientalism somehow seems to have gone through the looking glass. Instead of appearing as traditional societies suspended in time, in the early twenty first century certain parts of the Gulf became forward-looking, dynamic, and hypermodern, the very Arab states, Thomas Friedman of the *New York Times* wrote in 2006, that the United States should be supporting as a counterweight to the other Arab states: "Dubaians are building a future based on butter not guns, private property not caprice. . . . Dubai is about nurturing Arab dignity through success not suicide." The category of "good Muslims" now no longer referred just to the state or the ruling family (sometimes known, in Washington's idiom, as the "moderate Arab state") but had somehow expanded to include the entire society, in this case Dubai.[4] This shift is a main part of the background of this book, and analyzing how its local hegemonic articulations and effects have gone into the project of creating Dubai's sense of urban place in the first decade of this century is one of my main aims.

In the case of Dubai, this orientalism in reverse has had two striking features. First, its main exponents, along with the typical neoconservative and imperialist traditional intellectuals such as Friedman, were experts of a different kind. Writing about a different context (postwar France), Henri Lefebvre called these "urbanists" (2003)—architects, urban planners, and real estate developers, along with various kinds of intellectuals, from academics to journalists. Although many of these, such as the star architects or "starchitects" who began to descend on the United Arab Emirates in the middle part of the decade, were Western-based, many were locally based. The latter included managers of real estate development firms, locally-based architects, and perhaps most importantly, members of Dubai's effective state, the Executive Council, which controls much of the urban development in the city. During the period of my fieldwork, the most important members of the Council (a body not unlike the *Signoria* in renaissance Venice) were the ruler Muhammad Al Maktoum and his main confidantes, Muhammad Al Abbar, Ahmad bin Bayyat, Sultan Ahmad bin Sulaym, and Muhammad Al Gergawi. While Sheikh Muhammad reshuffled some of the important posts held by these men in 2009 (for example, demoting Al Gergawi as head of the Maktoum subsidiary Dubai Holding and replacing him with bin Bayyat and removing Al Abbar, Al Gergawi, and bin Sulaym from the board of the holding company Investment Corporation of Dubai), for almost the entire preceding decade they played a supreme role in Dubai urbanism, chairing the Maktoum parastatal firms EMAAR, The Media and Technology Free Zone (Tecom), Dubai Holding, and Dubai World, respectively.[5] These parastatals were founded in the late 1990s and early 2000s by Muhammad Al Maktoum as a sort of spearhead for the project of a socalled New Dubai, in which free zones, resorts, themed architecture, and massive enclaves—zones of "neoliberal exception," in Aihwa Ong's words (2000; 2007)—would carpet the city and, eventually, lead Dubai into a multinational, "flexible" (Ong 1999) global urban future.

A second feature of orientalism in reverse was how important this discourse became in the creation of the New Dubai of the 2000s, a city that was (and often continues to be) incessantly imaged and represented as new, futuristic, and a response to deep questions of human urbanity. The rise of the modern, postindependence city of Dubai, characterized by banking, ports, infrastructures, entrepôt trade, and platform utilities for Western (and, increasingly, Middle Eastern and South Asian) multinational corporate actors and institutions, coincided with the rule of Rashid bin Said Al Maktoum (1958–90), father of the current ruler, Muhammad. However, while Rashid initiated important, ambitious infrastructural projects, it was under Muhammad (who, although officially the ruler only since 2006, has been the effective ruler since his father's death) that the city became an eminence of global marketing. It is in this "Muhammedan era" (*al-ḥiqba al-Muḥammadiyya*), as the Emirati intellectual Abdul Khaleq Abdulla has put it, that Dubai became "Dubai," the fantastically photogenic city of skyscrapers, seven-star hotels, and city-sized special economic zones and residential–entertainment enclaves (Abdulla 2006). Until the 2008 world financial crisis sobered many erstwhile boosters, it was this "Muhammedan" city that cast a spell on most journalistic (and some scholarly) writers. The city, it was interminably asserted, was a radical break from "Arab traditions and pathologies" (pace Friedman), politics, and modernist and postmodernist urbanity.

These two features, reverse orientalism as an urbanist project (in the Lefebvrian sense) and as discourse of the New Dubai, coincided most strikingly in the middle of the first decade of this century, when Western architects and architectural theorists began taking Dubai seriously. The following are typical examples of the ways many of the metropolitan West's more sophisticated or creative classes were writing about Dubai as recently as 2007 and 2008. One writer, in the cultural magazine *Bidoun,* which in the first decade of this century became an influential venue for cultural and urban theory on Middle East cities, asserts the following:

> A major metropolis was and is being constructed by a nouveau riche tribal village whose goal is to make Dubai as a world-class city, . . . everything is new. . . . Dubai has passed into its latest phase of mega development; a phase that is difficult to pin down with one label but that might find its home with the notion of "supermodernism." . . . Much of the city's architecture seems to fall into the category of non-place [which has] established a new sort of authenticity; . . . it destabilizes our understanding of authenticity. [Ackley n.d.]

Another writer, a major architecture critic for the *New York Times,* wrote in connection to a Koolhaas–Nakheel project, the Dubai Waterfront City, that Dubai offered the star architect an unprecedented opportunity to create his own version of the famous Generic City theory (Ouroussof; see also Koolhaas 1978). Koolhaas himself has on various occasions, and with varying degrees of explicitness, discussed why Dubai and other non-Western cities have been attractive to him. Even after the disillusionment of the economic crisis, he argued at the 2009 meeting of the Sharjah, UAE Biennial, Dubai remained a city of experimentation and a "certain kind of beauty" connected to its accommodation of (urban and social) liminality or in-betweenness (Koolhaas 2009). Dubai is, in this reading, an example of the adventure and new possibilities offered by cities of the global south, an attraction felt by Koolhaas for a long time. Africa and Asia, he told an interviewer in 1996, felt much newer and more vigorous than the West; they are an antidote to the blasé sense that globalization makes everything homogeneous. African and Asian cities "are representative of the future"; building there is a "daily pleasure" (Heron).

Such enormous claims were all too common in the past decade. As elite local urbanists, the Maktoum state and parastatals along with other large firms, marched Dubai toward a modernity of a certain kind, there appeared no shortage of (increasingly more prominent) Western urbanists enraptured by this image of the city. The language used by urbanists is ostensibly different from older discourses about the traditional character of Gulf societies, the orientalism of the old school with its conflation of a kind of culture talk with politics and history. No longer is the non-Western other traditional, timeless, and mysterious. But culture talk still persists, if in a different form. The joint creativity of the ruler and the architects "made it possible for our small film team to get close to the characters throughout the year as we documented a process that reflects the entrepreneurship found in this Middle Eastern corner of the world," writes the director of an (admittedly excellent) PBS film on an architectural competition in Dubai's neighboring emirate, Ras Al Khaimah (Gjørv). The notion that the ruler is a creative genius has been asserted even more loudly by urbanists working with Maktoum and in Dubai. The political question, "what gets built and for whom" (Ghirardo), however, is not often asked in urbanist discourse. Like the orientalism of the old school, reverse orientalism excises history and politics from its representations. Now, not only the ruler but all of "Dubai" (or Abu Dhabi, Qatar, or Ras Al Khaimah, etc.) is modern, even supermodern (whatever that means). Only those characteristics of the ruler, state officials, and state institutions that these urbanists recognize as similar to their own—neoliberalism above all but also an assumption that they as actors are exempt from politics and history—are elevated to the level of cultural qualities evidencing the Gulf's modernity. As Gjørv suggests, it is a temperamental sympathy, rather than politically and economically conditioned contingency, that connects the local and foreign urbanist.

Urbanists think they are generating theory independently. As I show in this book, however, they are in practice, and perhaps unwittingly, aligning their theory with preexisting structures of political power and cultural representation in Dubai. In an excellent recent survey of urban theory, John Rennie Short has written that in the twenty-first century, "almost all city governments promote growth aggressively on a scope unimaginable just a decade ago. We live in an era characterized by . . . 'place wars'" (112). Short goes on to show how this period has witnessed the rise of increasing numbers of "wannabe cities," cities both in the developed and developing worlds that seek to achieve a world-city cachet and command function centrality. This they attempt to do through various strategies, such as dispersal of industrial infrastructures from urban centers, organizational streamlining of urban management, and cultural boosterism (113–15). The latter two are particularly relevant to Dubai. "Wannabe cities," writes Short, "are cities of spectacle, cities of intense urban redevelopment, and cities with powerful growth rhetoric" (115). They are cities with "an edgy insecurity about their roles and position in the world that gives tremendous urgency" to their "desperate scramble for big name architects, art galleries and cultural events" (115).

The main questions that I ask in this book are the following:

- What voices and social formations are both enabled and displaced when a city takes part in "place wars?"
- If "place wars" is a kind of globalization, and we no longer think of globalization as a top-down process of coordination of local worlds with the dictates of global capital, what are the local structures of power and meaning shaping Dubai's engagement in this transnational urban competition for real and symbolic capital?
- How do hegemonic representations of the urban ideal and the urban future draw upon local structures of meaning, and what are the slippages and tensions in such hegemonic projects?

In subsequent chapters, I will strive to provide concrete answers to these questions. But for the moment, it is important to dwell on the question of global cities. How might the study of Dubai reveal new insights that can inform global cities theory?

Much if not most of the work on so-called global cities has tended to apply a priori models of globalization to case studies with the aim of identifying which cities are really global and which are not. As Short points out, correctly in my opinion, this is misguided. Many if not all cities engage in globalization; global processes act in and through most cities. Any city "can act as a gateway for the transmission of economic, political, and cultural globalization" (74). In the United States, increasing integration of cities, particularly former smokestack or industrial cities, into the neoliberal era of globalization has been associated with the aforementioned strategies of city marketing and governance, as well as with rewriting the city as "green" (rather than "rusty") and as a good place to live. This process of rewriting, so to say, constitutes the point at which the economics, politics, and symbolism of urban globalization meet. In the North American case, the redefinition of the good life in this urbanist project has entailed foregrounding the possibilities for "individual consumption rather than collective welfare, private attainment rather than social justice, and the city as private pleasure rather than collective good" (124).

These are typical values of the post-Reaganite moment among the U.S.-American classes who most benefited from neoliberalism and who have largely been in charge of rewriting the narrative of the U.S. city. Although this emphasis on privatization over publicness, capital over collective life, can also be seen (with some variation) in Europe and in many parts of the global south, not least in Dubai, the variation can be significant. To understand how cities engage in projects of, as it were, topographical warfare, we must look at cities in their particularity rather than just comparatively (as global city studies tend to do). We must, moreover, balance an ethnographic sensitivity to symbolic processes and to everyday negotiations of larger political and economic realities with a feeling for the historical development of globalizing cities. This balance I try to achieve with this book.

Success in transnational place wars is not the only objective in the rewriting of the city (123–24). The process of rewriting, of constructing narratives about a city's identity, is also more localized in its objectives. Cities can often play a central role in national or class agendas, as was perhaps most clear in the case of Brasilia, a new city in the 1950s envisioned by the state to be both an emblem and crucible of Brazilian modernity (Holston 1989). Dubai, in particular the New Dubai, is a quite interesting case because since its establishment in the 1830s, it has been ruled by the Al Maktoum family. In the official view, the town's identification with the royal family is unchallengeable and absolute. The Maktoum, moreover, claim rights to what the political scientist Waleed Hazbun has called "total territorial control," a system established in 1960. The Maktoum considered land settled before this time as belonging to its inhabitants, "while all remaining territory, the vast majority of the emirate, was claimed by the ruling family, giving the al-Maktoums and the state complete control over urban planning" (Hazbun, 217). As Abdul Khaleq Abdulla has argued, the Emirati royals have attempted to monopolize definitions of modernity and sovereignty ever since the British recruited them to be imperial protégés in the nineteenth century (1984). Not surprisingly, this has not gone unchallenged, especially during the period of the Dubai reform movements between the 1930s and the 1950s. There is, therefore, and contrary to recent assertions about Dubai's novelty and radical break with the past, continuity between the New Dubai and the project of the state (or, as I shall be calling it in this book, the Maktoum "family-state"). This continuity is shaped by the local struggle over ideals of modernity and independence, fought over more visibly in the reform period than today, but which continue as the family-state attempts to consolidate its version of New Dubai. By extolling the supposed vision and generosity of the royals, and by foisting a very Westernized, neoliberal notion of modernity onto local society, urban ists such as starchitects perhaps unwittingly legitimize royal ideologies and claims to local historical memory.

Background of the Study and Research Methods

Toward an Urban Anthropology of the Arab World

I conducted the main research for this book between the summer of 2002 and early 2007, during which I spent in total nearly a year and a half in Dubai. My initial research question related to how representations of "the city," particularly those produced by institutional settings such as architectural and real estate firms, related to everyday Dubayyans' understandings of identity. My preliminary research on the social and political contexts of the built environment and urban space in Dubai and other Gulf countries mostly turned up work that tended to conflate notions of architectural iconicity, political and national identity, and the ideology of the ruling family-state. These were pieces of scholarship characterized both by an empirical rigor (of a sort) and by a lack of interest in the ideological and political contexts that made possible, in the first place, specific assertions about identity and the association between, for example, architectural façade and culture. This work left me dissatisfied, especially since I was simultaneously grappling with writers, on Middle Eastern and non–Middle Eastern urbanism, who were both critical of the investment into architectural façade of too much (or the wrong kind of) social meaning and sensitive to the social–processual, ideological, and political contexts of urbanism and the built environment (Abu-Lughod; Benjamin 2002; Eickelman; Harvey 2001; Lefebvre 2003). Another tendency of the Gulf literature of which I was skeptical was the marginalization of noncitizen perspectives. Only recently have scholars begun devoting serious attention to these perspectives; at the time I began my research, the literature was considerably smaller.

What struck me in my subsequent field research was the diversity, in terms of both perspective and ideology, of everyday engagements with the city and the related issue of identity. Both citizens and noncitizens constituted diverse groups whose perspectives often aligned with, but also often diverged from, the official and institutional representations of the urban that have taken the lion's share of scholarly attention in the literature. One of the contributions I therefore hope to make with this book is to the recent scholarship attempting to grapple with this diversity.[6]

A related contribution I aim to make is to the ethnography of the city in the Arab region. Although larger than the contributions to the cultural anthropology of the Arab Gulf, anthropological scholarship that takes the Arab city as a central theme of research, as opposed to its mere setting, is far from vast. Moreover, since Barth's path-breaking study of an Omani coastal town, ethnographic work on Arab urbanism has tended to focus on Cairo (Elyachar; Ghannam; Ismail; Kuppinger; Singerman; Singerman and Amar). Other Arab cities, such as Amman, Beirut, Damascus, and Tunis have received limited attention, albeit by very strong contributions (Collins; Monroe; Salamandra; Sawalha; Totah). Two other studies, while not focused on the city, nevertheless provide brilliant analyses of the embodied, temporal, and memorial experiences of Beirut and Baghdad, respectively (Al-Ali; Deeb). In spite of the strength of this work, in comparison to other global regions such as Latin America, East and Southeast Asia, and North America, Arab world urban anthropology is an embryonic field.[7]

But aside from simply adding another case study to the literature, what conceptual contribution can a study of Dubai make? One is an expansion of our concept of what an Arab city and Arab identity are. Even more than other cities of the region, Dubai is multiethnic and multinational. Along with being outnumbered by foreigners, the designation of "local Arab" Dubayyan is itself (as I show in subsequent chapters) a multiethnic, fluid category. Moreover, as others have shown, Dubai, like other port cities of the Gulf, has been characterized by a mixing of African, Arab, Persian, and South Asian cultures since the region came under British control in the early nineteenth century (Fuccaro 2009; Khalifa; Onley 2005).

Older Dubayyans often speak Arabic, Persian, and South Asian languages; local cuisine is largely Indian-derived; and local dress, at least in the pre-oil era, was a mix of Indian Ocean and Persian influences rather than Arabian, as it is today (Onley 2005). Arab identity in the post-oil period has been constructed largely in opposition to other identities increasingly categorized, officially, as non-Arab, a shift from the pre-oil period.

Second, over the last decade, Dubai has been central in the shifting of regional influence in matters related to urban-design and architecture (Elsheshtawy 2009; Forthcoming). Arab globalizing cities like many others have been engaged in the aforementioned place wars, undertaking redevelopment projects that emphasize tourism, consumption, and the construction of distinctive signature buildings. Although it would be an exaggeration to say that Dubai has been responsible for this, there is an undeniable "Dubai effect," as architecture scholar Neyran Turan puts it, being felt across the region. While Kuwait and Saudi Arabia in the 1970s, and even Abu Dhabi more recently, have been more aggressive in recruiting star architects for signature projects, no city in the region has been as comprehensive in its architecturally driven redevelopment as Dubai during the decade between the late 1990s and the financial collapse of 2008. During this period, when skyscrapers turned up in Amman, shopping malls in Cairo, or tourist enclaves in the Maghreb, the success of Dubai was often invoked (Elsheshtawy Forthcoming).[8] The study of Dubai's architectural development and redevelopment, and local engagements with these, therefore speaks to work on similar issues, for example, in Cairo (Ghannam; Ismail; Kuppinger) as well as to the analysis of the intersection between expertise, development, and cultural representation in the Arab world (Elyachar; Nagy).

Data

Much of my data I gathered from conversations, interviews, and daily interactions with Dubayyans of various nationalities and classes, from multinational corporate managers to government officials to everyday citizens and noncitizens from different classes and occupations. Although I conducted between forty and fifty interviews, primarily with Emiratis and South Asians (the groups on which I focus in this book), this number does not accurately capture the dozens of other more informal conversations over coffee, drinks, or meals, at *majālis* (formal receptions) and in offices, and in tours of New Dubai projects with real estate agents or architects, in which Emiratis, South Asians, non-Emirati Arabs and Iranians, and Westerners generously engaged me during my field research.

However, fieldwork in contemporary, supermodern, rapidly urbanizing Dubai quickly exposed the limitations of both verbal data and its complement in the toolkit of the anthropologist, participant observation. As traditionally conceived by Malinowski and other pioneers, anthropological participant observation was intended as a means for the researcher to better understand the practical contexts of what her interlocutors said and how they presented themselves in public, to place the said and the performed in its wider social setting. Regardless of how globalizing or modernizing Dubai is, most Emiratis are still reluctant to open up to outsiders. The sorts of relationships assumed by traditional participant observation, as I see it, I could not develop with most Emiratis. Non-Emiratis were quite different; South Asians and non–Emirati Arabs were much more comfortable inviting me out and conversing in a relaxed, informal way. Also, interestingly, I found naturalized Emiratis who were, for example, of Egyptian, Levantine, or other non–Gulf Arab extractions to be much more casual and relaxed than their Bedouin or Persian compatriots. I discuss intra-Emirati ethnic differences and the ways they shape subjectivity and identity in chapter 4.

In general, I met Emiratis at their offices or over coffee or lunch at a local shopping mall, meetings that had the feel more of business than social interactions. This is in no way to suggest that I resented the ways in which Emiratis managed my presence as an outsider. Often with good reason, many Emiratis feel that outsiders, especially Westerners, tend to misunderstand their society.[9] Moreover, although I am of Iraqi background, my U.S. citizenship and affiliation with U.S. research universities during my fieldwork no doubt positioned me both as an expert and as a representative of the United States, far from an uncomplicated or desirable situation in the age of George W. Bush, the Iraq invasion, Abu Ghraib, etc. Along with this, most Emiratis whom I met were fairly busy people, and it was not uncommon for phone calls or e-mails to be responded to months after the initial contact, if they were responded to at all. This was very frustrating for me but wholly understandable in its social context: Emirati society is richly and elaborately kinship based. Local people's social networks are, in this sense, closed to outsiders, who are functionally unnecessary for social interaction. As with most foreigners in Gulf societies, the anthropological researcher is, from the perspective of many locals, morally nonexistent. This is exacerbated by local concerns over *sum'a,* or reputation, which make it dangerous to openly discuss any remotely or possibly controversial issue with an outsider.

This should not be understood as a complaint, just a description of an important part of Emirati reality. In fact, contrary to outside perceptions of an exclusive and closed society, many of the Emiratis whom I met were generally open and generous with their time as they patiently sat through interviews and explained to me aspects of their experiences and histories which helped me immensely in the project of contextualizing how Dubai has urbanized over the past decade. But ultimately, Dubai was not an ideal place in which to form long-term relationships with interlocutors, build a deep intimacy, and gather data from an insider's voice or emic perspective (in this it is probably not very different from other parts of the UAE and the wider Gulf). It was not an ideal place, for example, to collect good data on Emirati family life, the Emirati home, and other such classic areas of ethnography. Moreover, in relation to the areas that most interested me—the intersection between the urban, the political, and representations of culture—much of the data I collected could only suggest interesting implications about Emirati daily life and attitudes. Much of the work of analysis in this book is not so much participant observation as inference and hermeneutics.

The great German culture critic Siegfried Kracauer is a helpful guide here. Although the context of much of his important writing, Weimar Germany, is obviously very different from that of contemporary Dubai, there is (as I discuss in more detail in chapter 3) one insight I think relevant to my case study. Kracauer, like Walter Benjamin, was suspicious of the truth-value and reliability of a society's "judgments about itself," the elements in a society which are generally deemed by its members to be important (75). This resonates with anthropological notions of participant observation. Participant observation, after all, was formulated because anthropologists started becoming aware that interlocutors tended to publicize aspects of their cultures that set those cultures in a positive light (not, in itself, something objectionable, and a practice that must be accorded a reasonable amount of respect). This tendency to positively frame culture for the researcher, of course, means that representations of culture become highly mediated and may develop into a way of diverting the researcher from the richness and complexity of the social process she is attempting to comprehend. Rather than investing such judgments with too much significance, Kracauer suggests that we focus on "the surface-level expressions" of cultural process, the "inconspicuous," even what the society deems to be trivial (75).

Because of the reticence of my Emirati interlocutors, I have tried to draw upon nonverbal and what Emiratis often considered trivial sources of data, such as images from architectural renderings of the ideal city of the future, newspaper reviews of future projects, op-ed pieces and comics from magazines and dailies, and insignificant elements of discourse, such as jokes or throwaway lines. Newspapers are an especially rich, and generally ignored (at least by anthropologists), source of data on the ways everyday people concretely engage and imagine more abstract, diffuse realities, such as the state and the community (Anderson 1991; Gupta 2006).[10] In attempting to grapple with the everyday processes of how a large, (in Gupta's words) "translocal," and abstract phenomenon such as the state is imagined, newspapers are an excellent source of "the raw material necessary of 'thick' description" (Gupta 2006, 222). I have drawn upon both Arabic and English-language Dubai and UAE newspapers, which address the different communities about whom I write in this book: Arabophone Emiratis, multilingual Emiratis, and South Asians. While certainly not ignoring Dubai's judgments about itself, the things it says and thinks about itself (often a useful source on ideology and performative identity), I have tried to complement these with the supposedly trivial.[11] For, as Kracauer says, by virtue of their unconscious nature, these surface-level expressions provide a more direct route to "the fundamental substance of the state of things" (75).

On Nomenclature

With this book my intention, as David Harvey has put it in Social Justice and the City, is to "relate the social processes in the city to the spatial form which the city assumes" (23). It is a case study in the tradition of what Harvey has called the "geographical imagination" or the "spatial consciousness" (23–24). This book is not an enthnography of the state. Nevertheless, it has proven necessary for me to make some perhaps simplistic claims about the state in Dubai. Throughout this book, I will be using the interchangeable terms "the family-state" and variants of "the Maktoum" or "Maktoum parastatals." I do not want to be misunderstood here. When I deploy the term "family-state," I am trying to point both to the hybrid character of the state in Dubai (simultaneously a family business, Dubai's largest, and something with an appearance and the functions of a state) and to the ways that its power insinuates itself into everyday, mundane cultural processes, such as narrative, imagination, and spatialization (a term discussed below). Family-state power is simultaneously formidable and contested (if almost always indirectly and euphemistically). Because contested, this power must both draw upon locally potent and persuasive symbols and narratives and constantly put a proregime construction on these symbols and narratives. This process of persuasion and contestation I try to highlight throughout the book. I am not suggesting that the state is unitary, coherent, or, as Michel Foucault might put it, "subjective." With recent critiques of the unitary state by anthropologists and political scientists (Brown 2006; Ferguson, Gupta; Herzfeld 1993; Herzfeld 2005; Li; Mitchell 2006), I am generally in agreement.

Timothy Mitchell has made the well-known argument that the appearance of a coherent, unitary, intentional state—the state as "subject" or "actor"—should not be taken literally but rather seen as an effect of modern practices of governance. This intentional-actor state is an appearance emerging from various practices—military drills, kinds of architecture, conceptualizations of space and spatial practices, etc.—that pattern a distinction between "the ideological and the material, . . . between meaning and reality. The state appears to stand apart from society in the unproblematic way in which intentions or ideas are thought to stand apart from the external world to which they refer" (174). For Wendy Brown, similarly, the state is not an "it," it is "a significantly unbounded terrain of powers and techniques, an ensemble of discourses, rules, and practices, cohabiting in limited, tension-ridden, often contradictory relation with one another" (191). Thus, the "state," the "it" that is the subject of common sense discourses about and of states, is an effect of practices, broadly conceived to include language and modes of visual representation.

A related theme is that of the social. Both Mitchell (2006, 176–77) and Brown (191) point to the social contexts that make it possible, in the first place, to imagine and represent the state.[12] Rather than viewing the state as the agentive headquarters of society, state and society stand in fluid, dialectical relation to one another. Brown, for example, argues that it is impossible to grasp the character of state power in the United States without taking serious account of the patterns of gender hierarchy in U.S. society. In the United Arab Emirates, the most important social reality is that of ethnocracy, a type of political power based on a logic of a ruling ethnie. The various family-states derive their legitimacy and impose their hegemony on historical and national-identity narratives because they (largely successfully) present themselves as responsible stewards of ethnic domination. How this system of ethnocracy came about, and its relation to the present spatial regime of Dubai, I attempt to explain in chapters 1 and 2.

Drawing on Michel Foucault, Mitchell proposes a notion of disciplinary power as a corrective of the unitary-state theory. Disciplinary power is not, as is assumed in much work on the state, external and constraining. Rather, it works from within, at the level of detail. It is "an internal productive power" (2006, 178). It produces rather than constrains individuals. One of the main assumptions about the relationship between state and society in the Gulf is that states, or more accurately rulers and other big men, are actors in history while citizens are passive objects of state paternalism. This assumption is reflected in, among other areas, the preponderance of scholarship on the region in which the only stories that seem to matter are the litanies of the acts of these important big men. Another assumption is that the relationship between citizens and foreigners only consists of victimization, oppression, and exploitation of the latter by the former. As I try to show in chapters 3, 4, and 5, citizens are not passive objects; foreigners are not just victims of ethnocratic hierarchy. Not only are they not passive in the more obvious sense, that of being at times critical of state ideologies and policies, they are not passive in the Foucauldian, disciplinary sense as well. They appropriate state-produced notions of space, territory, and identity and adapt them to socially relevant contexts. Citizens readapt ethnocratic mappings of space and identity to generate multiple outcomes, such as narratives of and identifications with a prelapsarian, ethnically homogeneous village of the past or a cosmopolitan, free-market city of the future. South Asian expatriates appropriate state-produced neoliberal constructions of Dubai and remake their place in the city as simultaneously agentive and systematically oppressed. In the process, both citizens and expatriates make their own identities and (re)construct the complex whole, territory-state-nation.

When discussing the state, whether in Dubai or elsewhere, I find it helpful to remember the following comment by Michel Foucault.

> *Power relations are both intentional and nonsubjective.* If in fact they are intelligible, this is not because they are the effect of another instance that "explains" them, but rather because they are imbued, through and through, with calculation: there is no power that is exercised without a series of aims and objectives. But this does not mean that it results from the choice or decision of an individual subject; let us not look for the headquarters that presides over its rationality. (Quoted in Brown 2006, 191–92, emphasis in the original)

The ambiguity that Foucault highlights between the fiction of the subjective agency supposedly residing in state power and the reality of this power's intelligibility is applicable to Dubai. Seeking the agency or coherence of the state is probably illusory, and my usage of the term "family-state" should not imply otherwise. But the intelligibility of state power can still be inferred from the daily cultural processes engaged in by everyday Dubayyans.[13]

Argument and Plan of the Book

The argument in this book consists of two main parts. In the first two chapters, "State, Citizen, and Foreigner in Dubai" and "'Going South' with the Starchitects: Urbanist Ideology in the Emirati City," I contextualize Dubai urbanism both in the city's local history and in the emergence of urban entrepreneurialism or place wars in the post-1980s period in global urbanism (Broudehoux; Short). In the three subsequent chapters—"The Vanished Village: Nostalgic and Nationalist Critiques of the New Dubai," "The City-Corporation: Young Professionals and the Limits of the Neoliberal Response," and "Indian Ocean Dubai: The Identity Politics of South Asian Immigrants"—I analyze the everyday appropriations, by both Emiratis and South Asian expatriates, of the institutional constructions of Dubai urban space discussed in the first two chapters. In making my argument, I have deployed two concepts adapted from the work of other writers, such as Henri Lefebvre, Akhil Gupta, and James Ferguson. These are, respectively, "spatial representations" and "spatialization." The concept of spatial representations underpins the discussion in the first two chapters while that of spatialization frames and organizes the subsequent three. Below, I elaborate on how I am applying these concepts to the case of Dubai.

Spatial Representations

Late or postindustrial capitalism is characterized by numerous interconnected features—labor flexibility, capital mobility, a crisis of profit accumulation and a consequent retrenchment of elite economic interests, and, more pertinent to my argument, the spatial representation and spatialization of symbolic processes of culture and political processes of hegemony (Harvey 2005; Jameson 1991; Lefebvre 1974/1991; Lefebvre 2003; Short). To introduce what I mean by the assertion that late capitalism is not just an economic, ideological, and cultural project but also a spatial one, let me take Fredric Jameson's celebrated example of the Westin Bonaventure Hotel in Los Angeles. Echoing Kracauer's interest in the trivial, Jameson takes this somewhat unprepossessing and architecturally undistinguished hotel (designed by John Portman in the late 1970s) as richly suggestive, in an oneiric way, of "postmodern hyperspace" (Jameson 1991, 44). Carefully noting his experience inhabiting and circulating through the hotel, Jameson argues that the space of the hotel is "both the symbol and analogon" of the individual subject's situation vis-à-vis an overwhelming, complex, and fluid late capitalist society (44). Disassociating itself by means of a scarcely perceptible glass skin from the rest of the city, immense in scale and comprehending (or, rather, allegorizing) multiple urban activities, such as crowding and the promenade, the hotel strives to be a total environment, a city within a city.

But it would be inaccurate to read this in a teleological fashion—the hotel does not literally replace the city. It suggests and allegorizes this replacement, and insofar as it does this, it is more organically connected to late capitalist society than is the prevailing cultural consciousness and perception, the society's conscious "judgments about itself," as Kracauer might put it.

> We do not yet possess the perceptual equipment to match this new hyperspace . . . in part because our perceptual habits were formed in that older kind of space I have called the space of high modernism. The newer architecture therefore . . . stands as something like an imperative to grow new organs, to expand our sensorium and our body to some new, yet unimaginable, perhaps ultimately impossible, dimensions. (38–39)

The allegorical and oneiric qualities of the space, Jameson continues, are a "dialectical intensification of the autoreferentiality of all modern culture" (42). The space of the hotel is therefore both a reflection and a naturalization of late capitalist society. Rather than subjectivating (to adapt a term from Judith Butler) only through ideology, hegemony, or coercion, late capitalist society subjectivates through space. The subject of late capitalist society—autonomous, compartmentalized in imagination and worldview, and, as Jameson might say, disoriented vis-à-vis an immense, manmade yet finally alien capitalist society—is a subject, ultimately, of the social space she inhabits.[14] What ideology only partially expresses about the normative relationship between the individual and capitalist society, is sensed as an imperative in spatial context.

This resonates with (and in some ways goes beyond) Henri Lefebvre, from whom I draw the concept of spatial representation. One of Lefebvre's great insights was to insist that the analysis of power in capitalist society must take account of space (Lefebvre 1974/1991; 2003). A main reason for this was that by the second half the twentieth century, urbanization had advanced to such a degree that it was erasing the old distinctions between the city and the countryside; the latter was increasingly becoming an appendage of the former. The coming revolution of late capitalist society, for Lefebvre, would be an urban revolution, shaped by the struggles of poor city dwellers. Taking control of urbanization would be the task of those who wanted to bring about a new kind of society (Lefebvre 2003; Harvey 2008; Holston 2009).

Elsewhere, Lefebvre makes a distinction between what he calls "representations of space" (or, as I have adapted the term, "spatial representations") and "representational spaces" (Lefebvre 1974/1991, 33–42). Representational spaces, argues Lefebvre, are complex, experiential, textural, and shot through with the oneiric and the bodily; they are "directly *lived*," "they speak" (39–42, emphasis in the original). Spatial representations, by contrast, are more conceptual. They are signified and, almost exclusively, the objects of instrumental rationality. They are the privileged domain of "scientists, planners, urbanists, technocratic subdividers and social engineers, . . . all of whom identify what is lived and what is perceived with

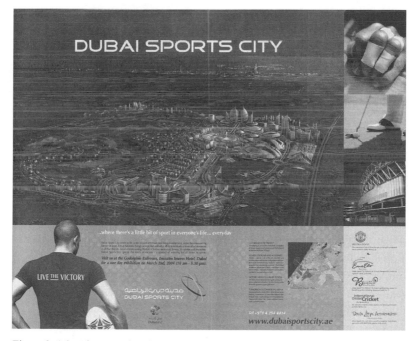

Figure 2. Advertisement showing an artist's projection of Dubai Sports City, a mixed-use project of a Maktoum parastatal, 2004.Jumeirah Hotels and Resorts.

what is conceived" (38). "Today more than ever," Lefebvre presciently wrote in a period, the 1960s, still transitioning from industrial to neoliberal capitalism and from high modernism to postmodernism, "the class struggle is inscribed in space" (55). Anticipating Jameson, Lefebvre is here suggesting that the abstract spaces of planners and other urban experts are products of a latent historical process and political, class struggle. The dominance of capital in (post)modern society is, in short, coded in the spatial representations of states, experts, etc.

Jameson and Lefebvre are, among other things, reflecting on the connection between spatial form and the contours both of ideology and subjectivity in (Western) late capitalist society. The resonance between abstract space (Lefebvre) or postmodern hyperspace (Jameson) and the ideologies of this social order (abstraction, scientism, numeric fetishism, disorientation, individualism) goes deeper than mere correlation. Space subjectivates; it escapes the confines of ideology; it is a more immediate opening into the "fundamental substance" things (Kracauer), the real power relations in late capitalist society. In the case of Dubai, I find this work helpful insofar as it brings space back into the frame of power and redirects the analysis away from culturally reductive, exceptionalizing emphases on rulers, tribes, and architectural iconicism (i.e., "culture talk") towards the political. This is a shift to analyzing how cultural representation, notions of tradition and modernity, and urban form are situated in the struggles and competing claims of different social groups over the memories, identities, and landscapes of the city; to how the spaces and spatial representations of the ruling classes are situated in the context of their struggles with these competing claims; and to how these representations are appropriated in the symbolic engagements of everyday people. As Akhil Gupta and James Ferguson have put it, space constitutes the (often unacknowledged, untheorized) arena in which the interconnections between different groups occur, interconnections that tend to be marginalized or concealed by the logics of the nation-state and bounded notions of culture (1997a).

While these insights are powerful, they must be approached with care, because both Jameson and Lefebvre are writing about Western (post) modernity. Their arguments cannot be neatly applied to non-Western contexts. Both the power and the limitations of Lefebvre's project appear in the case of David Harvey, perhaps the leading exponent of Lefebvre in Anglophone social science (Harvey 2001; 2008). In a recent article, Harvey argues (as he has done for a generation) that urbanization is central to the development of capitalism because it both absorbs surplus production and labor and quells potential revolt through the opiate of consumerism. From Haussmann in Napoleon III's Paris to suburbanization in the postwar United States to the rise of China and the "astonishing if not criminally absurd mega-urbanization projects. . . in places such as Dubai and Abu Dhabi" today (2008, 30), Harvey sees a continuity—urbanization is one of the strategies through which capital stabilizes itself. In turn, urbanization brings with it new financial institutions and new ways of life, from the Credit Mobilier and Credit Immobilier to finance Haussmann's infrastructural projects to the debt-financing of urban development in the contemporary world; from Haussmann's "City of Lights" to neoliberal, spectacular urbanscapes in Shanghai, Dubai, and beyond (26 30).

More than any other writer, Harvey has shown how integral a grasp of urbanization is to a wider appreciation of the ways modernity works. He has made accessible the writings of a philosopher, Lefebvre, the power of whose insights is often in direct relation to the esoteric quality of his linguistic formulations.[15] Moreover, much of Harvey's view of urbanization (and, by extension, that of Lefebvre) is directly applicable to the case of Dubai (and not only the comment about the absurdity of its megaurbanization). For example, as discussed below and in the subsequent chapters, local voices have for a long time been critiquing Dubai's turn toward the Westernstyle free market. This book in fact bears the imprint of one of these voices, in particular, that of Abdul Khaleq Abdulla, who has argued that Dubai elites and their Emirati counterparts are a *peir-olsle* that equates a Western upper-class lifestyle with modernity (1984, 137, 175–76).

Nevertheless, Harvey's concept of urban culture is not wholly satisfactory. For example, he writes that a consequence of capital's enrollment of urbanization is the impoverished (not just literally) urban life in the cities of the capitalist world.

> Quality of urban life has become a commodity, as has the city itself, in a world where consumerism, tourism, cultural and knowledge-based industries have become major aspects of the urban political economy . . . Shopping malls, multiplexes, and box stores proliferate, as do fast-food and artisanal marketplaces. We now have . . . "pacification by cappuccino." (2008, 31)

There is perhaps an even stronger equation of contemporary culture with alienation in Lefebvre. As we have seen, for Lefebvre, representations of space are conceptual, disembodied, and abstract. Abstract space is the space of technocrats, the space of the state, which "expresse(s) itself through the void: empty space, broad avenues, plazas of gigantic proportions open to spectacular processions" (2003, 109). Abstract space is space subordinated to the sign, a term that, for Lefebvre, stands in both for the arbitrariness of language in modern, capitalist society and for instrumental reason, or, as he puts it, "knowledge." "The power of the sign is . . . extended both by the power of knowledge over nature and by the sign's own hegemony over human beings; this capacity of the sign for action embodies what Hegel called the 'terrible power of negativity'" (1974/1991, 134). "Signs have something lethal about them," he continues; they are violent, forcefully introducing abstraction into "nature," what Foucault might term "the irreducible" (Afary and Anderson, 15, 85). Signs "strike, slice, and cut" irreducible reality, "and keep doing so until the purpose of their aggression is achieved" (Lefebvre 1974/1991, 289).

Not many anthropologists have directly engaged with the work of Lefebvre.[16] Of those who do, Erdreich and Rapoport's critique is the most relevant to my argument. They contend that Lefebvre's "semiological" notion of space, by which I take them to mean his analogy between the sign and abstract space, is too monolithic. This implies that space "embodies a code of signification, which can be decoded by reading" (120). But space is not read; it is "perceived, lived, and produced by means of embodied experience"; thus space as code, or abstract space, is rejected by Lefebvre.

Erdreich and Rapoport argue that Lefebvre's analogy between space and text is undermined by his erroneous concept of the text. He sees the latter in too teleological a fashion, as a closed system that unilaterally generates meaning. Texts, they write (correctly, in my view) are open to the reader's experience; readers, as we now know well from literary critical scholarship, actively make meaning while engaged in reading. While Erdreich and Rapoport are engaged in a project that is different from my own—to salvage an open-ended notion of reading for use in spatial politics—their point about Lefebvre's semiological analogy is germane. It is underpinned by a Romantic Marxist alienation theory implying that spatial representations mask reality, nature, etc. The spaces of states and technocrats, this suggests, can only be repressive and are lacking in open-endedness. Throughout the book we will see various actors invest their experiences with meaning and otherwise appropriate spatial representations in ways that imply a far less clear demarcation between institutions of power and everyday actors. Spatial representations of capital and of ethnocracy (discussed below) are appropriated by differently situated actors and drawn into these actors' respective quests for meaning.

State, Citizen, and Foreigner in Dubai:
Spatial Representations of Power

Dubai is the largest city in the federation of seven principalities, or emirates (*imārāt*), called the United Arab Emirates (*al-Imārāt al-'Arabīyya al-Muttahida*).[17] Situated near the gate of the Persian or Arabian Gulf, along the southeastern stretches of the Arabian Peninsula, the city is the seat of the larger, eponymous emirate and is the financial center of the federation.[18] While one should not be reductive in reading Dubai's history, much about its trajectory can be grasped by looking at the history of empire in the Arab Gulf. In the late eighteenth century, the British started taking an interest in the Arab Gulf as a result of Napoleon's plans to attack India through the region (Halliday, 427). Then, as today, there were two major ruling tribes (*qabā'il,* sing. *qabīla*) in the area around what is today's UAE, the Qawasim and the Bani Yas. During the first decades of the nineteenth century the power of the Qawasim began increasing as Ottoman and Persian imperial power began to weaken. This tribe, whose seat was (and still remains) the emirates of Ras al-Khaimah and Sharjah, controlled "63 large vessels, 800 smaller boasts, and up to 19,000 men" in 1800, according to Fred Halliday (428). The British saw this emerging regional power as a threat to their designs on securing the approaches to India. To the British, the Qawasim therefore became pirates, a theme that would shape the entirety of the nineteenth century history of the Arab Gulf. "Piracy may have been an old profession, but it was now infused with a new meaning" (Bose, 25).

As nationalism would be in the mid-twentieth century, piracy was a British obsession in the nineteenth century (Al Qasimi 1986; Bose). For the British, the Qawasim, like the Sulu sultanate in Southeast Asia, represented "the quintessence of an Islamic world whose activities centered about piracy and slavery" (Bose, 45). Between the 1820s, when they first intervened in the Gulf, and the late nineteenth century, the British imposed on the region's sheikhdoms or emirates a draconian system of treaties. These treaties forbade foreign relations between the sheikhdoms and other states without prior British approval and created a network of rulers wholly dependent on the British for protection. Other scholars have written in great detail about the history of British imperial rule in the Gulf (Bose; Davidson 2008; Halliday; Onley 2007; Zahlan). For my purposes here, I shall only point to what Sugata Bose has called the unitary system of sovereignty entailed by British domination of the region. To pacify these ostensibly unruly territories and to ensure a continuous supply of reliable proxies, the British enlisted the collaboration of prominent tribal chiefs in the Gulf emirates and reinvented them as unitary, hereditary, and absolutist sovereigns. In turn, territories that had heretofore fluid boundaries, and over which were made competing and relatively equally legitimate claims, came under the control of unitary, hereditary ruling dynasties.

In Dubai's case, the new, invented dynasty, the Al Maktoum, both successfully ensured territorial pacification and supplied protection to the activities of merchants, primarily Persians and Indians. Important and relatively large numbers of Persians started immigrating to Dubai in the early twentieth century, and are generally regarded as having given a cosmopolitan merchant cast to the town (Al Sayegh; Heard-Bey). During the nineteenth century, the primary Gulf trading ports, such as Lingah, were on the Persian coast, and most trade occurred on this side of the Gulf. In the early twentieth century, however, the Persian king raised import and export duties, which ruined trade in Lingah and most other Iranian Gulf ports. The then ruler of Dubai, Maktoum bin Hashar (great-grandfather of the current ruler), seized the opportunity and enticed the merchants of Lingah to move their trade to Dubai with cheap land and a tax-free policy. These merchants were followed by craftsmen, traders, and pearl divers (Heard-Bey, 245).

Although Dubai at this time had become, in Heard-Bey's words, a home for exiles (244), Persian immigration was still small-scale, the primary merchants remaining Arab and Indian. By the 1920s, Maktoum bin Hashar's son, Said, offered Persian merchants a more permanent residence in Dubai. A large number of these merchants came from Bastak in the Iranian subprovince of Lar. The area of Dubai that they settled became known as the Bastakiyya, and this also became the town's port.

These Persians were Sunni and belonged to various ethnically Arab tribes based in Persian towns such as Lingah, Bandar Abbas, and Charak. They were therefore eventually integrated into the local population, which was also Sunni and ethnically Arab. According to James Onley, intermarriage between Arabs and Persians was not unusual in the pre-oil Gulf (2005), although concrete figures on Dubai itself are, to my knowledge, nonexistent.[19] Indeed, for writers such as Onley and Frederick Anscombe, the Gulf's Arab coast was, before the time of oil, characterized by "Arab–Persian hybridity" (Onley 2005, 65) and was even an "a-national society" (Anscombe).[20]

This Arab–Persian (and to some extent, pan-Indian Ocean) identity was probably always more characteristic of the elites—rulers and merchants—than it was of people in more modest positions. But by the second half of the twentieth century, one notices in the Gulf emirates a marked shift in state self-representations and discourses towards a more European-style, ethnic nationalism. In Dubai, the reasons for this were both interconnected and not without contradictory results. One of the factors was mobilization against the Maktoum dynasty. By the late 1920s, merchants began to question the ruler's monopoly of rents and state income. A major cause of merchant dissatisfaction was the ruler's dependence on the British, a critique that would again be leveled against the Maktoum in the 1950s by a more nationalist movement of reformers. While the reform movement of the 1920s–1930s did succeed in checking the power of the ruler, their ambitions were less far-reaching than those of the 1950s nationalists. Inspired by Nasserism and Third World independence discourses, the 1950s nationalists both advocated independence from the British and had an ambiguous relationship to ethno-nationalism, often culturalizing or ethnicizing the ruler's motivations as being unduly influenced by Persians and Indians.

The threat posed by the nationalists to the Maktoum should not be minimized, as tends to be the case in the most highly regarded literature (Davidson 2005; 2008). The ruler's fears of an imminent and radical change in the status quo can be gauged by the fact that when the British indicated in the late 1960s their intention to leave the Gulf, Dubai ruler Rashid Al Maktoum and his Abu Dhabi counterpart Zayed Al Nahyan were the "two [Emirati rulers who] most vehemently opposed British military withdrawal from the UAE" (Abdulla 1984, 95). "We have taught the rulers to rely on our support and protection," the Orientalist J. B. Kelly reflected. "And they have undoubtedly benefited from this relationship, but it would not be reasonable or just to blame them now for sheltering under our umbrella when for generations we have encouraged them to do so" (Abdulla 1984, 95).[21]

Oil changed the Maktoum's fortunes, as it did those of other Gulf dynasties. Whatever leverage merchants had against the dynasty disappeared. Coffers bursting with petrodollars, the ruler could co-opt citizens with welfare state benefits and opponents with exclusive rights to selected sectors of the economy. The dynasty fashioned a so-called ruling bargain in which valuables distributed by the state would be exchanged for political demobilization. Nationalism was no longer seen as necessary in the 1970s. Ideology (the conventional story goes) was replaced by a market-oriented and consumerist pragmatism. The usual argument about the ruling bargain is that it was a sensible response to dramatically shifting economic fortunes and that it was, in general, widely seen as a good thing by all the parties involved (state, merchants, citizens).

The ruling bargain's ideological character is, in short, ignored. Yet everyday Emiratis are, in fact, quite ambivalent. While Emiratis generally celebrate what they see as the progress and prosperity their society has achieved since independence, there always seemed a double-voicedness, an undercurrent of doubt, to such assertions. Along with the structural nostalgia common to all societies (Herzfeld 1991), in which older generations always seem to find fault with younger ones, many Emiratis besides the elderly and middle-aged suggested that much was lost in the post-oil period. This can be summarized as the ethic of the pre-oil period entrepreneur, a man (usually) with a nearly superhuman work ethic, a clear and simple moral code, and (to adapt a phrase from Max Weber) a worldly asceticism. This might seem like structural nostalgia and therefore unremarkable, but I suggest a different reading, one more situated in local history.

By the middle 1950s, the nationalists had enlarged their platform to a multiethnic, plural anticolonialism. Against the dynasty's ideology of dependency, protection, and co-optation they proposed a conception of national sovereignty resting more on a pillar of rights-based citizenship. This third world–influenced conception of sovereignty was perhaps the most significant casualty of oil and the ruling bargain. Instead of citizens, the oil-rich family-state called forth dependent subjects, who exchanged all political rights for extensive welfare state goods, "the ruling bargain" (Davidson 2008, 139–58). The ruling bargain was no bargain at all, however, but an ideological and political project of state building by the Maktoum dynasty. As I argue in the first chapter, the ruling bargain had an important consequence. It appears to have consolidated an ethno-national, not to say ethnically purist, sense of citizenship and claim to national territory, something new (although, in the example of the nationalists of the early 1950s, not unanticipated) in the history of an ethnically plural Indian Ocean city. In turn, critiques of this state-building trajectory came to be expressed in ethnicized terms, as complaints about threats to national identity, undue foreign influence on Emirati culture, and, significantly, as a dependence on foreigners and foreign capital. Thus, mid-twentieth-century nationalist discourses of self-determination became transformed into late twentieth and early twenty-first century discourses of economic autochthony and ethno-nationalism or "ethnocracy" (as Anh Nga Longva puts it). Oil and the ruling bargain certainly expanded the material welfare of Emiratis, but the discourses of many Emiratis suggested a constriction of political horizons.

To represent itself as the guardian of these ethno-nationally inflected values, the family-state among other practices increasingly began manipulating the imagery and ideology of ethno-nationalism, especially when intervening in the mobility and spaces of less privileged economic actors. In this way, the family-state could present itself as protecting the citizenry from the threats posed, for example, by South Asian working-class foreigners. The current political order and landscape of Dubai depends not only on the supposed ingenuity of the ruler and important merchants (much in question since the recent financial crisis) but also on this more rigid distinction between (a certain class of) foreigner, on one side, and both citizen and privileged foreigner, on the other. Cities do not "emerge from the sands overnight" without huge, expendable armies of workers lacking any claim to protection from the state. Citizens do not acquiesce in the "total territorial control" (Hazbun) over their polity without exclusive gifts from a paternalistic state and the successful hegemony of the political–cultural claims made by that state.

As I show in chapters 1 and 2, the ruling bargain should be read both as an ideology and as a central element of spatial representation, in the Lefebvrian sense. Like abstract space in many parts of the postindustrial West, spatial representations in post-oil Dubai imply a specific kind of spatial politics, in which Dubai generally and certain privileged spaces within the city specifically, become elaborations on the theme of the ruling bargain (and its entailments, the otherness of certain foreigners, paternalist state domination, etc.) Migrant worker spaces and mobility come to be identified with moral and aesthetic degradation and pathology, seeming in turn to invite state intervention. Neoliberal enclaves and zones of exception (Ong 2007) come to symbolize the supposed "openness" of the "New Dubai" to the movements and activities of privileged foreigners.

In turn, the conceptualization of the large gentrified enclaves in the 1990s and early 2000s, the typical spaces of New Dubai, has taken place by representing the territory of the polity as homogenous, its boundaries as lacking in porosity in certain respects (vis-à-vis working-class migrants) and porous in others (vis-à-vis Western and other "social instruments" of "capitalist dependency") (Abdulla 1984). In turn, what I call the "spaces of the ruling bargain," spatial representations that reaffirm the ideology of the ruling bargain, articulate with the visions of Dubai created by the urbanists and starchitects of the first decade of the twenty-first century.

The Intersection of Neoliberal Urban Politics, Cultural Representation, and Urbanism

One of Henri Lefebvre's insights into the processes of late capitalist urbanism lay in pointing out how urban experts, or "urbanists," (2003) such as architects and urban planners reflected the ideologies of capitalist modernity in their urban imaginations (1974/1991). They practiced a "politics of the eye," as Stefan Collini has written (referring to a different context)—disembodied, abstract, and numerically reductive (see also Holston 1989 and Scott 1998). Modern architecture has developed in a complex dialectic between an intra-disciplinary, immanent logic and historical contingency. As early as the fifteenth century, European architecture began emancipating itself from the related practices of crafts and "mere" building (Frampton 1991). Architecture increasingly began to see itself as exclusively concerned with aesthetic form, the architect as an artist rather than a builder. The figure of the architect as an autonomous genius, so central to the high modernist tradition, was immanent in the development of architecture as one of the central practices of Western modernity. By the late twentieth century, building technologies had advanced to a degree that obviated the need for architectural input on projects. Instead of signaling the demise of the autonomous architect, however, these advances exacerbated the notion of the autonomous genius. This process articulated with simultaneous shifts in global urban politics and culture (the aforementioned place wars of neoliberal postmodernity), a conjuncture that created a new space for a certain kind of architect, the so-called starchitect: the self-styled aesthetic and theoretical genius whose very name became a highly sought commodity in entrepreneurial urbanism (Frampton 1991; McNeill).

In the context of the Gulf, Dubai is a latecomer to the recruitment of starchitects.[22] Kuwait, Saudi Arabia, and even Emirati neighbor Abu Dhabi preceded Dubai in hiring major architects for their urban entrepreneurial projects. Moreover, because of the financial crisis of 2008–9, the projects of starchitects such as Zaha Hadid and Rem Koolhaas were short-lived, either suspended (at the time of this writing) or cancelled. Yet Dubai's experience (and that of other Emirati cities) with starchitects is instructive nonetheless. The discourse of big name architects and other professional agents of urban representation (whom I call, after Lefebvre, "urbanists") about Dubai, Abu Dhabi, and other Emirati cities during the past decade aligned in determinate ways with the politics of cultural and urban representation already discussed. Starchitects (whose case I take, in the second chapter, to be typical of urbanism in the early twenty-first century UAE) constantly spoke about rulers as visionaries, and emirates and Emirati cities as "blank slates" and "laboratories" in which architects had unprecedented opportunities to experiment with urban and architectural form. These urbanists often invoked local culture in ways that resonated with local elites' constructions of local culture. Contrary to the myth of the autonomous architect, starchitects seemed to be greatly and unwittingly influenced by local political and symbolic structures that had evolved to justify family-state political domination. As I show in chapter 2, starchitects and various other kinds of urban experts in effect practiced a representational politics that articulated all too well with the local politics of antireformism, authoritarianism, and ethnocracy. Architectural and spatial form came to echo the contours of local family-state hegemony and the ruling bargain ideology. Like the latter, the former assumed that the territory of the polity and society was a blank slate, uncritically suggested that the "exotic" or "quaint" local people could only be given voice by an "articulate" and "modernizing" family state, and implied that elite claims about "local culture" and ethno-nationalism were identical to local culture itself.

Spatialization: Anthropology and the Politicizing of Space

How do the politics of the family-state articulate with the everyday cultural milieu in Dubai? What is the role of the spatial regime of the "Muhammedan era" (Abdulla 2006)? What voices and perspectives are displaced by this regime, and how are contemporary Dubai identities and voices shaped by it? A key concept I deploy in the third, fourth, and fifth chapters is that of spatialization, by which I mean the ways in which people almost unconsciously assume that key aspects of their worldview are spatial and how these assumptions shape the metaphors and identities thereby entailed. Both space in the physical, urban sense and space as an imaginary, metaphorical, narrative, and bodily process is profoundly shaped by the political context of the society in question.

In a classic and highly suggestive essay, anthropologists Akhil Gupta and James Ferguson (1997a) make an argument that strongly resonates with and expands upon insistence of writers such as Lefebvre and Harvey on politicizing space in the social sciences. Gupta and Ferguson argue that writing on culture in the social sciences, not least in anthropology, is dependent on images of break or rupture. Anthropologists, for example, have traditionally represented themselves as traversing cultural worlds, making an arduous journey from their own culture to another culture. Moreover, anthropology has tended to uncritically territorialize and bound culture in ways similar to how post–Westphalian atlases have territorialized and bounded nation-states. Thus, while a certain kind of space (modernist, national, and culturally homogenizing) was always a central organizing assumption in anthropology, this spatialization remained largely untheorized. Such a spatialization has, in turn, concealed the ways in which societies and peoples were interconnected (33–36).

The territorialization of culture is disrupted by the various features of modernity. Neither the border crossings of migrants, nomads, professionals, refugees, etc., nor the cultural diversity within localities, nor the hybrid character of the postcolonial experience fits into this notion of distinct cultural worlds. Although it imposed notions of unitary sovereignty on the peoples it came to rule and helped to refashion cultural identities into ethno-national ones, colonialism too is an example of these processes, merely displacing one form of interconnection with another (35). Echoing Lefebvre, Gupta and Ferguson argue that rather than assuming these naturalized and territorialized representations of culture, anthropologists should investigate how difference is *produced* in shared spaces of interconnection. The seeming given-ness of a world "in the first place divided into 'ourselves' and 'others'" must be subjected to analysis and critique (45).

Family and Hierarchy in the Idealized Village: Constructing the Ethnically Homogeneous, Dynastic Polity

Like other Gulf states, Dubai is neither an autocracy nor a democracy but an ethnocracy, as Anh Nga Longva has argued in a seminal article about Kuwait. It is (or, as I suggest, has increasingly become) a polity in which the "defining feature is not race, language or religion but citizenship conceived in terms of shared descent," a society governed by an exclusive, ruling ethnie (119, 126). The demographic imbalance between citizens and foreigners is the primary reason why citizens worry about "cultural integrity" (122).

> Ethnocratic regimes draw their *raison d'etre* from a peculiar state of mind, widespread among the ruling ethnie, in which a vivid awareness of being under threat combines with an equally vivid experience of empowerment derived from control over subordinate groups. (126)

Demography, linked in turn to the global oil economy and the neoco-lonial relationship between the Gulf States and the capitalist West, consti-tutes the structural basis, so to say, for the politics of the ruling bargain. In the post-oil period, this conjuncture of global forces with the family-state agenda favored the emergence of a discursive field in which a certain kind of ethno-nationalism (ethnocracy, in Longva's word) and an Arabized neo-liberalism were flip sides of the same coin. In the third and fourth chapters, I analyze the narrative constructions and symbolic negotiations of identity by everyday Emiratis. This provides an aperture into the ways the family-state's construction of modernity is appropriated and reproduced by every-day Emiratis. If the politics of protection and the spatial representations of urbanists are the means by which the family-state maintains its hegemony, narrative and symbolism are a means by which everyday Emiratis invest the turbulent twenty-first century with meaning.

The demobilization of the populace was a main consequence of the politics of the ruling bargain. Along with this, and integral to the process of demobilization, went a depoliticization of contemporary Dubai time and space. In turn, practices such as a family-state governance of neoliberal exception (Ong 2007) and urbanism constructed an unproblematic identi-fication between the territory of the polity, culture in the reified, museum sense of the term, collective memory, and the ruling dynasty. This process operated by means of a family-state–centered (re)interpretation of potent local symbols, among others, the family, the village, and gender. The fam-ily, for example, constructed as hierarchical and gender-segregated, came to fill in for the political. I call discourses and spatializations that draw upon such images and symbolism of family, traditional village life, etc., neoorthodox both to differentiate these discourses from other tendencies in contemporary Dubai (chapter 4) and to point out that they are not tra-ditional at all, but very contemporary responses to problems of Dubayyan modernity. Above all, neoorthodoxy consists of a set of spatializations of Dubai that both resonate with the politics of the ruling bargain and have profound implications for identity politics in Dubai. Neoorthodoxy reaf-firms the spatialization of Dubai, implicit in the ruling bargain, as an ethni-cally Arab territory with borders lacking in porosity. Deviations from rei-fied models of family life and cultural expression tend to be seen, from this perspective, as threatening to the culture and values of the UAE. Critique of the status quo tends to be expressed in terms of cultural authenticity and bounded territory.

Since the reformist struggles of the early and middle twentieth century, the family-state has faced a political conundrum. It has attempted to consolidate two kinds of projects, each of which was in tension with the other. The first was to demobilize potential critiques and non-state–sanctioned popular movements. This was achieved through controlling and setting the limits to the discourse of identity. The second project consisted in adapting a free-market absolutism to local lived experiences. A different constituency needed to be cultivated for the success of the second project, a social formation more adaptable to global economic conditions and for which overt expressions of cultural authenticity and cultural threat would be anathema. This was a seemi n g l y progressive shift beyond the politics of the ruling bargain. But there were also limitations to this project.

Neoliberal (In)Flexibility: The Limitations of Dubai's Arabized Neoliberalism

Like the modernist Modigliani style of map critiqued by Gupta and Ferguson and others (e.g., Malkki), theories of neoliberalism have tended to spatialize culture by deploying the organizing metaphor of the rupture; like the modernist map, they have territorialized culture. Consequently, it is common to read ahistorical accounts of neoliberalism as a culturally neutral and global phenomenon that makes contact with local worlds. Presumably, these local worlds were not globalized or connected with other parts of the globe before this contact. After this encounter, the local worlds are assumed to adapt to the far more powerful attraction of the global/neoliberal. My argument in chapter 4 emerges from recent developments in the anthropological analysis of neoliberalism that take issue with this assumption.

The assumption that neoliberalism is simply a "package of policies, ideologies, and political interests" (Hoffman et al., 9) that are mechanically applied across the globe is too simple. It ignores two processes that are better captured by the metaphor of interconnection than by notions of cultural contact or encounter. These pertain to the role of local structures of meaning and symbolism in reshaping neoliberalism, and to how everyday people cultivate selves and subjectivities in contexts of neoliberal

Many of my insights in this argument I have drawn from anthropological critiques of package theories of neoliberalism (Ong 1999; 2007; Wilson). But the Arab Gulf is unlike the recent classical loci of these anthropological critiques of neoliberalism, East and Southeast Asia. Aihwa

Figure 3. New Dubai, late 2004. Near the Media and Technology Free Zone ("Tecom"), a Maktoum parastatal.

Figure 4. New Dubai luxury villa development by EMAAR, June 2004.

Ong has persuasively argued, for example, that the Southeast Asian neoliberal state tries to engineer economically valuable citizens by calling upon them to question traditional identities and values (Ong 2007, 4, 185, 189, 219–39). In Dubai, where citizens are vastly outnumbered by foreigners and are, relative to foreigners, economically unproductive, economic value is not the primary organizing metaphor guiding neoliberalization. Like neoorthodoxy, neoliberalism in Dubai emphasizes themes of cultural authenticity and virtuous citizenship, but gives these a new twist. Values of entrepreneurialism, individual creativity, and even scepticism of neoorthodox nostalgia are aligned with notions of calling and a national struggle for modernity. In the fourth chapter I focus on a group of young managers at leading Dubai firms, such as the Maktoum parastatals and Majid Al Futtaim. Following Ong (1999) and Wilson, I call these managers Dubai's "flexible citizens." Fluent in Arabic, English, and sometimes other languages, well-educated (in a Western-style business curriculum), and often well-travelled, flexible citizens reject the nostalgia that characterizes much neoorthodoxy. Flexible citizens do not, however, reject Emirati and Muslim identities. They appropriate and enact them in ways consciously different from what they see as those of their more conservative compatriots.

The ascendancy of Maktoum-led neoliberalism, in the style of what Abdulla has called the "city-corporation" (2006), succeeded in the early twenty-first century because the Maktoum and other city-leading corporations successfully aligned free-market values with local cultural attitudes and dispositions (see also Abdulla 1984, 191–92). Yet this was not a smooth or automatic process. Gender, especially, has been a focus of contention over what kind of neoliberal modernity should be pursued. While female flexible citizens were in general agreement with their male compatriots and coevals about the positive aspects of Dubai's modernity, they were also more likely to point to the importance of balancing the modern with local traditions (*taqālīd*). This highlights the extent to which the neoliberal project in Dubai has been a gendered project, and in turn, how it has been structured not only by the explicit cultural knowledge and desires of everyday Dubayyans, but also by tacit, perhaps unconscious structures of hierarchy.

Ironically, there is another, tacit cultural knowledge (for lack of a better term) that goes into the making of neoliberalism in Dubai—ethnocracy. Neoliberal discourses in Dubai are organized to a great extent by the notion of a cultural openness that envisions Dubai's future as moving beyond neoorthodox anxieties over cultural authenticity. Many flexible citizens emphasized that what they valued in Dubai was its openness to individuality and entrepreneurial creativity. For them, the future lay in a vision of a market-oriented meritocracy. This entailed a notion that Dubai was a consumer polity open to all regardless of their identity (a view shared, not coincidentally, by middle-class South Asians, on whom I focus in chapter 5). Yet the image of the city they so strongly identified with was just that, an image. The reality it attempted to transform was more complicated.

Indian Ocean Dubai

In chapter 5 I attempt to connect the experiences of South Asians with those of Emiratis. In this, I try to show how the identity of each group is shaped in the shared space of the city and in dialectical relation to the other group. The lives and experiences of South Asians in Gulf societies have tended to be minimized in the literature on the Gulf. As already discussed, recent scholarship has attempted to remedy the situation and with my fifth chapter I hope to contribute to this conversation.[23] In doing so, I am also implicitly responding to Gupta and Ferguson's call for an anthropology in which representations of cultural process move beyond territorializing assumptions and toward capturing cultural and social interconnections within shared spaces.

Dubai's South Asian population is one of the largest, in proportional (and perhaps absolute) terms, in the Middle East. Fully one in two Dubai residents is from South Asian countries. Regardless of class, South Asians generally come to Dubai for better economic opportunities than can be found in their native countries. This has tended to entail the assumption, in Gulf scholarship, that the category of expatriate encompasses the experiences of all South Asians.[24] Instead of bundling nationality with class, however, I separate them analytically. Here I take up a thread introduced in chapter 1, where I argue that the ways in which foreigners are subjected to the governance of the Gulf state are determined not only by one's foreignness but also by one's class. This is not to doubt the fact that being a middle-class South Asian in Dubai means one is subjected to systematic kinds of discrimination, based especially on ethnicity. But this discrimination differs significantly from the kinds of surveillance and governmentality to which working-class migrants are subjected. Working-class South Asians perhaps suffer the most extreme forms of Emirati governmentality—expropriation of passports, incarceration in worker camps, broken contracts, etc. (see chapter 1).

Although middle-class South Asians both protest against perceived racism by Emiratis and Westerners and voice solidarity with the plight of working-class South Asians, there are ironies and slippages conditioned by their structural position (see also Vora 2008). For example, middle-class South Asians' views of Dubai are often quite similar to those of Emiratis, especially the so-called Dubai flexible citizens. Both middle-class South Asians and Dubai flexible citizens tend to see the ideal Dubai as a neoliberal, market polity in which economic merit should go along with material rewards. Both are allergic, so to say, to the kinds of overt ethno-nationalism characterizing much of the neoorthodox tendency. South Asians certainly and justifiably chafe under perceived discrimination based upon nationality or ethnicity. As anthropologist Neha Vora has put it, middle-class Dubai South Asians enact two simultaneous and contrasting identities, as global neoliberal participants in a free-market economy and as a disenfranchised racial group (2008, 392). But, significantly, when discrimination is felt, middleclass South Asians tend to criticize this discrimination in economic, free-market terms, not political terms. Discrimination compromises Dubai's promise of economic, not social or political belonging, for them. Political and social belonging appear to be a matter of indifference to most middle-class South Asians.

Working-class South Asians tend to see things differently (Human Rights Watch 2006). According to Davidson, while such workers have indeed experienced poor working conditions, their employment in Dubai was "voluntary, was normally for a short term of two or three years, and was usually paying wages several times greater than could be expected in South Asia" (2008, 187). While I owe a debt to Davidson for his research, here I weigh this part of his argument against the ethnographic evidence. I believe that Davidson, like others, conflates the experiences of middleclass expatriates with those of working-class migrants. Middle-class expatriates may have the luxury to be opportunistically mobile, but for working-class migrants, the politics and ideology of the ruling bargain translate into serious, unnecessary, and systematic discrimination and diminished life chances. As I discuss in the book's conclusion, Dubai is a city in which worker demonstrations and work stoppages are common. It is far too facile to see this unrest as a result of worker irrationality (as I think Davidson and others tend to do). Only by looking at the structured hierarchies that are reproduced by prevailing ideologies, and how these in turn qualify and conflate nationality and class, can we begin to move beyond analytically unpersuasive stereotypes of worker unrest.

It might seem ironic that middle-class South Asians tended to share with their Emirati counterparts a neoliberal identification with Dubai. This

Figure 5. Near the Defense Roundabout, Sheikh Zayed Road, 2004. Sheikh Zayed Road is Dubai's main thoroughfare and passes through New Dubai into Abu Dhabi.

I contextualize both in middle-class South Asians' experiences with mobility and with the hegemonic Emirati notion of ethnocracy. Unlike working-class South Asians, middle class South Asians experience transnational mobility as an emancipation from relatively worse economic, social, and other kinds of circumstances. In turn, they often view and experience their stay in Dubai as temporary, their home in South Asia as secure, their mobility as conforming to the liberatory, pragmatic, and individualistic narratives of neoliberalism. Along with this, they must negotiate Emirati ethnocracy, which tends to bundle non-Western foreigners, especially South Asians, into broad categories such as cultural threat, unskilled labor, etc. Thus, as I show in the fifth chapter, middle-class South Asians usually emphasize their middle-class identity in situations where they feel they are prevented, by dint of their nationality, from participating in the supposedly egalitarian economic opportunities promised by neoliberal Dubai.

New Dubai

As it did for many Emiratis, especially flexible citizens, for middle-class South Asians the so-called New Dubai seemed to promise an opportunity to realize this consumer citizenship. New Dubai's landscape of shopping malls, gated communities, and other bourgeois consumer landscapes seemed to represent, in spatial form, an approximation of an egalitarian consumer citizenship (Vora 2008), an image of Dubai as an ideal free-market space of economic opportunity. New Dubai stretches from the wall of skyscrapers on Sheikh Zayed Road west into only recently developed desert with spectacular landscapes, giant shopping malls, luxury residential enclaves, and reclaimed land projects past the upscale neighborhoods of Jumeirah. This part of the city, which began taking shape in the mid-1990s, is probably what most outsiders think of when they think of Dubai; it is the part of Dubai that has been seemingly interminably photographed and propagandized during the past decade. Its immense enclaves and daring buildings seem to represent a progressive vision and futuristic orientation for the city, in apparent and explicit contrast to what I call the neoorthodox discourses of a prelapsarian village. But New Dubai is, I argue, a typical urbanist project, governed by an exclusionary, ethnocratic logic that in fact strongly resonates with conservative discourses. The irony is that urbanists such as starchitects see themselves as global actors, generally unencumbered by local baggage. In reality, however, New Dubai projects, for example the gated communities of EMAAR and Nakheel and the shopping malls of the giant holding corporations, but also, I suggest, the more recent examples of starchitectural whimsy, resonate with and reinforce local hegemonies and structures of ethnic and class exclusion. In short, local systems of hierarchy are a strong influence on starchitectural and other urbanist spaces, shaping both their conceptualization and social effects.[25]

New Dubai did not turn up out of the blue. The recent emphasis on large projects should be contextualized in the aforementioned global urban place wars but also in the local context, where the utility of large infrastructural projects has been a strong assumption of urban development for a long time. Soon after Rashid bin Said Al Maktoum became Dubai's ruler in the late 1950s, he began implementing a program of infrastructural modernization. This included dredging and expanding the creek, spanning the creek with a bridge, and building an airport in collaboration with the British engineering firm Halcrow. This was the beginning of what the historian of the UAE, Frauke Heard-Bey, sees as the vast modernization campaign that transformed the village into one of the major Middle Eastern entrepôts. Both the airport and the bridge, argues Heard-Bey, showed that Dubai infrastructure planning was not just a pragmatic response to contemporary needs, but rather anticipated future development (261).

Dubai went from a town of about 59,000 inhabitants in 1967 (263) to a city of about 1,250,000 people about four decades later. In the 1970s, newly prosperous Emiratis began moving out of the old population centers around the Creek (Khor Dubai) in the neighbourhoods of Deira, (Bur) Dubai, and Shindagha, and into compounds of modern villas further out from the village center. These compounds continued, like their village predecessors, to be organized on familial and tribal lines. The first shopping malls, the Al Mulla Center and the Al Ghurair City, appeared in the late 1970s, but, as several locals informed me, they were not seen as destinations to spend leisure time. Al Ghurair City, for example, was seen as a disreputable place, associated with prostitution and other shady activities. "We used to spend all our [free] time doing things with family. We would go to the mall only rarely, to go to the Baskin-Robbins," said one of my friends, an Emirati in her mid-thirties, as she reflected on her childhood in the 1980s. In short, in spite of the ambitions of Rashid, Dubai remained at the time of his death in 1990 a fairly provincial, if not obscure town, at most a stopover for travellers headed to more interesting places beyond the Gulf (Parker 2005, 133).

Under Rashid's successors, his sons Maktoum (d. 2006) and Muhammad, the city began its explosive urban transformation. During the 1990s, more than thirty shopping malls and other massive real estate projects emerged. As the cliché had it, the city became a construction site. By the turn of the twenty-first century, observers began to remark the insanity of architecture and building in Dubai (Parker 2005).

There are two salient aspects of this development—the reduction of its objectives, seemingly, to the profit motive alone, and its speed. By the first decade of this century, Dubai developers under the leadership of Muhammad Al Maktoum and other major corporate heads such as Majid Al Futtaim and Saif Ahmad Al Ghurair had begun to reject more conventional understandings of real estate development. These they considered too long-term, appropriate perhaps to U.S. and European markets, but out of step with Dubai's standards and ambitions. Instead, Maktoum, Futtaim et al., would schematically sketch out their vision and immediately make a public statement about their intentions. The master planner and the architect would be invited in at this point to massage the vision into something more feasible than the original vision. One architect close to the Dubai ruler estimated that it takes about ten days for the whole process to take place, from original sketch to final master plan and architectural projections.[26]

Because of Dubai's relative independence from oil (*Economist,* 26–28) and its political evolution as a free-market state, the principal modes of revenue generation are rent, consumer spending, and the reexport trade. This has led, since the mid-1990s, to the development of increasingly large mixed-use commercial real estate developments. While the Old Dubai still retains some public and informal spaces, such as some quite well-groomed and accommodating parks and the various, labyrinthine sinews of the spice, gold, and fish *aswāq* (markets), New Dubai has virtually none of these. Rather, New Dubai developments tend to be gigantic, gated, mixed-use commercial and luxury residential properties. These include, for example, the Maktoum parastatals such as the Media and Internet Cities (the free zone "Tecom," discussed in chapter 4, part of Media City), Majid Al Futtaim's Mall of the Emirates (a shopping mall completed in 2006 and featuring an indoor ski-slope), and Saif Al Ghurair's refurbished Burjuman Shopping Centre, which in late 2003 expanded its retail space from 300,000 square feet to 1.1 million square feet (Middle East Council of Shopping Centres, 78–79). By 2003, according to my estimate from the available literature and anecdotal, on-the-ground evidence, there were about thirty-five shopping centers in the city, thirty of which were built since 1990 (74–93). The newest and largest of these shopping centers are, invariably, part of the much larger conglomerates owned either by Maktoum or by other large corporate chiefs. Each of these, in fact, are large holding corporations with numerous retail, real estate, and investment interests both in Dubai and globally. The most prominent of these holding corporations are the Al Futtaim, the Al Ghurair, and, of course, the ruling Al Maktoum. Sheikh Muhammad's interests are the best example of a Dubai holding company.[27]

Sheikh Muhammad, who calls himself the "CEO of Dubai," is a larger-than-life figure in the city. He is frequently depicted, along with his late father and the late UAE president, Zayed bin Sultan Al Nahyan, in portraits around the city, often seated atop a white Arabian horse. (Sheikh "Mo," as he is often called, is a world-class endurance racer as well as an ambitious poet.) In this capacity, he has taken it upon himself to will Dubai into the status of a global city. The fact that much of the emirate's land and most of the undeveloped part of this land belongs to him, rather helps in this enterprise. Thus, most of the brand names that have become associated with the New Dubai—EMAAR, Nakheel, the free zones, Dubai Holding, Dubai World, Dubai Ports, the World Islands, the Palm developments, the Burj al-Arab Hotel, the recently completed Burj Dubai/Burj Khalifa, and the Dubailand mega-project—are Maktoum parastatals.

In late 2005 and early 2006, I wrote that, "the New Dubai is still more of a fantasy in the fevered dreams of Sheikh Muhammad and his allies in the merchant class, but what Dubayyans have been promised in the near future is still revealing of the ways in which the ruling class map and interpret the space of the city" (Kanna 2006, 23). While I still find this to be correct, reading this now is an odd experience. Much has happened in intervening years, a period shorter than half a decade. Many celebrated (or notorious) projects came online—Futtaim's Mall of the Emirates with its indoor ski-slope; Nakheel's Ibn Battuta shopping mall with its (supposedly) 1:1 replica of the Taj Mahal and other gigantic halls carrying the theme of Ibn Battuta's travels from the Maghreb to China; Sheikh Muhammad's Burj Dubai (Dubai Tower), the world's tallest skyscraper. Other projects came and have already either encountered major setbacks or have been scrapped altogether—Nakheel's Palm Islands, for example, which were just beginning construction in 2005, are now struggling with structural problems and delays and have generally disappointed their investors and residents; major starchitectural projects, such as the Koolhaas Waterfront City and the Hadid Dubai Opera House, which were not even anticipated (at least publicly) in late 2005 and early 2006, have now both come and gone. To speak about New Dubai as a fantasy, a projection, a spatial representation, is now to refer to something like an antique phase in the city's history. Much of the fantasy has foundered on the sobering reality of 2008–9.

It was, I think, the atmosphere of optimism then prevailing in Dubai that makes that period now seem so remote. My interlocutor Maryam, a Dubayyan from the social position I will be calling "flexible citizenship" (chapter 4) and an employee of one of the Maktoum parastatals, captured this mood well in a 2004 interview.

> I think, when you look at the Arab world, you thank God for a place like Dubai, really. Thank God for a place where you have temples and you have mosques, and [where] you have churches. Thank God. Thank God for a place where you have more than one language.... *Al-ḥamdu-lillāh* [Thank God].

Rana, an Emirati of similar social background, put it another way (also in 2004). A few years before, Dubai was not as interesting or diverse, "there weren't all these. . . projects around." She added that what she found so exciting was the feeling that she and many of her compatriots were actively taking part in making Dubai's future, "It is a country adventure."

I did not at the time anticipate how true Rana's comment would become, nor indeed, do I think Rana did either. If Dubai's trajectory over the past decade contains any lessons at all, it is perhaps that those wishing fame for their city in global place wars had better be careful what they wish for. The game is rigged. "Our [Western] reading" of the non-Western city, Rem Koolhaas correctly pointed out recently, tends to be both self-serving and seductive (Koolhaas 2009). Emulating Western models can produce immense rewards. But these can be illusory, fleeting, and destructive (of the city and of the lives of many of its inhabitants). Images of cars abandoned in parking lots by laid-off expatriates hurrying back home may be exaggerated, but for me and many of my Emirati interlocutors, they conformed to a pattern we witnessed many times before—evidenced by the passing racist comment about lazy Arabs and South Asians in a Dubai English pub; by the Western desire, heedless of local perceptions, for sun, no taxes, and easy consumerism on display at the shopping malls and beaches of the city; by a complacent identification among many expatriates of local accommodation of Western intolerance with modernity ("It's like we're in London, but with sun and a housekeeper"). Under condition of anonymity, several Emiratis, and not only older or more conservative ones, told me about feeling colonized by Western expatriates. They chafed at their city being treated as ephemeral, a guilt-free consumer resort, as disposable. The images of the abandoned cars need not reflect a common reality. Variants of this image have been experienced for a long time, perhaps since the counterhegemony of the mid-twentieth century reformers was defeated by the hegemony of Maktoum market absolutism. Maybe those who extol Maktoum stability over the past 170 years have a point.

CHAPTER 1

STATE, CITIZEN, AND FOREIGNER IN DUBAI

> Let us decide not to imitate Europe; let us combine our muscles and
> our brains in a new direction. Let us try to create the whole man,
> whom Europe has been incapable of bringing to triumphant birth.
>
> Frantz Fanon, *The Wretched of the Earth*

> [Capitalism] merely requires a way in, a foreign but colluding social
> hierarchy which extends and facilitates its action . . . the connection
> is made, the current transmitted.
>
> —Fernand Braudel, *The Perspective of the World*

Shortly before I traveled to Dubai in late 2006, there appeared a report by the New York–based, nongovernmental organization Human
Rights Watch (HRW) entitled "Building Towers, Cheating Workers."
The report accused the United Arab Emirates (UAE) construction industry of systematic abuses against workers, including breached contracts,
wretched living conditions, and usurious financial practices. Focusing on
Dubai, which at the time of the study accounted for a disproportionate part
of the UAE construction sector, the report argued that state authorities and
agencies—those of the federal UAE state but also, by implication, those of
Dubai emirate—were complicit in these abuses, if more by omission than
commission. Not surprisingly, a lot of locals were incensed. One interlocutor suggested that the report was part of the larger neoconservative agenda
targeting the Arab world. Another simply denied one of its main pieces
of evidence (a fact that I had personally confirmed), that there are vast
labor camps on the outskirts of the city in which workers are effectively

imprisoned. Others, such as an Indian friend living in Dubai at the time, were pleased. It was about time, he said, that the situation of the workers in the UAE was publicized. Until that point, there seemed to be nothing that could dent many locals' sense of triumph in *mithāl Dubai,* the "Dubai model," the myth of the laissezfaire utopia being advanced by the family-state and its friends.[1] While the report is indeed devastating, and in my opinion perhaps one of the better works on the political economy of a Gulf state, there is more to the story of the HRW report and its ramifications than my Indian friend at first appreciated.

Foreigners constitute approximately 95 percent of the workforce in the UAE (Human Rights Watch 2006, 6). Of these, the majority are migrant workers (as opposed to more well-to-do expatriates) who labor in the construction and service sectors. It is usually assumed that work in these sectors is voluntary and temporary, engaged in by South Asian and other foreign workers making purely economically rational decisions and having the liberty to seek better alternatives elsewhere should conditions in the UAE prove unappealing. One of my friends, a middle-class Indian and long-term resident of Dubai, spoke in a way typical of many more-privileged Dubai residents, "No one puts a gun to the [expatriates'] heads. If they don't like [the working conditions] here, they can go elsewhere." Part of the power of the HRW report was the way it exploded such complacent assumptions. It showed, for example, how common are such practices as non-payment of wages and *contract switching*, where employers change contracts any time they wish and/or force workers to pay for their own visas and travel expenses. Those practices are illegal according to UAE law. But the state agencies, such as the Ministry of Labor, charged with overseeing treatment of workers, are understaffed and what staff they do have are often owners of the very businesses they are supposed to be overseeing (36, 53).

There is another theme in the HRW report that has been less remarked upon, and it is the jumping-off point for this chapter. The report lists a set of demands on the UAE government, such as establishing independent commissions of inquiry, public reporting of labor disputes and their resolution process, the removal of bans on human rights organizations, and banishment of corrupt companies (16–17). On September 28, 2006, Abdulaziz Nasser Al Shamsi, the permanent representative of the UAE to the United Nations, conveyed in a letter to HRW the UAE Labor Minister's response to the organization's report, to whit:

> Workers hosted by the UAE and other [Gulf Cooperation Council] countries cannot be considered migrant workers [which would entitle them to rights stipulated in the UN's Migrant Workers' Convention of 1990], as they work on a temporary basis and according to fix-term employment contracts. . . . Therefore, the immigration laws applicable in the western countries cannot be applied to these workers. [20]

The patent nonsense of this response,[2] along with the UAE state's otherwise feeble reaction, is puzzling in light of the UAE's, and in particular Dubai's, desire to craft a reputation for an appealing, wholesome modernity. The ambassador's response is best understood in the context of Dubai's shifting historical role as a protection hub. More than its challenging of assumptions about the character of migrant labor in Dubai, the report directly attacked the finely cultivated line between economic sectors and activities protected by the state and those that are not. Moreover, while it is tempting to read this interpellation of the state in a literal sense, as a call on the state to enforce or reform its laws (and certainly, this is one correct reading), one may also see the HRW event symbolically. In a sense, the report was asking the state to extend in significant ways to all residents of the country the logic of governance it applies to its citizens and privileged members of the expatriate community. This perhaps inadvertent conflation of the symbolic domains of citizen and noncitizen, more than the surface aspect of the interpellation, carries particular significance in the context of the contemporary UAE where the political stakes in defining citizens and non-citizens have a specific and fraught history. Dubai's case, while in some ways unique within the context of the UAE (Fenelon, 66–67; Heard-Bey, 239), is consistent with other examples from the Gulf in terms of the struggle and eventual triumph of its family-state against reformist and nationalist tendencies of the middle twentieth century (see, for example, Vitalis on Saudi Arabia). This struggle is characterized by a trajectory in which the discursive space of rights-based citizenship, a main goal of the Dubai reform movements of the period between the early 1930s and middle 1950s, was constricted and eventually tapered off. It would be replaced by the family-state ideology of dependent citizenship, the so-called *ruling bargain* in which citizens exchange all political rights for extensive welfare state goods distributed by the state (Davidson 2008, 139–58). In eclipsing a definition of citizenship based on a logic of self-determination, the ruling bargain notion of citizenship more efficiently secured the family-state's monopoly of the political sphere. But it had an important unintended consequence—it came with and indeed seems to have exacerbated an ethnically purist, or ethnocratic, sense of citizenship and claim to national territory. This is a novel phenomenon in the history of a traditionally Perso-Arab and Indian Ocean city. Therefore, in today's Dubai to suggest that citizens are dependents of the state is politically uncontroversial. To suggest that migrant workers might be is politically very dangerous, challenging not only the state's sovereignty over its labor market but also hegemonic modern sensibilities about who belongs to the national community and who does not.

It is commonly assumed that economic globalization directly led to the peculiar relationship between citizens and foreigners in the Gulf. At a certain point in the twentieth century (the story usually goes), the Gulf country in question "discovered" oil, became instantaneously wealthy, and began a modernizing development program. Because the population of the country in question was so small, it did not have the demographic capacity to develop this oil wealth and therefore needed to import vast numbers of unskilled foreign workers. The resulting disproportion between foreigners and locals led to resentment among the local population, which began to see its culture being threatened by these foreigners.

While this story is not entirely incorrect, the lack of context in which it is usually told can tempt us to assume that the suspicion of foreigners in Gulf societies is based on cultural antipathy to foreigners, or that Gulf citizens are resentful of and unable to adapt to globalization. In this chapter I aim to contextualize the relationship between Gulf citizens and foreigners. I focus, in particular, on the development during the twentieth century of the ways the Dubai family-state came to envision and enact this relationship. During the nineteenth century and the first few decades of the twentieth century, the Dubai family-state (under the protection and instigation of the British) deployed an ethnically pluralist mode of governance in which mainly Persian and South Asian actors (primarily merchants) made equally legitimate claims on the market and political protection of the state. This system of governance narrowly defined pluralism as an openness to economic practices and actors who did not actively challenge (and in the case of Indian merchants, or *Banians*, actually advanced) British supremacy (Al-Sayegh, 88). As such, it was secured by British power and embodied in the person of the Dubai ruler, who by the 1930s monopolized rent income and leveraged British protection to his own advantage against the merchant class. Starting around the late 1920s and early 1930s, a protonationalist formation of Arab merchants, whom the collapse of the pearl trade affected more acutely than the Persian and Indian merchants, began challenging the ruler's monopoly of state income and his fealty to the British, as well as calling for a social modernization program in which citizens would have a greater role in their governance (94–96). By the early 1950s, a new reformist challenge, inspired by Nasser's Egypt and the rumblings of anticolonialism in the wider Arab world, began more assertively to advance a notion of participatory citizenship over dependent citizenship. Faced with these challenges, the family-state began constructing an ethnocratic conception of Arabness to represent itself as a legitimate expression of the *vox populi*. The family-state's conception of nationalism was different, logically and discursively, from that espoused by the reformists. While the latter envisioned a socially robust and reformist, participatory, and ethnically pluralistic nationalism, the family-state attempted to defang reformism by appropriating its socially modernizing, "internationalist nationalism" (Prashad, 12) and reframing this as a European-style ethnic nationalism. In the process, and aided by the oil wealth of the late 1960s and 1970s, the family-state coopted the reformists and secured the hegemony of a cultural nationalism disconnected from logics of self-determination and active citizenship. In post-oil Dubai, as in the rest of the UAE and much of the Arab Gulf, ethnically purist cultural nationalism became a guiding logic of state domination and was increasingly seen as identical to a type of citizenship in which the state stands as protector of dependent, apolitical citizens.

By contrast to the pre-oil era, the boundary of the post-oil UAE came to be seen as lacking in porosity, keeping the territory internal to this boundary as homogeneously "Arab." Although as in the pre-oil era, the Dubai family-state continued to privilege segments of the foreign population, discourses of modern, European style ethno-nationalism and related logics of ethnocratic space and time came to be deployed to manage the spaces and movements of other segments of the foreign population. Whereas the Dubai family-state continued to protect the activities of many foreigners, for example, treating Western corporate managers in the oil period as it did Persian merchants in the early twentieth century, it increasingly used the imagery and discourse of ethnocracy when dealing with the spaces and mobility of less privileged actors, such as South Asian or Iranian small merchants and unskilled workers. In doing this, the family-state attempted to represent itself to its citizens as primarily interested in citizens' welfare and in protecting citizens against foreign threats. Historical practices of market and merchant protection entered the oil era as the guiding *style* of state governance. By employing protection as a style of governance, the family-state reaffirmed the impoverished, depoliticized, and "culturalized" version of nationalism that had served its monopolistic agenda so well. It is therefore neither fair nor sufficient to see the antipathy against some foreigners among some Gulf citizens as an example of simple, unthinking cultural resentment or racism. In the constricted contemporary discourse and symbolic field of nationalism now hegemonic in Dubai, ethnocracy is above all a family-state affair, an instrument of political domination by the state and its privileged allies in the multinational capitalist class. All other interpretations of nationalism have either been erased from the public memory or rendered politically dangerous.

On the "Ruling Bargain"

There are two assumptions about the UAE that should be noted as problematic so that we may more clearly appreciate the connections between the state, space, and cultural politics in Dubai. The first assumption is that the ruling regimes of Abu Dhabi and Dubai are overwhelmingly popular among their people. Admittedly, they cannot but appear to be when compared to their counterparts in other parts of the Arab region (Davidson 2005). But this should not tempt us to assume that Dubai is not a politically diverse, even fractious, society. Among the population of nationals, or Emiratis, in Dubai, one often senses frustration with the direction Dubai's modernity is taking under the ruling Al Maktoum. This frustration is usually expressed indirectly, through discourses of ethnocracy.

The second assumption, or more accurately, set of assumptions, pertains to Emiratis' perceptions and treatment of expatriates and migrant workers, especially those from South Asia. Apologists for the status quo tend to argue that foreign workers should not complain about discrimination or abuse because "they can always vote with their feet." Not a few interlocutors, of various nationalities, told me that foreign workers would not have come to Dubai were conditions in the Emirati city not patently superior to those in foreigners' home countries. This book is partly an attempt to puncture this neoliberal myth. On the other side, however, there is an equally problematic assumption, which is more closely connected to the issues introduced in this chapter's introduction. Critics of locals' attitudes and labor practices often assume, as did many of my middle-class South Asian interlocutors, that locals are simply being racist when they voice antipathy toward foreigners (see chapter 5). These critics assert that the locals feel this way because of fears of South Asian or Iranian hordes overrunning their country.

An Emirati businessman made an interesting remark as we chatted one day. He had asked me what my job was in Dubai and when I told him that I was a social science researcher interested in relations between locals and foreigners, he responded to the effect that the UAE could have become like Switzerland had it developed in the right way. When I asked him what he meant by this, he said, "we imported too many foreigners." This was not a random, contextless comment, nor was it an unusual one. This is a common theme of discourse on foreigners and the trajectory of Dubai (see chapter 3), but it is not always simply motivated by racism.

Critique of foreigners in Dubai is sometimes redolent of ethnic antipathy and ethnocentrism, but more often it emphasizes the frustrations of citizens' dependence on the state and implies that this dependence infantilizes citizens. Voicing a very common sentiment among adult and elderly Emiratis, my friend Salim, a forty-something administrator at a local university, told me that today's Emirati youth are feckless and lacking in ambition. They spend all day at the shopping malls, smoking, drinking tea, and talking about cars or premarital escapades with the opposite sex. They lack the entrepreneurialism and willpower of their elders. Ahmad, an ambitious artist in his thirties who both works for the Dubai Municipality and runs his own business, was scornful of what he saw as the complacency of his Emirati coworkers in the government job. (As I show in chapter 4, this perceived dependency on the state has triggered neoliberal style critiques among emerging, self-styled entrepreneurial young elite among Dubai citizens.) With over half of Emiratis of working age receiving social security benefits (Davidson 2008, 179), even the former UAE ruler Zayed Al Nahyan and Dubai ruler Muhammad bin Rashid Al Maktoum have reluctantly admitted a connection between the ruling bargain and what Christopher Davidson has called the UAE's "domestic" or "rentier pathologies" (2005; 2008, 178–79). This is all counterintuitive, because few Emiratis would gainsay the material prosperity of the oil wealth period. By the same token, however, few Emiratis seem totally oblivious to the fact that oil wealth has been both a blessing and a curse. The comment of my acquaintance, the businessman enamored of Switzerland, can therefore be read not as part of racist discourse, but as part of a discourse of autochthony common in the contemporary UAE. This is a discourse about the ideal character of citizenship that is different, perhaps radically so, from the state's ruling bargain ideology. Unlike the ruling bargain, autochthony is a species of a larger genus, self-determination (although, admittedly, in Dubai the former has turned out to be a somewhat impoverished, sometimes narrowly ethno-nationalist version of the latter). Unlike the state's ideology, autochthony suggests that citizens, not the state, should guide the direction of the polity. Autochthony discourse is a distant and distorted cousin of third world independence and self-determination discourse, in which notions of dignity, rights, and the intrinsic connection between meaningful labor and participatory citizenship were salient (see Prashad for an excellent summary). The ruling bargain, by contrast, is a construction of citizenship based on notions of protection, hierarchy, and charity. In this logic, the state controls the national wealth and citizens can only access it at the pleasure of the state.

The very term *ruling bargain* implies the genteel atmosphere of the boardroom, of individual-to-individual negotiation, the sensible cultivation of accord between two parties. Each player arrives at a point of mutual interest through rational choice. This assumption about politics minimizes the extent to which the current order in Dubai was achieved through conflict and suppression. I prefer the frame of social conflict, with its connotation of social worlds made or constructed in political struggle, to that of bargaining and rational choice, which (unlike Dubai, whether today or in the past), is too bloodless and tranquil. Between the 1930s and the 1950s, Dubai was convulsed by conflicts between the ruler (and, indirectly, the British), on one side, and what might be called reformist movements, on the other side.[3] By the 1960s, the emirates of the lower Gulf, still under the nominal domination of Britain, were among the poorest, least developed parts of the Arab region. While oil, discovered in the late 1950s in Abu Dhabi and late 1960s in Dubai, along with the federation of the seven emirates, would lift the UAE out of poverty by the 1970s, Dubai citizens during the first half of the twentieth century were not simply sitting around waiting for black gold to develop their society. At various points during this period, they attempted to mobilize organized social reform to improve their conditions. In this preoil period, Dubai reformists saw issues of equity and self-determination not simply in economic terms but as embedded in political relations.

Between 1929 and the late 1930s, the collapse of the pearl trade and the onset of the Great Depression began changing the power dynamics in Dubai—merchants, on whom the ruler was dependent, began to lose leverage. In an attempt to regain some of their former power, a group of village notables began lobbying the ruler to sever his ties to Britain and advocating for a judicial body controlled by locals, not by the British. Implicit in these demands were an awareness and critique of the fact that, under British protection, the ruler held a monopoly of all rent income paid by the British for a new airbase in Dubai and for oil exploration concessions (Al-Sayegh, 94). The so-called *majlis* movement of 1938–39, led by notable families such as the Al Ghurair, Bin Dalmuk, and Bin Thani, similarly demanded rent sharing, but it went further. Under their pressure, the ruler allowed the formation of a consultative council, the majlis, while the reformists agreed that the ruler should head the body. The ruler, Davidson tells us, agreed to distribute 85 percent of rent income, the expenditure of which would be subject to the council's prior approval. Fatma Al-Sayegh adds that all air and oil rents were now to go to the state's treasury, not that of the ruler (95). Davidson's implication is that the ruler did this because of his magnanimity and foresight. I am less certain about this. Davidson notes, for example, that an anxious British Political Resident regarded the 1938–39 movement as a "democratic wave that aimed at putting more power in the hands of the people" (2008, 33). This kind of language suggests that the reformists were more threatening to vested interests than is implied by a narrative about the ruler's magnanimity and the meekness of citizens who saw themselves as his dependents. The language of the Political Resident suggests that this may have been a proto–Third World independence movement. So does the recollection of one Dubai notable. The British, according to him, "had fears about what they saw as the emergence of *progressive* tendencies demonstrated by the *separatists* . . . and the establishment of an assembly which was actually representative of the community; . . . it would be easier to keep dealing with traditional tribal structures than the more diffuse, less predictable activities of popular assemblies" (2008, 35, emphasis added). The use of the terms *progressive, representative,* and, especially, *separatists* is striking, implying that the ruler and the British equated reformism with a radical movement aiming at national independence. Again, the metaphor of bargaining, with its connotations of rational choice and mutual accord, is not sufficient to interpreting these events. A struggle between different social formations, with its implicit divergence of perspectives on ideals of governance and the meaning of citizenship, was likely brewing.

This irreconcilable divergence is also suggested by the fact that by 1939 the Dubai ruler Said Al Maktoum and his son and deputy Rashid (father of the current ruler, Muhammad), along with their British protectors, had begun to tire of the reformists and to suppress them by force. Although the fatalities were few (only about ten individuals were killed by the Maktoum, with prisoners blinded in one eye), the symbolic impact of the suppression was large, with the pan-Arab press in the Middle East treating the event as an example of British and family-state injustice. In spite of being short-lived, however, the majlis movement did leave a significant modernizing legacy, its agitation leading not only to the aforementioned consultative council but also to the establishment of social security for the elderly, an elected body of customs officials employed by the state (as opposed to the ruler), and an education department with powers to appoint the director of schools and to recruit teachers from the local population. The scholarly literature minimizes these accomplishments and disconnects them from the global intellectual and political currents of the time, but these achievements are evidence of the reformers' probable awareness of, and commonality with, other progressives in the Third World movement. The reformers' aims and vision of a polity that was not simply a feudal appendage of the empire were modernizing and even radical in the stifling political context of their Dubai.

If the family-state's intention in crushing the majlis movement was to destroy reformist tendencies, as the colonial parlance of the time had it, the following decades would prove frustrating and even frightening for the Maktoum. During the 1940s and 1950s, Dubai was awash in an atmosphere of Arab nationalist resistance to British rule in the lower Gulf. For the British and their Maktoum protégés, this could only have been the result of "infiltration" by expatriate Nasserist sympathizers, "imported ideologies, foreign newspapers, and in some cases even *agents provocateurs*" (Davidson 2008, 40). The Iraqi-staffed al-Falah school, where the teachers encouraged students to parade through the streets carrying the Arab nationalist colors and chanting nationalist songs, was singled out as a particularly dangerous example of this supposed provocation. That Dubai citizens and parents were witnessed to be encouraging the students contradicts colonial and family-state assertions that nationalist sentiments were simply a result of "false consciousness" and imported ideologies. By 1960, the schools were openly nationalist and Nasser had become a figure of veneration.

Increasing Nasserist sentiment led in 1953 to the formation of the socalled Dubai National Front. It was initially narrowly ethno-nationalist, formulating a platform consisting largely of opposition to the influence of non-Arabs, especially Indian and Persian merchants. As means to this end, the Front sought to reduce the ruler's power and British interference in domestic affairs. In this ethno-nationalism, the Front was similar to other post–Great Depression indigenous nationalist and protonationalist phenomena in the Indian Ocean arena, including the wider Gulf region, as well as British East Africa, Malaya, and (most spectacularly and sadly, in the form of the millenarian and anti-Indian Saya San rebellion) Burma in the 1930s (Bose, 72–121). The leaders of the Front numbered among the emirate's most prominent Arab families, such as the Al Futtaim and the Al Ghurair. Juma bin Maktoum Al Maktoum (crown prince Rashid's uncle), was among the fellow travelers, and Rashid exiled him to Damman, Saudi Arabia in 1955.

The Front tried to broaden its base by the late 1950s when it began to perceive common interests among Dubayyans of all ethnicities against British domination and family-state fealty to their protectors. This broader agenda and strategy, according to Davidson, worried Rashid a great deal (2008, 49). The British responded by removing the "more troublesome" expatriate teachers from the schools and appointing pro-British expatriates (especially Sudanese and Zanzibaris), as well as increasing funding to Dubai schools. This was a reversal of British policy, which up until this point had concurred with the views of the ruler and other members of the ruling family that formal education may lead to demands for political reform. The Political Resident was similarly fearful of formal education, which, he theorized, would lead to demands for changes in the "existing patriarchal forms of government" (52).

The Said and Rashid faction within the Maktoum therefore entered the 1960s with great anxiety over the direction of their less than pacified feudal town. The wider Arab region was lurching to the left. Colonialism was seen by most of these other "darker nations" (Prashad) for the shabbily exploitative and racist affair that it actually was. Yet the Maktoum (and their Abu Dhabi counterparts, the Nahyan) were attached to the British with unflagging fidelity. Were they going to be forced by their people to sever ties with their imperial masters? Would their people simply dispense with them? Dubai reformists for the previous three decades had come perilously close to the sentiment that monarchs, in general, were retrograde, and that their own monarchs in particular were a false and unpersuasively "invented" example of the species. Many of the reformers would likely have concurred with Sugata Bose's more recent assessment: "the sovereignty accorded to some of the Gulf sheikhdoms was . . . no more than the other side of the coin on which the supremacy of British power was clearly engraved" (25–26).

Oil saved the family-state. Income flowing in from oil concessions freed all Dubai citizens from taxation and "a frenzy of consumerism began" (Davidson 2008, 53). Rashid, now the ruler, co-opted the leaders of the Dubai National Front with exclusive licenses in the import and construction sectors. These erstwhile nationalists became the largest Dubai private concerns, next to Rashid bin Said's and Muhammad bin Rashid's own holding corporation. By the late 1960s, nationalist sentiment in Dubai was receding into memory and myth. Today, these aspirations continue to live on, but only in the faintest form, in the distorted and spectral discourse and symbolism of Emirati Arab ethnocracy.[4]

The current political order of Dubai, in which the ruler's appointed Executive Council exercises near-monopolistic control of politics and urban policy, owes its emergence largely to this co-optation and crushing of the reformist tendencies and their replacement with a Western-style consumerist orientation.[5] Thus, the political scientist and Dubai native Abdul Khaleq Abdulla's analysis from the mid-1980s, although expressed in a now dated idiom and referring more broadly to the UAE, is still a largely valid critique of Dubai. "As a periphery (the UAE's) narrow specialization was to produce and export crude oil and import goods manufactured in the advanced capitalist countries of the center" (1984, 96–97). Three social groups, who historically have directly benefited from the collusion between the local dynast and the British, have maintained this dependency. Abdulla calls these the "social instruments of political dependency": (1) the ruling families such as the Al Nahyan of Abu Dhabi and the Al Maktoum of Dubai, which retained at the time of independence in 1971 a monopoly of oil revenues and public land (land without deed at the time of independence); (2) a local elite from among the merchant class (among them the former nationalists), who through royal concessions came to hold a monopoly on financial, industrial, and commercial activities; and (3) a class of largely Western-based managers of local corporations who received preferential treatment in the labor market (124). Abdulla also describes the ideology of the ruler and his elite merchant allies: "(this group) thinks of itself as the most modernized social segment and empathizes with the Western upper-class consumer life-style" (176). They identify modernity with consumption of Western luxury goods and espouse a free-trade ideology (124–25). Abdulla's conclusion about the wider UAE a quarter century ago can almost directly be applied to Dubai today. The UAE, he writes, is "characterized by an invariable tendency towards an authoritarian and politically marginalizing system, which closes all possible channels of political participation and systematically suppresses opposition movements" (181–82). This has entailed a "political deactivation of the populace" (182).[6]

In the late 1950s and early 1960s, writing from the Algerian national liberation front, Frantz Fanon with characteristic flair expressed the aspiration of Third World liberation movements to "create the whole man"

(Fanon, 313). Drawing on German romantic and early Marxist themes of alienation and self-actualization, Fanon argued that European colonialism had both socially and psychologically malformed the colonized. Part of the project of colonial subjugation was to get the colonized to identify progress and enlightenment exclusively with European models, specifically liberal bourgeois capitalism. To build a new society on the basis of a concept of citizen as a monadic individual, isolated from society and governed by the profit motive, was to Fanon an impoverished vision. The new, liberated society should be a radically new model of liberation, a society in which the political participation of the masses, along with socially constructive, rewarding labor and national self-determination would be intrinsically connected. Abdul Khaleq Abdulla's (1984) critique of the UAE state seems to be a great (if valedictory) reaffirmation of this sentiment from an Emirati and Dubayyan perspective. Since the early 1970s Emiratis have become materially prosperous in unprecedented ways. Yet there is an oft-expressed frustration with the direction of family state led modernity. This frustration must be contextualized in the fact that the intrinsic connection between labor, mass political participation, and self-determination was severed by the various family-states' ruling bargains. Because the reform movements have disappeared from the political landscape, this frustration became channeled in an ethnocratic direction.

"Protection" as Practice and Style of Governance

Among other things, the reformist movements of the mid-twentieth century threatened the hierarchy of tacit protection agreements between the British, the family-state, and foreign merchants.[7] The reassertion of family-state control required not only intervention at the institutional level but at the political, and eventually, the ideological level. The twentieth century in Dubai is largely the story of the impoverishment of the public sphere in the late pre-independence and post-independence periods. With increasing family-state control came the eclipse of a substantive sense of nationalist reform, based on the idea of self-determination by a much narrower, dependent notion of citizenship, the ruling bargain. In the process of making their legitimacy and promoting the ruling bargain, the family-state represented itself as protector of its citizens—increasingly constructed as homogeneously Arab—and defender of (national, urban) boundaries, and represented as lacking in porosity.

At least until the economic crisis of 2008, neoliberal writers routinely celebrated Dubai (*Economist*; al-Malifi; Friedman 2006). The small laissez-faire state, it was argued, was better adjusting to and even benefiting from the demands of the global economy because of its self-discipline and comparative advantage in the knowledge, communications, and tourism markets—a nimble and clever little entrepôt between much larger states. This "success" was attributed to the supposedly minimal and intelligent role of the state in the economy. Even Abdul Khaleq Abdulla seems to have come around to a more optimistic view of things. In 2006 he expressed what was, and even in the wake of the crisis seems to persist as, a commonplace of much of this commentary: "Non-interference by the state in the economy is the law for all aspects of life in [Dubai,]. . . a city which offers a pool of skilled, cheap labor, full profit repatriation, [and] non-interference in any way by the UAE state" (15). In this case, he is referring specifically to Dubai's free zones, but the general point is that these zones are (or should be) in the vanguard of the city's development agenda.

On the surface, Dubai does (or, at least until recently, did) seem like a free market utopia. As the state continues to attempt to liberate itself from the oil economy, sectors such as the free zones, tourism, and real estate development become increasingly important (ironically, the very sectors most vulnerable to a financial downturn). Looked at more closely, however, the state plays a much more interventionist role in the economy than is apparent at first (Marchal 2005). Dubai's adaptation to its regional and political-economic contexts has traditionally been based on a set of carefully crafted tacit protection agreements. Often, these have been protection rackets, but there are also examples of "legitimate" or formal economic activities that are protected. The most obvious example, of course, has been the security of and stability of the family-state, which was ensured by British and American naval power. Political protection, in turn, is intimately connected to markets. As Carolyn Nordstrom has pointed out, the distinction between the "formal" and the "informal," "legitimate" and "illegitimate," is arbitrary. Trading networks are, after all, markets, and markets do not distinguish between the two types of trade. Let us take Nordstrom's example of the shipping container to clarify.

> A shipping container can "contain" arms, cigarettes, and the latest pirated DVDs, along with a host of other commodities ranging from the seriously illegal to the merely mundane; . . . such transits work more smoothly than they would if all routes were separate: arms buyers find an easy market for cigarettes, videos,

and information technology (or Mach 3 razors, 4 X 4 all-terrain vehicles, or pornography). (8)

Dubai has become one of the world's top ten transshipment hubs (Deutsche Bank Research 2006, 8). Dubai Ports was recently estimated to have processed approximately nine million twenty-foot equivalent units (TEU) of the total of 455.9 million TEU shipped globally, a figure that was officially forecasted, before the economic crisis, to be increasing (*Dubai Ports World*).

Nordstrom adds, "More than 90 percent of world trade is conducted by the international shipping industry. Around 50,000 ships registered in 150 countries are manned by more than a million sailors from virtually every country in the world" (115). Moreover, "the most sophisticated ports in the world can inspect a maximum of only 5 percent of the cargo passing through customs" (118). It is impossible not to deduce from this that much of the shipping going through Dubai is not tracked, and that this is either because of agreements or tacit understandings between shippers and the family-state or, perhaps more likely, as Nordstrom suggests, because the volume of shipping through a port such as Dubai is simply so immense as to be impossible to track. As an entrepôt, Dubai is probably similar in this respect to many other major shipping hubs across the globe. What is important to point out is that the territorial boundaries of the city-state are clearly, at times, porous. Yet, it is also the case that discourses of legitimate and illegitimate mobility, "legal" and "illegal" movement within and without Dubai's borders, are a prominent part of public and official discourse. It is interesting to note that the subject of these discourses is often foreign workers, and that such discourses precisely map the class hierarchies of contemporary Dubai. Looked at from another angle, certain kinds of mobility (of capital, humans, and goods) are either protected or at least tolerated by the family-state. Other types of mobility are subject to elaborate surveillance and discursive focus.

Protection is an ostensibly curious label to apply to the relationship between the state and economy in Dubai, which is commonly seen, as already mentioned, as a laissez-faire city-state. In fact, protection has been an uncontroversial part of the economy of Dubai for a long time. Before the oil period, this was mainly because of the political clout of the merchant class, which was traditionally integral to the maintenance of power by ruling families both in Dubai and in the wider pre-oil Gulf (Herb; Onley 2005). At least since the late eighteenth century, Gulf societies have been stratified into classes of Bedouin and urban dwellers, with merchants constituting a prominent subclass of the latter (Field; Herb). Before oil, rulers drew their income largely, if not primarily, from trade; "the merchants subsidized the rulers, while in turn the rulers protected the merchants' trade" (Herb, 57). The nationality or religious identity of merchants was at most a secondary concern for the ruler. In fact, Dubai rulers often favored foreigners when crafting protection agreements, something that led to the resentment fueling the nationalist reactions discussed above.

Thus, the term *Weltmarkt* (world market), employed by Fernand Braudel to describe cities such as late medieval Bruges and Hanseatic Lübeck, applies in some ways to Dubai; "most of the ships in the harbour belonged to foreign owners, . . . [the cities'] inhabitants played only minor part in active commerce. They were content to act as intermediaries for the merchants who flocked into the town from every direction" (101). Not quite a world city of the level of imperial capitals such as Amsterdam or London, a world market nevertheless anchored networks of mobility and capital from vast surrounding regions and was a hub for what Braudel called world economies.

The first foreign merchants to make connections to Dubai were Indian and Persian. In the pre-oil era, these British Indian (or Banian) and Persian traders made up, along with the Arab merchants, a cosmopolitan merchant community (Al-Sayegh, 88). Although embedded in the broader capitalist world system in various ways, these merchants occupied what has been called an "intermediary capitalist" level, largely, if not fundamentally, autonomous of the level of the European-dominated capitalism of the colonial period (circa mid-eighteenth century to mid-twentieth century) (Bose, see also Onley 2005). Crafting networks of kin and community across the Indian Ocean and its tributaries, such as the Gulf, these merchants operated within a highly lucrative capitalist arena between European high capital and economies of subsistence, and dealt in both the commodities of trade and finance (Bose, 74). Well-known are the Bhatias, Memons, Bohras, and Khojas of Gujarat, who established networks connecting India with Muscat, Aden, and Zanzibar between the second half of the nineteenth century and the 1920s (75). As Sugata Bose shows, the trade of these Indian merchants was protected by local potentates in the Indian Ocean ports where they had set up their businesses. In turn, these potentates were both creations and protégés of the British Empire, which in the latter half of the nineteenth century attempted to establish centralized states governed by "traditional" principalities (24–25, see discussion in Introduction and above). What Braudel wrote about the emergence of capitalism in renaissance Europe is therefore apposite to our discussion; "it merely requires a way in, a foreign but colluding social hierarchy which extends and facilitates its action; . . . the connection is made, the current transmitted" (65). The means through which Dubai was integrated into capitalism was, of course, the British Empire, which saw protection as intrinsically connected to hierarchical governance presupposing a "unitary," European style of state sovereignty (Bose).

Let us take a closer look at Dubai's foreign merchants. Two important events in the town's early formation as an entrepôt attest the interplay between protection and capital flight. As discussed in the Introduction, the Persian Emperor's raising of duties on imports and exports at the turn of the twentieth century drove Persian Gulf merchants to Dubai, where the ruler Maktoum bin Hashar welcomed them with free port policies (Lorimer 455–56, Heard-Bey, 243–45). Lorimer notes that, at this time, the re-export trade began to take on more importance in the local economy (456). A more significant number of Persians followed when, in the 1920s, Reza Shah passed the *kashf-e-hejab*, a law outlawing the woman's headscarf. Many Sunni Persian merchants from Persia's Gulf coast fled to Dubai.[8] These again were predominantly merchants whom the then ruler of Dubai, Said bin Maktoum, invited to remain permanently (as opposed to the temporary residence offered to their predecessors by Said's father, Maktoum bin Hashar). Like his father, however, Said gave the merchants favorable land deals and a duty-free zone in which to conduct their import–export trade. Among other things, these merchants built the first architecturally sophisticated town center in Dubai, importing wind-tower (*barjīl*) and other construction technologies from Persia. Many of the prominent Persian merchant families, such as the Darwish, the Galadari, the Al Mulla, the Al Ansari, and others, came to Dubai through such connections with the rulers (Davidson 2008, 156). Attesting the wider, Indian Ocean city-region of Dubai were South Asian merchants, such as the Al Belushi, the Bin Lutah, the Al Nabudah, and the Al Majid who also made similar connections (156). As any traveler to Dubai today will immediately discover, these Persians and South Asians founded some of the city's most prominent corporations, which often took the names of their respective founding families.

The smuggling trade is another example of a protected market. In 1970, according to Michael Field, 259 tons of gold flowed from cities such as London and Geneva, through Dubai, and primarily into India (61). Field estimates this to have been over 20 percent of the non-Communist world's new gold supply "and represented some five kilos for every man, woman, and child in the emirate" (61). Field maintains that most of the elite merchants of Dubai, including the Al Ghurair, the Al Majid, the Owais, the Al Mullah, and the Galadari were involved in smuggling (62), although what the ruler got in return is unclear. By mid-1970s, however, the gold trade collapsed, owing to dramatic price rises and the Indian government's more energetic efforts under Indira Gandhi to crack down on Bombay's gold agents (63). The merchants, however, seemed to have weathered the change in fortunes relatively well, developing re-export trade in other types of contraband such as cigarettes and cloth, which they exported to southern Iran and Pakistan (63). Today, the smuggling trade seems alive and well, and much higher in stakes, although it has often caught the attention of governments far more powerful than India's. Since September 11, 2001, for example, the United States has been pressuring the UAE government to monitor the so-called *ḥawāla*, or cash transfer, flow from exchange offices primarily located in Dubai, as well as Dubai's role as a clearing station in the international arms trade.[9] The European Union and the United Nations have also cited Dubai and Sharjah as key nodes in the international trade in illegal diamonds, endangered species, and stolen cars.[10]

Others have covered the smuggling, human trafficking, and weapons trade through Dubai and other emirates fairly well, so it is not necessary to dwell on the issue (see Davidson 2008, 277–97). By now, we have a good sense of what types of activities are protected or tolerated by the family-state. We should focus on what types of mobility and economic activity are not protected and how this lack is imagined (or, in James Scott's words, "seen") and spatialized by the state. It is important, contextually, to return for a moment to the aforementioned merchants, who in many cases eventually became naturalized Dubai citizens (their Persian and South Asian origins now taking a secondary position in relation to their UAE citizenship). As Davidson points out, the Dubai polity categorizes its citizens (or, more accurately, nationals *muwāṭinūn*) in two, not unrelated, ways: by ethnicity and by relative political allegiance to the royal family. This in turn is connected to the British-imposed system of hierarchical, unitary sovereignty already discussed. Elaborating upon this, Davidson writes that the British strove to keep Dubai, as they did many of their Indian Ocean and Persian Gulf colonies, "primitive" and "under a more colonial character" (59), thus necessitating a centralized system governed autocratically by invented "traditional" dynasties (25–26).

Once in place, such dynasties incorporated politically dependable affiliated clans, as well as foreigners, such as the Persians and South Asians. In Dubai, the first group, the closest to the apex, consists of members of the ruling family's Al Bu Falasa section of the Bani Yas tribe, often co-opted through exclusive concession deals, with the Persians, South Asians, and others further from these in terms of political leverage and access to governmental offices. (See Abdulla 1984, 138; Davidson 2008, 153–58). The Al Bu Falasah families and the prominent merchants form an elite relative to the remainder of Dubai nationals, but the latter are still, structurally, in a privileged position vis-à-vis non-nationals (expatriates and migrant workers). The entirety of the general group, Dubai nationals, is incorporated into the family-state's ruling bargain.

With the onset of the oil economy, the rulers no longer needed the merchants as allies. They could co-opt them like any other citizen and force them into a dependent position. This brings us back to the issue of Dubai's demographic imbalance, alluded to in the businessman's comment that the UAE could have been more like Switzerland. With oil Abu Dhabi and Dubai became majority foreigner societies and consolidated themselves as "the purest examples of rentier states" (Davidson 2008, 151). In the post-oil period, the demographic imbalance became favored by the family-states as a means of political stability (151). The market protection of the merchant capital period evolved into the ruling bargain mode of governance in the post oil period. Protection went from a literal to a figurative mode of governance, its transformation reflecting the emergence of a style of state domination in need of symbolizing, rather than necessarily always practicing, the protection it provided.

The Condition of the Working Class in Dubai

Migrant laborers in the UAE constitute a casually employed and legally unprotected group that runs the country's day-to-day operations. In spite of their numerical importance and centrality to the UAE economy, the scholarly literature has tended to marginalize them. The politics of identity and otherness in the UAE and the broader Gulf have not been much interrogated in the literature, let alone the ways in which these politics are spatialized and spatially represented.[11] Neither racism nor globalization (or, "oil-driven modernization," if one likes) is a sufficient explanation of the peculiar position of migrant workers in the UAE. As the family-state transitioned from the merchant capital period into the oil period, it developed the ruling bargain strategy to co-opt its citizens. This strategy and the ideology that justified it required the setting up of a more inflexible boundary between who belonged to the state and who did not. Not all foreigners, however, were treated equally as outsiders. A globalized, largely (although not exclusively) Western-based, middle-and upper-middle-class technocratic elite was incorporated into the economy through privileged access to jobs, salaries, benefits, and property. This strongly echoed the protection practices of the merchant capital era. On the other end of the class system, workers from South and Southeast Asia (and, to some extent, the Middle East) were increasingly represented as absolute outsiders. This was a function neither of racism nor of globalization only, but (perhaps most importantly) of the ideology of the ruling bargain, and it articulated with cultural and spatial representation in complex ways.

As already mentioned, foreigners make up about 95 percent of the workforce in the UAE, with the majority of these being migrant workers.[12] Whereas on average, a UAE resident has a comfortable income by any standard,[13] in reality, a large fraction of the UAE population toils under unnecessarily exploitative conditions. Statistics on the breakdown of income according to nationality or occupation are not available, but one can get a general idea of migrant living conditions by glancing at an average classified section from any of various Dubai daily newspapers. Full-time maids, according to a typical classified section I collected during a fieldwork visit in mid-September 2003, could hope to earn between $190 and $270 per month, as much as about $3240 per year. "Part-time" housemaids or houseboys, who work between four and six, and sometimes as many as ten, hours per day for a single family, can usually expect between $80 and $140 per month. The average income of a construction worker, according to the 2006 HRW report, is $175 per month, more than ten times less than the UAE per capita income (7).

Repayment of labor agents is a significant expense for migrants, and shows how arbitrary the UAE and Dubai states are in both formulating and enforcing their labor laws. When a Westerner or a well-to-do non-Western expatriate (an Indian MBA, for example) takes a job in management with a company that operates in the UAE, he or she can expect the company to arrange for visas for everyone in the family, as well as for their travel to the UAE. Very often a company car is provided as well as accommodations in one of the better neighborhoods of Abu Dhabi or Dubai, along with a paid holiday home for a month or more. Although it is illegal, employers of migrant laborers in the UAE often force workers to arrange for their own visas and travel. Moreover, a UAE income regulation prevents low-income workers from bringing family with them. David, a bartender from Goa, told me how he and his peers had to pay a labor agent in India Rs 40 000 (about $1100), to arrange for a UAE visa and a local *kafil* or sponsor. While he claimed that the salary of an average worker in his occupation is about $100 per month (in late 2004), I assume that this is too conservative a figure. Based on anecdotal evidence from daily classified ads and the 2006 HRW report, let us assume that the average monthly salary is twice the figure David gave me. Even with a "high" salary of about $200 per month, it would take about half a year of spending on nothing except repayment of a labor agent to extricate oneself from this burden (assuming the loan is not accumulating interest, not a safe assumption). Given the UAE state's and laborexporting countries' inability or unwillingness to enforce existing laws against labor agent extortion, migrants are usually forced to borrow to cover travel and visa expenses. Recruitment agencies in turn offer workers loans at as much as ten percent monthly interest to cover these expenses (Human Rights Watch 2006, 29).

Exacerbating the situation of migrants are other illegal company practices, such as *contract switching,* in which the employer suddenly changes a contract to reduce or even avoid payments of agreed upon wages. Other onerous expenses include visa and work permit renewal fees and health insurance, which, again, UAE labor law requires employers to cover. As one construction worker put it,

> The company . . . deducts fees from my salary for expenses that the company is supposed to cover under the law. I have to pay 900 AED ($245) to renew my visa. The company takes this out of my salary in increments. Also, every three years, 500 AED ($136) is deducted for renewal of my work permit. The health card costs 300 AED ($82) and the company takes this from my salary every year. (29)

Another worker summed up this situation well, "We can't just go back. Each of us owes a lot of money to recruiting agents back home. How can we go back when we have taken such huge loans?" (35–36).

The case of domestics, although in some important ways different from that of other migrants, is particularly significant because this group, perhaps more than others, reflects the informal, indentured nature of labor in the UAE. Estimates of the number of domestic workers are wildly divergent, but seem to be consistently on the order of several hundred thousand.[14] These women, who are recruited in their home countries by often corrupt agents, are an important source of hard cash for their home countries.[15] Therefore, migrants' home countries are reluctant to intervene in cases where maids allege abuse or breached contracts, to name two of a panoply of injustices suffered by these workers.[16] Compounding matters, national labor laws, such as they are, do not apply to domestics in the UAE, because domestics are categorized by the state as falling under the sovereignty of the family for whom they work. The family is considered the maid's *mu'īl* ("guardian," literally family provider, sustainer, or breadwinner) as opposed to her *kafīl* ("sponsor"). Most other guest workers enter into a *kafāla* ("sponsorship") relationship with an Emirati national, and thus are covered by labor laws, anemic as they are (Hilotin).

Although I did not personally encounter any of the more serious examples of abuse that are beginning to be more publicly aired (usually outside the UAE), I did frequently overhear employers, both Emiratis and expatriates, referring to their maids as *girls*. (The term *house boy* or *tea boy* is used almost exclusively for the South Asian men who work as office assistants, custodians of buildings, gardeners, etc.) One time a Western-Arab expatriate made a rather telling off-the-cuff remark. Her Filipino maid had wanted to join friends for a Sunday visit to a local church. "I'm not sure," said the *mu'īla,* "that I really want her mixing with her kind. I am afraid that they would corrupt her" (*ykharbūha,* literally, to "break her," or "ruin her," a word that also applies to the use of tools, instruments, and other such objects). To inoculate prospective domestic workers against bad habits such as protesting their working or living conditions, some labor exporting governments, such as Sri Lanka's, have set up schools to prepare and indoctrinate these workers as to their appropriate place, "The teacher held up an electric cake mixer and told the class of wide-eyed women before her to clean it properly. If it smells, 'Mama' (as the aspiring maids were instructed to call their female employers) will be angry and she will hammer and beat you" (Waldman).

Migrant laborers in Dubai seem to inhabit a space over which the state has assertively extended its control, drawing the boundaries for political-economic reasons between insiders (Emiratis and elite expatriates) and outsiders (migrants from relatively weak states, often economically dependent on labor export, and others from the surplus global army of labor). The situation is not just random, a mere side effect of globalization. It is embedded in localized structures of meaning and power, specifically, the aforementioned ruling bargain between the state and its national subjects, as well as the tacit protection agreement between the local capitalist elite and global capitalist actors. The construction of the boundary between insider and outsider, the legitimate and nonlegitimate, the legal and the illegal, discussed in the remainder of the chapter, suggests that in the case of Dubai the politics of protection is connected to the spatial representations by which the state governs it territory and populace.

Constructions of Legality and Illegality

Dubai, like most of its Gulf neighbors, has felt diverse pressures to its sovereignty since the oil era began in the late 1960s and early 1970s, when migrant laborers, mostly from South and Southeast Asia, began immigrating in large numbers.[17] Emirati nationals, such as the Swiss-oriented businessman, often refer to this pressure as a "demographic problem" or "demographic distortion" (*al-khalal al-sukkāniyy*) which is, in turn, ethnically marked. One Emirati observer recently put it rather frankly, "[The Indians] cause, and continue to cause, a distortion in the population structure that is felt by the people. This imbalance . . . has become a threat" (Hussein, 123–24).[18]

This perceived threat to national identity and state sovereignty has increased since the attacks of September 11, 2001, and yet again since the financial crisis of 2008. The pressure brought by the United States on the UAE government to monitor its smuggling trade, a staple of the local economy, intensified after the terror attacks on New York and Washington, D.C. The aforementioned scrutiny by human rights organizations has also been seen by many locals as a threat to the status quo. As a result, we witness a subsequent increase in the amount of discourse about cracking down on illegal activities. Such discourse should be contextualized in the foregoing discussion about mobility of goods and people within and without Dubai. On the one hand, as a major transshipment hub, Dubai processes an immense volume of shipping through its port facilities. Only a small percentage of this is tracked, and much of the untracked material is probably illegal. On the other hand, those groups, such as Western technocrats and other social instruments of dependency, in a privileged enough position not to require state protection against usurious or abusive labor practices are permitted wide latitude in entering and leaving the city-state. The opposite holds for migrants. In the context of increased scrutiny and threatened sovereignty, migrant labor becomes a main target of state discourses and a spatial politics that Henri Lefebvre might call "urbanist ideology" (Lefebvre 2003, see discussion in chapter 2). Representations of migrant labor and its mobility symbolize the effective management of the ruling bargain by the family-state, in turn reaffirming assumptions about dependent citizenship and the absolute otherness of working class foreigners.

Spatial and discursive constructions of illegality apply to many different activities, such as drug smuggling, smuggling of other contraband, and the *ḥawāla* trade. The state's actions to crack down on illegal activities and clean up the country of individuals and behaviors that run counter to "the UAE's rules and the region's Islamic values" are attested frequently and seemingly arbitrarily by local newspapers as well as informal conversations.[19] Dhows (small sailing vessels used by Gulf and Indian Ocean traders) are "barred from selling bargain goods," according to a typical headline. As the subtitle explains, "most of the products are brought in illegally," which reassures the reader that the boundary between legal and illegal is being kept under close surveillance (Arbab). Rereading this article reminded me of the time when I attended a Ramadan *majlis* (reception) at the home of a local notable, where a guest noted how efficient the Dubai police were in keeping the peace and conducting traffic during the Dubai IMF–World Bank meetings in September 2003. "I once saw a police car chase another car which was speeding," reminisced a second guest. "*Subḥānallah!* (Praise the Lord!) It was like Los Angeles! It was like a Hollywood film!" This was a comment that drew laudatory remarks from the assembled guests. Elsewhere, certain kinds of smuggling were constructed as illegal and decontextualized from the reality and pervasiveness of similar kinds of illegality that are commonplace in a major entrepôt city; "Drug peddlers caught with narcotics, face life in prison"; "Man gets death sentence"; (Zaza 2004b); "Drug dealers sentenced to life in prison" (Zaza 2004a).

The movement of migrant laborers (as opposed to that of privileged expatriates) is of the utmost concern, and interpellative utterances in state-sanctioned media remind the populace of the need for constant vigilance. Classified ads called notices reminiscent of Western movie "Wanted" posters appear from time to time in the local newspapers. "Notice: This is to inform all concerned that the persons, whose photographs appear above, are under our sponsorship and are absconding. Any person/firm dealing with them will do so at his/their own risk. Kindly inform us or the concerned authorities of their whereabouts if known." So reads one of these "notices," which, helpfully, also gives the offenders' passport numbers.

Although "absconders" are not always so successful in eluding the law, migrants signify a near-constant source of threat. "The UAE Coast and Frontier Guards seized hundreds of Asian migrants who tried to enter the country illegally last month in search of jobs. Most of the 579 infiltrators are from Bangladesh, India, Pakistan, and Iran and were captured as they landed at mountainous areas near the northern border with Oman."[20] This was in February 2004. By May, the central government in Abu Dhabi was reporting "a drastic increase in the number [of illegal immigrants] arrested. . . . They soared from 215 in March to 701 last month."[21] Such accounts are sometimes spiced with a dash of adventure, "The immigration authorities in Abu Dhabi have further intensified their crackdown on illegal residents by carrying out more raids on their hideouts" (Hoath 2003). The illegal residents were guilty of moving from Dubai to work in Abu Dhabi after the Dubai authorities carried out "tighter security measures. . . for the ongoing World Bank and IMF meetings." "These people," the authorities are quoted as saying after another series of raids, "were arrested from their hideouts in residential buildings in several parts of [Abu Dhabi] city during the four days [of the raid]."[22] Months later: "In the continuing crackdown on illegal immigrants, law enforcement agencies arrested 980 people attempting to sneak into the country in June" (2004). "A growing number of illegal immigrants have been sneaking into the country through our international borders and the coastline," according to an official statement. "The strict vigil and enhanced security on the borders and the coast, however, have prevented them from succeeding in their attempts to take refuge and stay here illegally."

Discourses of hygiene are often a subtext of these representations. The body politic must be seen to be "clean." The aim in the cases of both discourses of illegality and hygiene is the well-maintained space over which the state has sovereign control, the successful performance and dramatization of the ruling bargain's spatialization of insider and outsider. UAE national Abdallah Humaid strikes a commonly heard note when demanding, in an Arabic daily, that the municipal authorities monitor the covered vegetable market in Ras al-Khaimah, a small coastal town northeast of Dubai. "What is at issue here is the fact that the vegetables are being stepped on by people's feet. No one cares about this, from the perspective of the [South] Asians and their nonchalance with respect to cleanliness." This situation, adds Humaid, will attract insects and vermin. "For cleanliness is a necessary and basic element in the life of peoples (*ḥayāt al-shu'ūb*), so it is not right that you have a people (*sha'b*) that does not care about cleanliness. The Department of Health must punish the careless Asians and introduce them to the concept that health is the most precious thing in existence, and that the Emirates are not India." In Dubai, meanwhile, the municipal government is monitoring the situation. "Some 360 expatriates were deported by the Clinic and Medical Services section of Dubai Municipality after being detected with communicable diseases . . . like AIDS, Tuberculosis, Hepatitis B, and Leprosy."[23] Such intensified surveillance measures are justified by the UAE interior ministry in the name of keeping the country "clean of illegal immigrants."[24]

The Ruling Bargain as Spatial Representation

The type of space that is figured here is clean, both literally and figuratively, and hierarchically structured. It is a space characterized by hierarchy, hygiene, and intellectual order. It is a space, moreover, that is both technicalized, represented as an object of bureaucratic order, and pathologized, represented as an ailing body in need of the expert intervention of the state (symbolized with medical and hygienic metaphors).

Like abstract space/spatial representation in post-industrial Western Europe, on which the class struggle is inscribed, according to Lefebvre (see discussion in the Introduction), spatial representations in post-oil Dubai are symptomatic of social conflicts. They signify the ascendancy of the ruling bargain and its various entailments—the dependent notion of citizenship and the absolute otherness of certain classes of foreigner, for example. The spaces that migrants are seen to inhabit are taken to be reflections of a moral and aesthetic decay requiring state intervention. Since the rise of the reformist movements in the late 1920s, and especially during and after the nationalist period of the 1950s, the family-state has struggled to represent itself as legitimate expression of the popular will. A countervailing pressure has been the attempt to ensure the city-state's image both as being open to foreigners (specifically to a Western-based bourgeoisie) and as a free trade zone. This openness has been symbolized in the imagery and urbanism project of "New Dubai," the planning and construction of large gentrified enclaves in the 1990s and early 2000s. The symbolic project of linking the family-state to legitimate national aspirations has been advanced by representing the territory of the polity as homogenous and its boundaries as lacking in porosity in the contexts of migration and commodity mobility from South Asia and Iran. This has been represented by what might be called "spaces of the ruling bargain," spatial representations that reaffirm the ideology of the ruling bargain.

Discursively and ideologically, the project of clearing space for development is connected to the project of cleaning the polity of troublesome elements (recalcitrant workers, progressive tendencies, etc.) Improvised or illegitimate dwellings, shanties, and worker camps exist in a sort of interstitial space developed neither by the state nor by its allied merchants and landlords. In 2007, I visited the Sonapoor labor camp.[25] A large ramshackle complex housing many of Dubai's construction workers, the camp lies outside the main city limits (about a ten-minute drive from the eastern or Deira district), a part of the city to which no respectable European or local Arab person would venture. Perhaps aware of this, the workers have given the camp an unrespectable name. "Sonapoor is a very bad word," said my guide, adding that it is Malayalam (the language commonly spoken in the Indian state of Kerala) for "vagina." In fact, the camp's name, as an Indian colleague recently pointed out to me, is a Hindi term meaning "city of gold." Another colleague, an anthropologist whose specializes in Pakistan, informs me that for many Pakistanis and other South Asians preparing to emigrate to Dubai, the city can seem to be a "city of gold," a dreamscape where fortunes can be made instantly. My guide may therefore have been honestly mistaken in stating that the camp's name originated in the Malayalam for vagina. Or he may have been (perhaps inadvertently) expressing the distance between workers' expectations of Dubai work and the reality of that work.

We turned off the main, paved road at a group of squat buildings and drove along unpaved roads crowded with men in the uniforms of different construction companies, returning from or going to their shifts. Large buses emptied their human contents and were refilled. We passed a couple of camps. "That one is Al Habtour," said my guide, naming a major Dubai construction firm. "That one is Al Abbar," an even more prominent firm. Habtour and Abbar are both large companies, with uncooperative security personnel and stricter surveillance of workers. They are too dangerous to attempt entry. We turned off again and finally reached our destination. The guard was not even at the security kiosk. We proceeded into a walled compound, past communal toilets. There were six or seven bedrooms on either side of the compound, a communal kitchen, and a TV area with easy chairs and sofas.

The bedroom we entered, which had two single and two bunk beds, was about 40 square feet. It had its own kitchen and toilet, a relative luxury at labor camps, as well as a TV connected to a satellite dish and a stereo box. We were greeted heartily by an Arab migrant worker, who offered us tea. "This is a very good room, relative to other worker accommodations," both at this company and at others, says my guide. Usually, he added, a room like this houses twenty workers, but this one houses only four. The relative luxury of this camp is uncommon for worker camps in the UAE, our host told us. Others cram many more workers into each room. At a camp in Sharjah, says my guide, who has long experience working with and agitating for the rights of migrant workers, there was no electricity for months. The owners of the company had switched contracts on their workers, effectively firing them. One of the owners, a Canadian, fled the UAE. The workers attempted to get the labor ministry to help them get back their passports and the back pay owed to them, but the ministry was unresponsive. The workers were stranded at the camp, and were forced to sleep on the roofs of their dwellings to avoid the suffocating heat inside.

It is not uncommon to hear protests by workers about cramped conditions, where flats "fit for only a single family [are] packed with 14 to 16 workers" (Al Jandaly 2004b). Indeed, it is widely assumed by both Emiratis and expatriate elites that this is as it should be, that workers willingly come to Dubai, and so should not complain. It is erroneously assumed that migrants are making much more money in the UAE than they would at home and therefore should put up with imperfect working and living conditions. Although Davidson's recent study of Dubai is generally a valuable contribution to our knowledge of the city-state, the following passages (interestingly, the only time in his nearly 300-page book where he discusses migrant workers) are a good example of taking at face value the ruling bargain ideology.

> While it is certainly important that all workers are treated humanely and that the emirate conforms to international labour conditions, many of the new [International Labor Organization] conventions that the federal government rather hurriedly and perhaps unwisely agreed to in 2002 . . . have led to the creation of several informal and worryingly confrontational workers' associations that the police do not yet seem to know how to control. (2008, 186)

In the time before this more "confrontational" period (in which the UAE government forbade collective bargaining by workers),

> Labour conditions never felt particularly repressive given that most workers in Dubai are essentially opportunistic Indian and Pakistani expatriates. . . . While such foreigners may have

Figure 6. Dubai's Satwa neighborhood with the Sheikh Zayed Road skyline in the background. This working-class neighborhood is now undergoing urban renewal with many residents scheduled for eviction to make way for a luxury development. Photograph by Yasser Elsheshtawy.

Figure 7. The Emirates Towers, headquarters of Maktoum's Executive Council, in the background of a Satwa alley. Photograph by Yasser Elsheshtawy.

experienced poor working conditions in Dubai, their employment
was entirely voluntary, was normally for a short term of two or
three years, and was usually paying wages several times greater
than could be expected in South Asia (about $3,000 per annum).
(187)

The "new ILO-inspired relaxations," according to Davidson, are responsible for increased worker aggression and violence. Rather than representing worker strikes as part of a wider struggle for dignity, Davidson de-
scribes agitation by terms such as incitement, violence, and rampage (187.
See discussion in conclusion). A work stoppage in 2007, in which workers
went so far as stopping traffic for several hours, was "a remarkable development given that all of the workers were expatriates, and only a few years
earlier would have been swiftly deported and replaced by a more pliable
contingent" (188).

The ruling bargain ideology, I have been suggesting, is based on two
assumptions, that the role of the citizen is that of dependent and that control
of economic policy and welfare state distribution is handed over by the citizenry in exchange for a tacit agreement that only citizens can make claims
on the state's protection. It is striking that the language used to describe
work stoppages in contemporary Dubai—confrontation, threats to stability, etc.—is similar to how the nationalists were described in the British colonial archives of the 1950s. Instead of the "infiltration" of the emirate by
expatriate nationalist sympathizers, "imported ideologies, foreign newspapers, and in some cases even *agents provocateurs*" during the 1950s
(39–40), which could have "exposed" the fledgling polity "to external influences and an unstable Arab nationalist movement" (59), today we have
ILO-imposed *relaxations* leading to threats to stability. The character of
this stability is not questioned, nor the spatialization of outside/boundary-
external as a source of baleful foreign influence and the inside/boundary-
internal as autochthonous, hierarchical, and subordinate to the unitary sovereignty of the family-state. Davidson's implication is that any attempt,
whether by citizens or foreigners, to question the naturalness or stability of
a system based on dependent and exclusive ethnocratic citizenship is inauthentic, in bad faith, or ideological.

This outside-inside spatialization can be read in the example of urban renewal, especially of so-called shantytowns or informal worker settlements. Al Ain, a town in Abu Dhabi emirate, and Satwa in Dubai during the last fifteen years demonstrate the process of spatial representation

under the ruling bargain regime. Informants sometimes spoke, in vague, nearly hushed ways, about Satwa, but my search for detailed information on what exactly happened during its urban renewal was mostly in vain. All I could gather from the Emirati informant who was most specific about the case was that a large section of this neighborhood, where the inhabitants are mostly working class and unemployed members of the Indian, Baluchi, and Bidoun[26] communities, living mostly in cinderblock and corrugated metal shacks, was razed almost entirely to the ground sometime earlier this decade.[27] The case of Al Ain, a town in Abu Dhabi emirate, was reported in a more detailed way in Dubai, and gives us a clue about the process of urban renewal in the UAE.

> A shantytown (here) has finally been demolished after its inhabitants were evicted from their homes. The country's largest settlement of medieval-style shacks and huts which sprawled across hills near the eastern industrial area was bulldozed in the presence of several hundred police personnel. . . . [A new development project for which the site was earmarked] will include . . . a network of roads, telephone and other main supplies, open spaces, parking lots, and pavements to meet the needs of an expanding population. The colony there had evolved without planning or permission largely for Afghan, Indian, and Pakistani bachelor labourers. It became known for its bazaars which resembled typical Afghan tribal market places featuring hawkers, kiosks, fruit stalls and traditionally decorated spice shops, earning it the sobriquet "mini Afghanistan." (Kazmi)

This passage, reported without analysis or editorial remark in a state-sanctioned Dubai daily, is an aperture into the way the family-state sees space and population in the city-state. A boundary is presupposed to exist between the legitimate and the illegitimate, the protected and the unprotected, which the family-state by implication is represented as policing. The space represented here is marked teleologically—temporally ("medieval" as opposed to the new, clearly modern development to come), ethnically (a quaint, exotic, and like Abdullah Humaid's aforementioned covered market, an "Asian" space), and legally (developed without planning or permission). In order to justify new, better, modern development, the space must first be represented as lacking a claim to protection by the state, which is to say, represented as subject to the unmediated sovereignty of the state.[28]

Related to this are representations of the family-state as consistent and fair arbiter of legality and protection, representations of the family-state from which, in other words, history and politics have been excised. This can be seen in examples in which the family-state is called upon to play the role of protector of migrant workers. The case of several hundred workers being forced by their employer to live in cargo containers was a notorious event during the period of my fieldwork in 2003–4. In late May 2004, it was discovered that the management of the whimsically named Romeo Decoration Factory, in an attempt to save money on transporting workers to their worksite, was housing the workers in steel cargo containers on the worksite. The ways in which the state becomes juxtaposed to the employer in this case is interesting: "The workers, who did not want to be named for fear of losing their jobs, said there are 17 containers with eight workers in each," wrote the investigative reporter (Al Jandaly 2004a). "Lodging workers on site and that too in containers is against the law. But what is even worse is that some containers that measure 18 sq metres do not have air-conditioners. The toilets are dirty, (the workers said). . . . Bunk beds are also cheek by jowl and workers can barely manoeuvre in the containers." Photos accompanying the piece show, respectively, the exterior and the interior of the cargo containers. The exteriors are rusting, windowless metal cubes strung with workers' laundry. Random items such as rope, oil can, shoes, and a bicycle surround the containers. Inside, more laundry is strung up. Something that appears to be an improvised kitchen counter jostles cupboards, a water tank, bundles of more clothes, and other personal effects. (The worker camp and quarters I visited in 2007 were reminiscent of this.) The manager of the company, a certain Nader Nashid, is quoted defending this situation, "The containers are healthy, they have doors and windows. There is also an air-conditioning system. I am not offending the law." Nashid allegedly later presented a letter to the Dubai Municipality protesting its ruling against Romeo. It was signed, he claimed, by the workers themselves, who, again according to him, were satisfied with their living conditions. "The workers are crying because they don't want to leave the place," he is quoted as saying. Mohammad al Tawhidi, the director of the building and housing department of the Dubai Municipality, asked to comment on Romeo's housing situation, said that the company had better move the workers to Municipality-approved accommodations or suffer penalties.

It was at about this time that another incident involving a South Asian migrant worker caught the attention of residents of the city. In early May 2004 *Gulf News* reported the death of one Shina Boomna, an Indian construction worker.[29] One of a group of construction workers who, the newspaper reported, had not been paid for six months, Boomna allegedly could bear neither the shame of poverty nor its material deprivations. He was found hanging from a rope by Dubai police early on the morning of May 5. Boomna's ordeal inspired some residents to contemplate the lot of workers. There are many letters to the editor at this time, not all of them dealing specifically with the two incidents discussed here. These can be contextualized more broadly within an atmosphere of intensified state discourses about the condition of workers. It was at this time, for example, that the UAE federal government in Abu Dhabi was making a great show of official concern about workers (Nowais, Salama 2004). Some reader letters are nevertheless revealing of the ways in which these narratives of exploitation reaffirm the notion that the family-state is above the political and historical fray, that it is politically neutral and, contrary to the evidence (Davidson 2008, 151; Human Rights Watch 2006), actually interested in a consistent, systematic regime of labor safeguards.

> The Labour authorities should check the status of labourers at cleaning and security companies. How can someone work for 12–16 hours daily without rest? . . . Employers exploit their labourers. The Labour authorities should help the labourers, and make Dubai a better place for all.[30]

> I refer to the article highlighting the heat stroke problems faced by workers in the construction sector. There should be government guidelines regarding work hours during summer . . . which should be strictly enforced. . . . All the rules seem to favour employers. . . .

> The authorities should take corrective action and promote better employee–employer relations.[31] The authorities should take action to prevent heat-related diseases and suffering of labourers in summer months.[32]

Such illocutionary acts effectively remove the family-state from a historical and political context of specialized privileges for a foreign bourgeoisie and a ruling bargain with citizens based on the very exclusionary logic that these illocutions recommend the state dispense with. Further, such speech-acts represent the state as a neutral, blind arbiter of relations within the population. Ironically, it was a construction worker who I met at

Sonapoor who put it in a way most congenial to the state, "The government is good, but the companies are bastards." The ruling bargain as a product of history and struggle is thereby erased.

It is such erasures that have enabled the family-state to replace more substantive interpretations of modernity with its version, the ruling bargain ideology fused with a consumerist, market notion of Westernization. The latter has been implicit in the project of the Maktoum for a long time (Abdulla 1984), but there was perhaps never so spectacular an attempt to incarnate this vision at the level of the urban landscape than the frenzy for luxury urban enclaves, resorts, Disney-fication, and "starchitects" during the prefinancial crisis period between the mid-1990s and 2007–8. At the time of this writing, in late 2009, the city is a smoldering ruin of casino capitalism. The ambitious projects of starchitects such as Zaha Hadid and Rem Koolhaas, meant to announce Dubai's arrival as a world-class global city, have either been put on hold or canceled. No one is certain whether the bubble has finally cratered. One imagines that had the reformers and nationalists of the first half of the twentieth century lived long enough to witness the collapse of the "Dubai model," they might have felt a vindication (albeit a joyless one), a feeling that they might have been right all along. The politics and economics of dependency have been a poisoned chalice. The reform period, they might justifiably feel, was a great missed opportunity. But that is another story. Dubai's success, until recently, seemed to vindicate the family-state. The city was on the verge of becoming, so it seemed, a new utopia of aesthetic and architectural experimentation. It is to this heady period, and its implicit, unstated politics, that I now turn.

CHAPTER 2

"GOING SOUTH" WITH THE STARCHITECTS

Urbanist Ideology in the Emirati City

> Most companies start with a clean sheet of paper.
> Ours was a city.
>
> —advertisement for EMAAR

> Every place has its own identity, and we have to create . . .
> a beautiful identity for Ras al-Khaimah. Naturally,
> environmentally friendly.
>
> —Khater Masaad, assistant to the ruler of Ras al-Khaimah

Driving along Dubai's Sheikh Zayed Road near the World Trade Center interchange is an uncanny experience in architectural remembrance.[1] A wall of skyscrapers, one to each side of the highway, gives the passerby the claustrophobic impression of traveling through an interminable tunnel of mirrored glass. Writing for the *New Yorker,* Ian Parker put it perfectly and cuttingly: "The highway has become a wall across the city: a kind of round-the-clock mugging of Jane Jacobs" (131). Parker's comment reminds us that in spite of the critical tradition initiated by Jacobs, modern architecture has yet to bridge the gap between its progressive political self-image and its sometime collaboration, if more by virtue of its immanent logic than active commitment, with politically regressive forces. What Margaret Crawford observed twenty years ago about American architecture remains strikingly unchanged in the contemporary global south.

As individuals, most American architects sincerely assert that they are deeply concerned about issues of social and economic justice. Yet, over the past twenty years, as a profession they have steadily moved away from engagement with any social issues, even those that fall within their realm of professional competence. (27)

Parker's observation and the drive down Sheikh Zayed dredge up specific images from architecture's past, such as Le Corbusier's Contemporary City. With its walls of skyscrapers on either side of an immense thoroughfare, the Contemporary City bears an uncanny resemblance, if only for the duration of the flash of recognition, to its Dubai avatar. Jacobs and others (Holston 1989; Scott 1998) have correctly perceived the pernicious logic of modernism's myths of reason, the autonomy of aesthetics from politics, and the cult of the expert. In this chapter, my contention is that contemporary architecture, especially, although not exclusively, in its guise as so-called *starchitecture* sometimes manifests a retrogressive move away from the insights of the Jacobsian critical tradition. Specifically, it is by "going south" to the global south, that contemporary architecture recreates the myth of the autonomous architect, the aesthetic genius unencumbered by local context and history. In other words, by going south, architects escape politics, and they, in turn, help local elites do so as well.

By politics, I mean something more than the truism that the built environment and monuments play an important role in state and elite political agendas. The acts of architectural representation and the visualization of space are intrinsically political, and each connects to and advances specific politics of representation. Moreover, the process is dialectical—just as architectural representation influences and shapes the spatial and cultural politics of states and elites, so do the latter structure and shape architectural representation. The politics of architectural representation are obscured by the myth of the autonomy of the architect. This myth is central to the modern tradition, but in fact it is much older, originating in the second half of the fifteenth century. It arose in parallel with the secularization of Europe and the reinvention of building as "design," in which built space became, primarily, visualized space. This was a turning away from what Henri Lefebvre has called "monumental space" and towards "abstract space" (1991/1974). Space increasingly became an object to be visualized and abstracted from its more complex, multi-layered, and symbolically imbricated social texture (to, again, adapt Lefebvre). Vision arose over and above embodiment (Frampton 1991; 1998; Lefebvre 1991/1974). For Kenneth Frampton, this was a sort of insidious forgetting of the tactile "capacity of the body to read the environment in terms other than those of sight alone" (1998, 31).[2] In other words, the rise of visualized space was an effect of the ascendancy of the *artes liberales* over the *artes mechanicae,* of the architect over the master craftsman, in late fifteenth-century Europe (1991, 17–18). As Frampton puts it, these developments resulted in the emergence of a discourse on architectural design as "a specifically modern, innovative, nontraditional procedure," carrying an assumption that the architect is a member of a specialized guild or even class of individuals outside and above the sphere of the everyday and of mere "building," whose mission is purely the elaboration of aesthetic form (17).

Since the 1970s, this has been reinterpreted in such a way as to result in the equation of architecture with fine art, a "revival of drawn representation" through which architects have sought to enter the art market (21). This is often called architectural "postmodernism," and its origins lie not only in the deep history and immanent logic of the *artes liberales,* but also in the specific conjunctures of the post-1970s period. Innovations in structural engineering enabled builders to put up edifices largely without input from architects, in turn increasingly confining the latter to competition over façade design and silhouettes (McNeill, 23). The 1980s witnessed the apotheosis of laissez-faire ideology in Reaganomics and with it the endorsement of conspicuous consumption, showiness, and display, all parts of a postmodern cultural dominant (to adapt a phrase from Jameson 1991) that trickled down to architectural practice (McNeill, 23). Architecture became reduced to architectural representation, architectural projects to monumental sculptures (Frampton 1991, 21). With this came a type of architectural critique that fixated on the formal and conceived of architecture as detached and ironical, a "silent witness to all the weaknesses, indulgences, and self-absorption characteristic of modern culture" (Ghirardo, 9). As Diane Ghirardo has put it, "as disengaged voyeur, architecture first and foremost came to be understood as an exercise in meaning, meaning that issued from the architect and emerged in the architecture, for example, in the form of witty comment upon earlier conventions" (9–10). The question of "what is built for whom?" is ignored or consigned to secondary status (15). This is the question that I will put to starchitecture and Emirati urbanism in this chapter.[3]

By noting the ways that the representations deployed by architects and other urban experts—*urbanists,* in Lefebvre's terminology—are applied to specific sociocultural and political contexts in the global south, we notice an intriguing set of shifts. Something interesting seems to occur when predominantly Western-trained architects and experts traverse the space between cultural worlds with which they are familiar and ones with which they are not. Their self-styled radical or reformist aesthetic aims suddenly begin servicing the not-entirely progressive aims of local elites. Claims about sensitivity to local cultural and ecological worlds somehow become appended to Orientalist stereotypes. A narrow focus on architecture as the exclusive concern with experimentation in aesthetic form becomes a means of collaborating in the erasure of local histories and the reaffirmation of the claims local elites make on the politics, histories, and spaces they already dominate.

Starchitecture

Along with China, the contemporary Arabian Gulf is undergoing an urbanization of massive proportions. Possessing a disproportionate share of the world's proven oil reserves, the six countries of the Gulf Cooperation Council were devoting hundreds of billions to trillions of dollars to construction projects before the financial crisis of 2008, which did indeed slow construction, especially in Dubai, the economy most affected by the crisis (Brown 2008).[4] Like China, architects view the Gulf, whose member states are run by tiny elites disposing of immense wealth and have nearly nonexistent labor and environmental regulations, as a liberating place in which to work. No Gulf country has been as aggressive in advancing top-down, large-scale, institutional urbanism (Lefebvre 2003, 79) as the United Arab Emirates (UAE). The rhetoric of government officials, architects, and the media, what Lefebvre has called *urbanists* (2003, 156–60), employs various discourses of progress and architectural radicalism to justify such projects.

Following places such as Riyadh, Jeddah, and Kuwait, which pioneered the practice of using big name architects in the Gulf, individual emirates of the UAE, especially the wealthiest two, Abu Dhabi and Dubai, have recently tapped so-called starchitects in a large project of urban entrepreneurialism (Broudehoux).[5] The list of the famous firms that were "rushing" (Brown 2008) to participate in the UAE's architectural "Xanadu" (Fattah 2007) was a who's who of global north starchitecture: Tadao Ando, Norman Foster, Frank Gehry, Zaha Hadid, Rem Koolhaas/OMA, Jean Nouvel, Skidmore Owings Merrill (already a veteran on the UAE scene), Snøhetta, and many lesser names. Looked at in the wake of the 2008 economic meltdown, in which many brand-name projects, such as Hadid's Dubai opera house and Koolhaas's Dubai Waterfront City, have either been cancelled or put on hold, this rush seems only to have been a brief flash of collaboration between the Emirati and global urban worlds. Serious scholarly observers have dismissed the Emirati use of starchitecture as superficial and merely profit-driven.[6] I agree with this, but regardless of its motives or "depth," the politics of starchitectural representation during this brief, precrisis moment remain of significant interest to the study of cultural politics in rapidly developing, globalizing cities. Moreover, such representational politics take on new meaning in an Emirati, and especially Dubai, context in which the main players in urban development are the family-states with their history of antireformism (see chapter 1).

The case of the master-planned Dubai Waterfront City (now on hold because of the economic downturn) is symptomatic of starchitecture specifically, and urbanist ideology more generally. Commissioned in 2007 by Nakheel and designed by the ubiquitous genius of contemporary global urbanism, Rem Koolhaas and his Rotterdam-based Office for Metropolitan Architecture (OMA), the project in its rectilinear plan is conceived as a 6.5 square-mile artificial island off Dubai's coast and is expected to be home to approximately 1.5 million people (Dilworth). The project is symptomatic of urbanism in the UAE and, perhaps, global south urbanism, in three ways. First, one notices a great deal of "culture talk" associated with it (see introduction). Referring to Al Soor, one of the Waterfront City's neighborhoods, OMA's website says that the project employs,

> The vernacular qualities of historic Arab settlements: an intriciate (sic) and varied composition of shaded buildings and alleyways where privacy is embedded and public interaction inevitable. The name Al Soor, meaning The Wall, refers to a large inhabited wall on the western tip of the site, jutting out into the Gulf. The dense building clusters, irregular streets, and pedestrian paths connect a patchwork of delights in this town, all of them walkable: beachfront resorts, souks, canalsides and waterfront promenades . . . and, across the water directly opposite, Waterfront City's second elemental geometric icon, the Spiral. This is an 82-storey coiling tower evoking classical Arabic architecture and serving as a beacon for the entire development.[7]

Second, there is talk of sustainability. The tall, densely spaced buildings, it is claimed, will create shade to reduce the need for air conditioning and encourage people to walk instead of drive, and it will connect with the city's monorail system (Dilworth).

Finally, the project supposedly reflects the architect's radical politics. Observers have, for example, connected the project to Koolhaas's "Generic Cities" theory (Koolhaas 1978), in which cities consist of repetitive buildings centered on an airport housing "a tribe of global nomads with few local loyalties." Generic cities supposedly critique late capitalism by "find(ing) optimism in the inevitable" condition of commodification (Ouroussof).

Renzo Piano and Richard Roger's Centre Pompidou arguably initiated the era of starchitects in the mid-1970s, establishing a prototype for urban development in the context of the emerging neoliberal consensus of the times. The Centre Pompidou showed how cities could recruit foreign architects to spearhead projects of urban renewal centered on spectacular spaces of consumption (McNeill; Zukin). According to Sharon Zukin, clients also saw this patronage of foreign talent as a way to display their sophistication and flare for the innovative. Since then, the starchitect has become a species of architect whose mere name is so enveloped in the mystique of genius that urban elites the world over now consider the commissioning of a building by a brand-name architect to be a municipal priority, regardless of the aesthetic or design quality of the project, its expense, or the demands it makes on local resources.

The rise of the starchitect as a global player indicates a quantitative if not (arguably) qualitative change in the urbanism of the last quarter century. Downtowns have become transformed from contexts primarily for functional centrality to centers of symbolic capital.[8] With the development both of information and design technologies, it has become possible to design increasingly radical and flamboyant (or "iconic") buildings and to disseminate images of this photogenic architecture instantaneously on a global scale. Images of downtowns replete with aesthetically fanciful buildings, instantly consumable for their vividness and superficiality, are now standard implements in the advertising toolkit both of established major urban centers and, like Dubai, cities attempting to establish a cutting-edge reputation for themselves. (How this fixation on the iconic will change in the post-crisis context is yet to be seen.) Starchitecture, which privileges the role of the architect as aesthete and genius of pure form and which elevates a few notable architects, investing them with almost superhuman powers of theoretical and aesthetic insight, is well suited to the demands of cities on the make. This is especially true in societies with little popular participation in the political sphere.

The invocation of dialectical theory ("finding optimism in the inevitable") in connection to the supposed radicalism of Koolhaas's architecture is intriguing. Arguments in dialectical theory about the mobilization of the materials of everyday mass culture for projects of radical critique are not new (Adorno 2005; Bloch; Jameson 1974; 2007; Lefebvre 1991/1947). Koolhaas's architecture is a *soi-disant* variant of "immanent critique," an architecture that, some have argued, makes visible the limitations of late capitalism by exposing its logic from within (Jameson 2003). But some questions remain, including these:

- In what specific ways are such projects radical?
- How do they relate to elite power and elitist agendas for urban spatial production?
- Can such elite projects be reconciled with architectural and urbanist discourses of progress?
- Do they critique prevailing clichés and stereotypes about urbanism in the local contexts in which they are commissioned, or do they reaffirm such stereotypes?
- Is starchitecture sensitive to the ways it excludes and includes, or is its approach to this issue simply a return to politically naive truisms about the autonomy of the architect?

Urban expertise, such as starchitecture, (what Lefebvre calls, with deceptive simplicity, "urbanism") is both a political and an imaginative process (2003). The production of space is a social process involving the confrontation and negotiation of various practices (architectural, institutional, and quotidian) that is determinate, embedded in concrete relations of power. Urbanism is thus an ideology and a set of discourses consisting of representations deployed in specific projects of the imagination of the urban. While the bulk of my analytical attention will seem to focus on starchitects, primarily because this group presents the most complex and contradictory case of urbanism in the UAE, I should emphasize that the term urbanism has a much wider application in my critique. Not only architects and planners, but technocrats, bureaucrats, and intellectuals more generally are involved in urbanism. I therefore follow Lefebvre in applying the terms "urbanism" and "urbanist" specifically to the intersection between local elites (the family-state and allied landlords, development firms, and various official and quasi-official technocrats and intelligentsia who share the family-state's and developers' spatial ideology) and transnational actors such as journalists, academics, and, not least, architects who work in the UAE. All of these might be called, after Gramsci, traditional intellectuals, manipulators, and disseminators of hegemonic representations, in this case of urban space. I have chosen to broaden the geographical context from Dubai to the wider UAE because urbanist projects in the latter can better contextualize those in the former. Obviously, each emirate of the UAE will have certain peculiarities. But urbanist projects and ideology across the UAE share enough similarities to make situating Dubai in its national context worthwhile.

Selective, ideological notions of history and culture are particularly visible, and the recourse to clichés particularly salient, in the case of starchitects "going south." For example, a sympathetic reviewer of Koolhaas's Waterfront City proposal notes that "the plan's geometric grid gives way to an intimate warren of alleyways, like a traditional souk" (Ouroussof), a cultural justification for the project also, adopted by OMA itself. As I show in this chapter, urbanists almost automatically reach for such cultural stereotypes when writing about or theorizing spaces in non-Western societies.

An effect of this dependence by architects and other urbanists on cultural and historical clichés is the erasure both of their own power and that of the local elites with whom they collaborate on urban projects. Unaware of its social and political determinations, urbanism reproduces some of the more elitist traditions in architectural history. Starchitecture, as mentioned, reduces architecture to pure aesthetic experimentation, in turn cloaking itself in the rhetoric of radicalism while unwittingly playing handmaiden to local hierarchies of power. This is ironic for two reasons. First, compared to less brand-name practitioners, starchitects are less dependent on client patronage and are therefore more autonomous than their more pedestrian colleagues. They therefore have more agency over which projects to take on and are less dependent on satisfying clients' desiderata. Zaha Hadid puts it this way:

> The avant-garde segment has quite a bit more space to maneuver than the mainstream commercial segment. This is because our work is considered to be a kind of multiplier. Economically our buildings operate as investments into a marketing agenda—city branding for instance. . . . [Our projects] are paid for by funds that have been extracted from the cycle of profit-driven investment . . . as designers we can enjoy and utilize the relative distance from concerns of immediate profitability to further our experimental agenda. (McNeill, 18–19)

The second irony is that prominent firms, whether led by starchitects or not, are increasingly interested in issues of local and cultural sensitivity.

Such firms, according to Donald McNeill, are, like law firms, "strong service" providers, whose services include both international expertise and "local knowledge and cultural sensitivity" (13). McNeill adds that cultural understanding is central to networking and bonding between firms and non-Western clients (39). Two assumptions are operative in Hadid's and McNeill's comments. First, that avant-garde design is inextricably connected to investment and city marketing (as Hadid implies), and second, that cultural understanding is a matter of transnational marketing, with the attendant bodily, linguistic, and spatial practices that help architects "bond" with local contacts (as McNeill suggests). Some critical anthropological questions should be raised at this juncture:

- Whose "culture" and what representations of it are being referred to here, and how are they deployed in the complex interplay between architects and other urbanists, such as clients, states, and state bureaucracies?
- How are these representations of culture shaped by the market-driven logic of urban entrepreneurialism and articulations between local elites and global urbanists?

While the rhetoric of starchitecture increasingly highlights cultural and local sensitivity, in practice it has tended instead to resort to cultural stereotypes and an almost total erasure of local power relations. Another irony, more specific to the UAE context, is that starchitecture does not overcome local urbanist discourses polarized between romantic notions of authenticity and local culture, on the one hand, and modernity, on the other; rather, starchitecture intensifies this polarity.

Urban Entrepreneurialism:
Global and Local Urbanists Meet

Although architects and clients in the UAE frame projects within discourses of cultural sensitivity, ecological awareness, and aesthetic and political progressivism, such discourses tend to be ex post facto justifications of a specific politics of space. The intersection between global architecture and local power produces depoliticized stereotypes both of architectural history and of local history.

Anne-Marie Broudehoux argues that recent urbanization in China is dominated by "urban entrepreneurialism." Her insights can also be applied, with minor modifications, to the UAE. Broudehoux notes the manipulation of the landscape to transform it into a "cultural resource that can be capitalized upon and repackaged for new rounds of capital accumulation and consumption" (383). Moreover, "designer buildings have become essential tools of city marketing. Motivated by what could be called the Bilbao effect,[9] cities around the world have embarked on a competition for global preeminence by building the tallest, most daring, and most technologically advanced buildings" (384–85). Broudehoux discusses the less well-publicized facts—from private-land confiscations by the state to forced internal emigration to public revenue losses—that are the social costs of urban entrepreneurialism. She also points out that this phenomenon has similar results independent of the formal political system in which it takes place (albeit taking an extreme form in China).

The urbanist production of depoliticized space and ahistorical culture precedes the arrival of starchitects in the UAE and is today a wider reality, although starchitects and their signature projects have a unique power to give such spatial representations an authoritative imprimatur. An early example of global-local urbanist interconnection from Dubai shows well the uses of historical and cultural stereotyping. In 1960, the then ruler of Dubai, Rashid Al Maktoum, commissioned a master plan for the city by British architect John Harris. A 1971 archival document I was able to access at a Dubai library in 2004, a modification of the 1960 plan, reveals cultural-representational and spatial logics that anticipate those of the more recent strachitects (Harris).[10] The document is, of course, a description of and a prescription for Dubai urban development. Less obvious, however, is the fact that it is more than a simple technical exercise. Rather, it makes unwitting assumptions about Dubai culture and history that resonate with more recent starchitectural and urbanist representations.

The 1971 modified plan begins with a history of Dubai—how the town was founded as a settlement by an offshoot of the Bani Yas tribe (the rulers of Abu Dhabi), how it became a haven for merchants in the Gulf, how liberal and visionary the rulers were, and so on (4–6).[11] To the reader unfamiliar with local history, it is a very bloodless, somewhat optimistic account of elite ingenuity and good policies through the ages. Those familiar with local history will recognize the foundation myth of the Al Maktoum embedded within this historical account. For example, there is a frequent conflation between the ruler and "Dubai," which comes to be represented as an extension of the ruler's will and agency. British imperialism is euphemized as "the British presence" and as a consensual relationship between Dubai and Britain (6, see chapter 1). The local political system Harris calls "traditional Arab desert democracy" (8). This "grants the leader ultimate authority. . . . His Highness the Ruler directs and controls all development personally with the help of informal committees and representatives of all the interests concerned in each project" (8).

This is quite similar to the tendencies of the starchitects more recently commissioned by Rashid's son and successor Muhammad. The analogy is not perfect, however. According to Yasser Elsheshtawy, who has looked more closely at the relationship between Harris and Rashid Al Maktoum, Harris was a modest and competent practitioner, not a preening "theorist" or self-styled "genius."[12] That Harris was far from a brand name architect was intentional. Rashid had someone like him in mind because in the 1960s the Dubai ruler could only afford to hire a relatively unknown architect. Moreover, according to Elsheshtawy, and unlike elsewhere in the Gulf, Rashid and Harris did not want to raze the old town and replace it with a modernist grid. Rashid and Harris wanted instead to integrate the old city with the new infrastructures and developments envisioned for the 1970s and thereafter. (One should, as well, avoid the temptation to homogenize the family-state. Rashid's vision and intentions for Dubai, while perhaps broadly similar to those of his successor Muhammad, were far more aesthetically modest than those of his son. Rashid was more concerned with modern infrastructures, Muhammad with global imagery and urban entrepreneurialism.) Harris, for his part, seems to have been genuinely sympathetic to local people, to local architectural vernaculars, and to Dubai's urban traditions. He was also serious about reconciling urban planning with local lived realities. The Dubai of the 1970s, according to Dubayyans to whom I spoke, had successfully integrated the old urban center with the new modern plan, a testament to Harris's ability.

Nevertheless, we must distinguish the intentions of the author of cultural and spatial representations from the structural forces that constitute the possibility of those representations. There is in the modified plan of 1971 a tendency to assume the naturalness and wisdom of the absolute monarchy, to neatly divide the *traditional* from the *modern* as well as a related affirmation of the trajectory undertaken by the family-state, and to culturalize the traditional as intrinsically linked to an almost autochthonous local society. The effect is (inadvertently and without any malicious intent toward local people) to affirm one interpretation of local history and culture—the ruling family narrative—as the authentic narrative. In this alignment between apolitical expertise and the family-state, there is a strong resonance between the unassuming Harris and the more recent starchitects.

An example of the latter, and a more overtly ruling-regime friendly case, comes from Eirin Gjørv, the director of the PBS film *The Sand Castle,* which aired in 2007. (In the interest of full disclosure, I was interviewed by the film's producers for contextual background and one of my articles is listed as a resource on the film's website.)[13] Though excellent in many ways, the film, which is about an architectural competition to build a city from scratch in the emirate Ras al-Khaimah, also exhibits the flaws of contemporary urbanism, specifically, the lack of serious interest by urbanists in the ways that power articulates with cultural representation. In the filmmaker's notes section of the website, Gjørv remarks on "the Sheikh's (i.e., the ruler of Ras al-Khaimah's) openness" to the presence of the film crew and the film's subjects, who are architects from the Oslo firm Snøhetta (*Wide Angle*). Gjørv's account of her experience strongly echoes Harris's from over a quarter century before, emphasizing the ruler's liberalism and entrepreneurialism and euphemizing the global architect–local elite relationship as a meeting of like spirits.

> We had the exclusive opportunity to follow some of the most outstanding architects of our time as they work[ed] with the progressive and powerful men of Ras al-Khaimah, working to create change at a speed we rarely have seen before. Though the main characters in the film have very different cultural backgrounds, they all share a creative desire that builds bridges despite cultural differences. This joint creativity made it possible for our small film team to get close to the characters throughout the year as we documented a process that reflects the entrepreneurship found in this Middle Eastern corner of the world. (Gjørv)[14]

Other recent intersections between architects and local elites have led to a (perhaps retrograde) redefinition of architecture as well. In the UAE the starchitect enacts some of the least egalitarian traditions from the history of modern architecture. The iconic and monumental quality of buildings demanded by urban entrepreneurs has often been noted (Broudehoux; Parker 2005). This is usually interpreted (correctly) as part of the capitalist transformation of urban space into commodified space. There are, however, reasons for iconicism and monumentalism that have more to do with the history of architecture and the formation of architects as self-styled artists exclusively concerned with aesthetic form than they do with capitalism per se. In a scathing critique of high modernism, Lewis Mumford referred to Le Corbusier's urban plans of the 1920s and 1930s (the so-called Contemporary and Radiant cities) as "pathological," exhibiting a Victorian obsession with bigness, a Napoleonic dream of centralization, and a Baroque insensitivity to time and functional flexibility (Fishman, 258–59).

Buildings, in this view, must manifest "authority" (237). They are the expression both of the architect's and of the state's genius (Scott 1998, 56). They represent a "geometric order [that is] most evident, not at street level, but rather from above and from outside, . . . in short, a God's-eye view, or the view of an absolute ruler" (57). Frank Gehry described the Saadiyat Island project, a large arts and museums enclave in Abu Dhabi (for which he is designing Abu Dhabi's branch of the Guggenheim Museum), in the following way, "It's like a clean slate in a country full of resources. . . . It's an opportunity for the world of art and culture that is not available anywhere else because you're building a desert enclave without the contextual constraints of a city" (Fattah 2007).[15] When Gehry talks about a "clean slate," he cannot mean this in the literal sense, because there is at least one source of constraint, the client. For example, when the Norwegian architecture firm Snøhetta proposed a convention center design to their client, the ruler of the emirate of Ras al-Khaimah, it was rejected because it was not iconic enough. As the assistant to the ruler put it as he literally sent the Snøhetta team back to the drawing board,

> In the end, you know, if you see history, the people who built the places, big places, what they have built, all these crazy kings, . . . if we take Ludwig, he built this Neuschwanstein in Germany. It is a crazy place, but today everybody is visiting it. . . . Versailles, everybody is visiting it; Tour Eiffel, everybody . . . it is a grandiose, something which impresses people. I think you can create more than this; . . . this is a costly structure, with the same cost, you can make something much more grandiose. (*Wide Angle* Transcript, 12)

The Production of Space as a Clean Slate

> When we started there was nothing but sand, birds, and sky. Today, lakes have replaced the sand. Tall towers reach out to the stars. Golfers sink birdies on world-class golf courses. . . . We

were the first to see the dream of Dubai as a modern, world-class city. And we were the first to see it through. We're changing Dubai's future.[16]

When Gehry and other urbanists mention the "clean slate," they are referring to the wider social world in which architect and client operate. It is a space evacuated of history (as human struggle) and culture (as richly-textured everyday practice). Such space in turn becomes the arena for the unlimited creativity of the architect-genius. Henri Lefebvre argues that the elitist collaboration between state, market, and architect is a major obstacle to the breakthrough to the urban revolution, in which space is liberated from "the imperialism of know-how" (2003, 59). Class urbanism creates inertspace, space as nothing more than a container for objects, be they animate or inanimate, and for fetishized "needs." The city, in this view, becomes "a simple spatial effect of a creative act that occurred elsewhere, in the Mind, or the Intellect" (28). Most disturbingly, "ever since its origins, the State expressed itself through the void: empty space, broad avenues, plazas of gigantic proportions open to spectacular processions" (109). Lefebvre's insights from over forty years ago are surprisingly perspicacious even today in the context of urban entrepreneurialism in the global south.

The case of Dubai is instructive. Like Los Angeles, it is developing into an extreme version of the polycentric city. Since the early 1970s, when it had a definite center around a natural inlet, the *Khor Dubai* (Dubai Creek), the city has exploded into its present form. Dubai's post-1990s sprawl into its surrounding hinterland, the area often called New Dubai, has been characterized by disconnected enclaves with their own amenities, security details, and infrastructures. The further from the traditional town center one goes, the more this is the case. Iconic architecture is not, moreover, always intended to announce Dubai as a world city but to signify the family-state's or the landlord's power, vision, and so on. Another aspect of Dubai urbanization is that land is not at a premium. Instead of, for example, clearing out entire neighborhoods for urban renewal, the city simply expands outward into the undeveloped terrain on what is, for the given moment, the existing city's hinterland, creating new poles for urbanization. This situation gives the impression that urbanism is simply about the unconstrained willing into being of new buildings and enclaves. In reality, a specific kind of city is created, in which space becomes increasingly fragmented, subject to privatized instrumentalities of control, and mobility without the use of superhighways becomes impossible. Therefore, Dubai sprawl is not a simple product of technical requirements, nor is its land-scape a canvas for politically innocent aesthetic experimentation. Sprawl enables and consolidates the political power of landlords and the class power of wealthier city residents. This reality is not reflected in starchitec-tural and urbanist discourse.

According to the conventional narrative, over the course of his ca-reer Rem Koolhaas has at most been permitted only to observe cities that seemed to demonstrate his theory of the Generic City. For a brief moment before the financial crisis, it seemed that he would finally "get a chance to create his own version," as one fawning reviewer wrote of his Waterfront City (Ouroussof). The reviewer continues: "Mr. Koolhaas's design proves once again that he is one of the few architects willing to face the crisis of the contemporary city—from its growing superficiality to its deadening sterility—without flinching." In this narrative, only Koolhaas and his aes-thetic quest are relevant. The local context where he intends to apply this vision—Dubai as a real, concrete city—is replaced by the cliché "the con-temporary city" and endowed with abstract qualities, "deadening sterility," and "superficiality." (Sterile to whom and superficial by whose standards?) The willful obliviousness of the architect, whose only experience of "the city" is managed by a local urbanist elite, is valorized as "unflinching" and courageous. The architect sacrifices himself and jumps into the void to res-cue this "pathological space" (Lefebvre 2003, 157).

This conventional understanding of the architect is shared by other starchitects. For example, Patrik Schumacher of Zaha Hadid Architects de-scribes the UAE in this way, "We are trying things out for the first time which we wanted to try out, but couldn't. . . . We have found an unusual de-gree of receptiveness to new ideas in the Gulf" (Brown 2008). For Schum-acher, "the Gulf provides a research and development lab for the archi-tectural industry." PBS's *The Sand Castle* describes the Ras al-Khaimah competition between Snøhetta and Koolhaas's OMA as a race to "invent a city on the sand dunes" of the UAE (*Wide Angle*). "The coolest thing about building in the desert," says Snøhetta's Kjetil Thorsen in one of the film's opening scenes, "is the desert!" The scene cuts to a meeting at the firm's Oslo office, in which Thorsen dumps a mound of sand on the table, presses a ruler into the mound, and says: "This is a section of the site. . . . This is the hillside. This is the water. And take something like this [the ruler]. And just make an imprint into that landscape. And that's the city" (*Wide Angle* Transcript, 1).

Once the clean slate is produced, a set of needs can be created. These needs, in turn, become identified with the so-called authentic local culture.

The former dean of the College of Architecture, Art, and Design at the American University of Sharjah, UAE, one of the Gulf region's top architecture schools, claims that "the experience of the vacuum, of the void" was central to the culture of "the Bedouin" (BBC Radio 3). He goes on to assert that contemporary UAE architecture is the Emirati culture's attempt to lift itself out of the void, to create a sense of permanence. Emiratis do this by emphasizing the colorful, extraordinary, and decorative in architecture, he argues. One of his colleagues agrees, suggesting that since the mid-1990s, Emiratis have looked to architecture to define their identity (BBC Radio 3).[17]

The Discourse of Sustainability: Power in a Shade of Green

Identity, conceptualized as a bounded culture's need for social cohesion, becomes reified, deployed as justification for urban entrepreneurialism and the politics of space in the contemporary UAE. One good example of the ways in which reifying spatial and cultural representations promote elite interests is the discourse of sustainability in the UAE.

Over the past five to ten years, the notion of sustainability has emerged as a priority for UAE urbanists. This is ostensibly a salutary development. The UAE is one of the world's largest per capita consumers of fossil fuels and emitters of greenhouse gases. "If the world lived like each individual in the UAE, we would need 5.5 planets" (AME Info 2005). Abu Dhabi, the federation's largest emirate, is the world's top emitter of greenhouse gases, per capita (Vidal). Moreover, UAE urbanists have recently referred not only to issues of ecological impact, but to economic viability and social equitability as goals which, they argue, their projects, not least, starchitectural brand-name projects, will help them achieve.

Urbanists in the UAE are beginning to make noises about each kind of sustainability—ecological, economic, and social. A 2007 workshop at Harvard's Center for Middle Eastern Studies, which I attended, was devoted to the theme of sustainability in the Gulf (CMES).[18] The workshop's organizer, a prominent Boston architect with a great deal of experience in the Gulf, declared in his opening remarks that in the context of rapid development, it is a moral, professional, and aesthetic quest to formulate a program of sustainable architecture. Among those in attendance were leading American and British specialists in sustainable architecture and two representatives (non-Emirati Arab expatriates) of a large Abu Dhabi–based real estate developer, Sorouh. What struck me about the discussion over the workshop's two days was the abstract, technical framing of problems of sustainability, and the conflation of orientalist or other ethnocentric stereotypes with locally situated problems of environmental impact that the UAE seemed to present. While expressing concern (doubtless sincere) for the sustainability of UAE architecture and urban development, many of the assembled experts almost automatically resorted to stereotypes about culture, politics, and economy to frame their urbanist programs.

Contrary to the technocratic, abstract myth of architecture fashioned by high modernists (Fishman, 238), "culture" is at the center of urbanist discourse on the UAE. The aforementioned workshop organizer attempted early in the proceedings to distance himself from Miesian modernism, which, he maintained, eliminates culture, considering it to endanger the purity of form. Culture, he went on, should be thought of as a passage from childhood to youth to maturity to old age. "Youth is the search for identity"; the UAE is a culture still in its "youth." The mission of architects is therefore to provide this youthful culture with its identity. "We are dealing with societies (those of the Gulf) that need iconography." He then proceeded to a slideshow of a recent project in Qatar, a 70-story building called "the Intelligent Tower." The tower, he argued, has a cultural inspiration, referencing the garden of traditional Arab houses (the tower has roof gardens that, he maintained, symbolize "traditional" house gardens).[19] The building is also an iconic structure, modeled on the cypress tree or *sār*, which is "a cultural symbol." It is self-fertilizing, incorporating the male and the female, as well as personal freedom and longevity or eternity, values that the architect sees as rooted in Gulf culture.

I deal with orientalism and culturalism in more detail in the next section. For the moment, I would like to focus on how UAE urbanism, in the guise of expertise on sustainability, erases local specificity and implicitly legitimizes the elite production of space. Like the Harris plan modification of 1971, with its uncritical uses of "Arab democracy" and conflation of the Al Maktoum foundation myth with the history of Dubai, the participants at the Harvard workshop generally conflated elite narratives of space and locality with local space and culture per se.

In the ideological and discursive work of sustainability, the development of large leisure and retail enclaves does multiple duties, allegedly contributing to economic, ecological, and sociocultural adaptation. Architects and real estate developers working in the UAE often make the argument that such enclaves, and most notably their "themed" or iconic architecture, are a rational, long-term adaptation to the economic demands of globalization. As one architecture professor at the American University of Sharjah argues in a paper on Dubai as a "global city," urban entrepreneurialism is what globalization is "all about" (Mustafa). At the 2007 Harvard workshop, the two representatives of the Abu Dhabi real estate developer Sorouh made a similar case for their enclaves. These were necessary for Abu Dhabi to join the global economy; developing such enclaves was a matter of urgency because the emirate was already behind. Abu Dhabi suffered 30 years of stigma "that they never developed anything." The political leadership is committed to moving forward, they said. Primary among Sorouh's desiderata are sustainable buildings and planning, they claimed. However, "with all this pressure to deliver, something has to give, and yes, sometimes we have to compromise." Interestingly, as an aside, one of the presenters added, "We only follow what (Western consultants) tell us." The implication was clearly that any deviation from the developers' sustainable ideal was the result of outsiders' extra-ecological (i.e., monetary) influence. Thus, the implication, often repeated by local UAE urbanists, is that the ruler, the landlord, or the real estate developer is agentive when the narrative is positive (Arab democracy, liberal policies, the UAE's visionary urbanists) and that they are passive when projects manifest flaws.

In spite of narrow-minded Western consultants, UAE developers are creating sustainable urbanism, according to the Sorouh public relations men. They gave the example of Nakheel, the Dubai developer that is owned by the ruler Muhammad Al Maktoum (and for which one of the Sorouh men had previously worked). Nakheel (famous for their brash iconicism, exemplified by projects such as the World, an archipelago of artificial islands mimicking the world map) "caters to a wide spectrum of society," by which the Sorouh man meant, simply, many nationalities. His implication was that this catering to diverse nationalities is somehow equivalent to "sustainability." Other Nakheel projects, such as the Ibn Battuta mall, a giant amusement park and shopping mall whose theme is based on the famous Arab traveler's journey from North Africa to China, blends cultural and heritage elements, thereby allegedly contributing to "cultural sustainability." In doing so, the Sorouh men argued, it also provides a valuable educational service. (This is a common theme of Nakheel's public relations; see chapter 3.)

"Sustainability" has recently become a theme shared by UAE urbanists and starchitects. Political, along with the aforementioned ecological, cultural, and economic, notions of sustainability are prominent here. As a member of the management consortium for Gehry's Guggenheim Abu Dhabi put it (echoing the Sorouh public relations men that Abu Dhabi is "moving forward"), the emirate's rulers are "very conscious here that [the arts and culture enclave at Saadiyat Island] can change the cultural climate in the region. . . . To be able to add high culture at the high end of international culture, this [is]a tremendous change" (Fattah 2007). Meanwhile, press materials for Norman Foster's Masdar ("the Source") project in Abu Dhabi, "the world's first sustainable city," list "equity," "fair trade," and "fair wages for all workers who are employed to build the city" among the priorities of the developers (Vidal).[20]

If the social reality of labor practices in the UAE is considered, the point about equity and fair wages is particularly difficult to take seriously. The 2006 Human Rights Watch (HRW) report on the UAE construction sector is a scathing critique of labor exploitation in the UAE construction sector, which is composed exclusively of foreign workers (see chapter 1). As I argued in the previous chapter, the abuses detailed in the report are systematic and structural, directly connected to the Dubai state's ruling bargain with local corporations and tacit protection agreements with foreign private interests. Not coincidentally, starchitects depend on these laborers to make their projects realizable within accelerated timeframes and at immense scale. These workers constitute the real social basis for the so-called industry laboratory celebrated by starchitects such as Schumacher. Among other things, the report, entitled "Building Towers, Cheating Workers," details widespread corruption among labor recruiters and employers, and practices such as expropriation of workers' passports and nonpayment of wages for months or even years, as well as the inertia of UAE state authorities in intervening on behalf of workers. The report also suggests that risk in the UAE labor market is borne almost entirely by the workers. Employers find various ways of evading serious government oversight (labor recruiters even more so). Worker revolts and suicides were also reported by HRW (as they are, to some extent, in the UAE press). Approximately one in five of the nearly 2.75 million migrant workers in the UAE (2005 estimate) is employed in the construction sector (7, see chapter 1). These workers are largely illiterate and from impoverished rural backgrounds. They are housed in dilapidated labor camps far from the city limits. The camp I visited in 2006–7, called Sonapoor, the Hindi word for "city of gold," actually a small town consisting of the camps for numerous construction companies, is at least five kilometers into Dubai emirate's desert interior. School buses transport the workers back and forth between work sites and the camps. For daily necessities, the workers shop at overpriced camp shops selling goods marked up even from the prices charged at upscale Dubai shopping malls. Although there is some anecdotal evidence (supplied mostly by the local press and therefore of limited reliability) that conditions in Dubai camps have improved (owing, among other things, to efforts such as HRW's), conditions in other emirates, according to a credible local source I interviewed, remained as of early 2007 abysmal (intermittent electricity, lack of infrastructure, and non-payment of wages, to cite a few examples).

As discussed in chapter 1, the permanent UAE representative to the United Nations argued against HRW's recommendations for reforming the construction sector. In a letter to HRW, he claimed that laws applicable in the western countries cannot be applied to workers in the UAE (70). For the ambassador, there is apparently no contradiction between drawing on the prestige and expertise of western starchitects while rejecting western human rights laws. The same can be said of UAE urbanists. A good argument can be made that with ventures such as Masdar, famous architects such as Foster are using the symbolic power of their names in genuinely progressive ways, ensuring that projects bearing their imprimatur contribute positively not only to a state's reputation but also to the social relations prevailing within that state. One should not gainsay the counterargument to the one I am making here, that if all architectural projects followed Masdar's lead, UAE urbanism may be far the better. It remains unclear, however, how far-reaching Masdar's sustainable innovations will be (simply an isolated enclave of relatively good conditions or encouragement to other projects to do the same) as well as how local authorities will seek to contain the project's progressive labor policies. However, even the most charitable reading of Masdar, which discounts the opportunism usually characterizing the sudden discovery of sustainability and justice by state-elite formations in the context of the recent global image economy of "green" symbolism, does not have a good response to the question: Are enclaves, with all that they imply in terms of elite political control, economic inequality, and the top-down rule of expertise, the best possible solution to contemporary urban problems that starchitecture can propose? Moreover, witnessing the repackaging by urbanists, such as Sorouh and Nakheel, of large enclave spaces of bourgeois gratification as "green projects," one cannot help but recall the following insightful observation by Donald McNeill (made in relation to similar efforts to "green" airports).

> As an envelope, yes, green airports are a possibility. But only if one ignores what is happening out on the runways and link roads and car parks that surround these light green structures. Indeed,

turning these environmental disasters into things of beauty has a parallel with some of the debates over the use of architectural monuments to prop up unpopular political regimes. (144)

In the UAE, the emergence of green ideology and the propping up of the political regime are not only analogous. They are often part of the same process.

The Spatial Re-Orientation of the East: Urbanism's Dubious Anthropology

Urbanist projects in the contemporary Gulf often begin with references to "culture." As we saw in the case of both OMA's Dubai Waterfront City and Doha's Intelligent Tower, this recourse to culture talk (Mamdani) is justified by urbanists as a progressive, positive critique. The architect or expert divines the supposedly authentic core identity of the society so that she may build in a more organic or humanly responsive way. This is certainly a laudable intention. But in practice things are more complicated, because most of the time urbanists end up reifying local culture rather than responding to it, in the process creating justifications of elite control.

Instead of perceiving the invented nature of the correlation between national identity and specific cultural icons, such as camels and traditional sports, dhows (Indian Ocean sailing vessels), desert landscapes, and Gulf national dress (Khalaf 1999; Onley 2005; 2007), urbanists usually take these icons at face value, assuming that they are expressions of authentic Emirati culture. One of the seemingly interminable debates through which UAE architectural practice is framed polarizes Emirati culture between tradition and modernity. The former is equated with authenticity, the latter with its opposite. Amr Mustafa, an Arab expatriate who teaches architecture at the American University of Sharjah, maintains that Dubai's architecture is generally inauthentic, aping foreign postmodernist styles, which is in turn a result of the nonparticipatory nature of urban development in the city (Mustafa). Echoing Harris's reference to "Arab democracy," he recommends "the tribal system" of the UAE as the basis for a more participatory public sphere. In this he ignores the inconvenient fact that "tribalism" is largely an invented identity of the post-1971 or nation-building era.[21] This formulation of authentic Emirati culture is ubiquitous among urbanists in the UAE, both local and foreign (BBC Radio 3). Among other things, it underpins recent projects of so-called heritage revival in various emirates of the UAE and other Gulf states (Khalaf 1999; 2000). Even those who reject the valorization of authenticity or vernacular in the Emirati built environment do so, almost exclusively, in the terms set by this tradition-modernity debate. In this debate, tradition signifies supposedly autochthonous aesthetic forms and cultural values, and modernity signifies the rejection of these and the embrace of western, especially neoliberal, notions of progress (see discussion in chapter 4).

The Boston architect who led the 2007 Harvard seminar echoes Mustafa's sense of ennui with the region's "modern" architecture and counsels a revival of the "traditional city" as an antidote both to urban anomie and to contemporary Gulf cities' disproportionate ecological impact. "You have to follow in the footsteps of your grandfather," he argues, holding out "the privacy-seeking, security-seeking world of the courtyard" as a model for future architecture. Sustainable architecture, for him, manifests a "coincidence between architecture and spiritual beliefs." For this architect, "spiritual beliefs" turned out to be exclusively (medieval, or, more accurately, "medievalist,") Arab and Persian in provenance.

Even immensely talented architects such as Tadao Ando and Jean Nouvel (both like Foster, Gehry, Hadid, and Koolhaas, winners of the Pritzker Prize, the profession's top honor, and the latter the designer of Paris's stunning Institut du Monde Arabe, a building of deep sensitivity both to the local urban context and to the Arab experience) cannot avoid the occasional use of culture talk. Taking the Emirati state's heritage revival project at face value, Ando incorporates the icon of the dhow as a signifier of the Arab authenticity of his Abu Dhabi Maritime Museum. (It is notable that this pan-Indian Ocean sailing vessel is converted into an Arab one in this narrative.)

> Dhows, Arab sailing vessels with triangular or lateen sails, float over the voids of the interior space and help create an intense visual experience by relating objects to one another and to the museum architecture as a whole. Below ground, there is a second space—a reception hall with an enormous aquarium. A traditional dhow floats over the aquarium and is seen from different perspectives. (Arcspace)

Nouvel's comment on the Saadiyat Island, where his and Ando's projects will be located, points to an urbanist notion of landscape as almost the opposite of urbanscape, landscape as a repository of the primal, the authentic, and the intuitive.

The island offers a harsh landscape, tempered by its meeting with the channel, a striking image of the aridity of the earth versus the fluidity of the waters. These fired the imagination towards unknown cities buried deep into the sands or sunk under water. These dreamy thoughts have merged into a simple plan of an archaeological field revived as a small city, a cluster of nearly one-row buildings along a leisurely promenade. (Arcspace)

For my final example, I return to the film *The Sand Castle* by Eirin Gjørv, which recounts the competition to build a new capital for the emirate of Ras al Khaimah (*Wide Angle*). The film is in many respects a good example of urbanist ideology as it pertains to developing countries in the early twenty-first century, exhibiting a perhaps inadvertent loss of critical perception as urbanism encounters the cultural other. In form and in content, the film tends to romanticize both the figure of the architect and that of local culture.

The film opens with a shot of the desert. As the audience takes in the landscape, a *mu'adhdhin* calls the Muslim prayer. As the *adhān* (call to prayer) continues, the scene shifts to a close-up of Kjetil Thorsen, head of the Snøhetta team, kneeling in the sand and sketching an imaginary city as his colleagues look on. After a short vignette (the mound of sand on the conference table in Oslo, described above), the film returns to the UAE to give more atmospherics. A scene from a Bedouin dance, performed for all visiting dignitaries and at heritage museums as an example of authentic Emirati culture, is followed by a scene from a performance of the *rimāya*, traditional rifle shooting, another recent invention of the Emirati heritage industry which is, however (the film implies), like the *adhan* and the dance, evidence of Emirati cultural "authenticity."

The camera then shifts to a position behind the four Snøhetta architects, the film's protagonists. They are depicted walking in the desert. The viewer senses that they are searching for something in vain, something not quite concrete or definable. A close-up of Thorsen's face comes next, indicating a sudden discovery: "Beautiful! Landscape, landscape, landscape, landscape!" (*Wide Angle* Transcript, 4). To emphasize the centrality of the landscape, the next two shots are again from behind the four architects. The viewer follows them as they climb a hill overlooking an immense, empty desert landscape. The last shot in the sequence is reminiscent of Caspar David Friedrich's *Traveling above the Clouded Sea,* with the traveler-architects' figures shrouded in darkness as they gaze out into the distance.

As the architects contemplate the ineffable Emirati *Landschaft* the narrator intones, "the Snøhetta team is not alone in delighting in the romance of the desert *and* bidding for the capital's master plan" (4, emphasis in the original). This brings Rem Koolhaas into the action. The landscape is also central to his attraction to the UAE. "It's heart breakingly beautiful" (4). As Koolhaas says this, the camera shoots the landscape through the windshield of the jeep he is riding through the desert. The soundtrack kicks in with Arab flute music. The shot through the windshield continues, again emphasizing the landscape. As the windshield frames the shot, the audience is given the impression that the landscape is divided into four bands—the blue-white layer of the sky above the tan layer of the desert above the silver strip of the car's hood above the black band of the dashboard. A different way to frame the previous, Friedrich-esque reading of the landscape, but the message is the same—the landscape is primal, consisting of simple, bare colors and emptiness. The Koolhaas vignette is completed with a close-up of the architect's face as he sits on an airplane gazing at the urbanscape of Dubai (the architect as a brooding genius attempting to penetrate from above the essence of the landscape in which he will realize his vision).

There are various other representations of the landscape and the figure of the architect, but each advances the unfailing message—the local culture is steeped in "tradition," iconically represented by exotic, aesthetic expressions of identity; the architect and his local elite client are visionaries who will excavate the landscape's hidden potential, transforming it from its intuitive, primal immanence into its concrete final shape. As the film closes, the narrator says, "Ras al-Khaimah today still boasts a pristine Arabian Desert landscape of sand and rock. Soon a new city will stand here, an architectural landmark to attract the world's businesses to this ambitious 21st century kingdom" (21). The final shot has Kjetil Thorsen, standing in an immense desert landscape at dusk, asking Khater Masaad, the ruler's assistant and main handler of the Snøhetta team, "Can you see it already?" (21). "Yeah," says Masaad, "I see it already. Yes" (21).

Culturalizing Spatial Politics

Although I am clearly skeptical of the phenomenon of starchitecture, this chapter should not be read as an indictment of individual starchitects, still less of architecture tout court. Nor do I believe that architects alone created starchitecture. The emergence of the architect as a marketable commodity (something with which, to be sure, individual architects are complicit) is a complex phenomenon, connected with the rise of urban entrepreneurialism in the era of neoliberalism. It goes without saying that, at their best, the starchitects discussed in this book can be by turns visionary, challenging, and deeply sensitive to aesthetic experiment and to the local conditions where they work (see Barber; Glancey; Lubow; Templer 1999; Tusa). Moreover, for many starchitects architecture is, or should be, socially conscious in ways that, set beside their more aesthetically radical projects, can seem prosaic. Here is Hadid speaking to an interviewer, for example: "What I would really love to build are schools, hospitals, social housing. . . . I wish it was possible to divert some of the effort we put into ambitious museums and galleries into the basic architectural building blocks of society" (Glancey). Gehry's first job was in public housing, a job he took, he says, because of his left-wing politics (Tusa). It is paradoxical that most starchitects would likely express solidarity with Gehry and Hadid yet not only work on politically dubious projects, but promote them as progressive.

Rem Koolhaas is, as is often the case with him, an example of the complexities and contradictions of contemporary starchitecture. Celebrated, justifiably, not only for his talent as an architect but also for expanding the profession's definitions of design and even of architecture itself, Koolhaas has cultivated a persona which he and his admirers situate within modern western traditions of radical cultural critique. For example, he criticizes the profession for being politically "lobotomized" (Freund), elitist, and out of touch with "the world" and "the other" (Lacayo; Lubow). A main theme of works such as *Delirious New York* and *S, M, L, XL*, as well as of the projects he led on the Pearl River Delta, Lagos, and shopping, is the embrace and critique from within of the supposedly generic and commodified character of cities and urban regions during the past three decades. This idea has a venerable pedigree within radical thought. Ernst Bloch, a founding figure of Western Marxism, argues that everyday cultural forms and modes of expression can conceal elements of radical critique of the status quo, an idea that would influence the thought of Adorno and other Western Marxists (Bloch, see also Jacoby; Jameson 1974; 1991). Henri Lefebvre reached similar conclusions in turning Heidegger on his head and composing a Marxist "critique of everyday life" (1947/1991). Yet Koolhaas's results are, at best, radical in a highly idiosyncratic way, requiring a great deal of interpretation even by Blochian standards to discern their radicalism. One example was the ill-starred Venetian Hotel Guggenheim project in Las Vegas. Intended by

OMA as a transformative collision of high art and leisure space, the project has become, less than ten years after its conception, a theater whose main function is the daily staging of *The Phantom of the Opera* (Hawthorne). Another is the collaboration with the Italian fashion designer Prada, which was drawn to Koolhaas as a result of his book on shopping.

> Capitalizing on the insight that people spend more money in spaces that are not seen as purely commercial, Koolhaas has designed the Prada store in New York to be adaptable to cultural performances. . . . OMA is reformulating not only the space in which you shop but also the way in which you shop. The office team compiled a list of annoyances in shopping and devised many clever improvements. (Lubow)

Is this radical critique or merely expertise making the prevailing power relations more efficient in securing their domination? These examples suggest at least that the line between political engagement and political accommodation is a blurry one and that encomia to the inevitability of neoliberalism may be different from immanent critique.

Particularly marred by a facile and dubious reasoning are Koolhaas's invocations of the other, culture, and related themes. Responding to an interviewer's question about the future of architecture, Koolhaas once asserted that,

> With globalization, we all have more or less the same future, but Asia and Africa feel much more new. I've been doing research on China recently, investigating cities that emerge suddenly, in eight years or so, seemingly out of nothing. These places are much more vigorous and representative of the future. There, building something new is a daily pleasure and a daily occurrence. (Heron)

Singapore, he goes on, has succeeded by "removing any trace of authenticity. . . . And many Asian cities are like this now, seeming to exist of nothing but copies." Elsewhere, he tells us that Asian markets and African cities remain spontaneous, alive, and richly social, while in the West these have lost their spontaneity, have become more regimented and cold, "You could say that the shopping project is . . . about nostalgia for a pre-modern condition" (Sigler).

Thus, although Koolhaas argues for an architecture that is more open to the world, such public utterances in practice end up increasing the gulf between architecture and its everyday contexts. Instead of a genuinely worldly architecture, we are presented with a way of conceptualizing space that relies on clichés about culture and globalization. Far from urban space becoming more open-ended and spontaneous, this approach strengthens power's claim over, and identification with, space.

The alignment between global expertise and local elite interests favors an apolitical representation of local culture. In Dubai, in which architecture and images of a hypermodern, Westernized urbanity are central elements in the political project of the family state to represent itself, depending on context, as vox populi, modernizing, or authentically Arab, starchitects and other urbanists are key producers of hegemonic cultural representations. Maktoum urban projects, along with those of other large firms (e.g., the Futtaim and Saif Ahmad Al Ghurair) are routinely presented in public as, on the one side, visionary and futuristic and, on the other, exemplary of the respective firm's noble, merchant Arabian roots, a background which in turn (it is argued) enables the firm to successfully meld the "modern" and the "traditional." Such representations redound to the credit of large holding company CEOs, such as the ruler himself. As the filmmaker Gjørv put it, the ruler of Ras al-Khaimah is creative, progressive, and, not least, powerful. Performances of Emirati culture by powerful men and their bureaucratic instruments (assistants, institutions, media) are conflated with Emirati culture and history in toto. Of course, such uses of Emirati culture are not unique to starchitects nor are they new.

In the late 1930s, the British Political Resident conveyed to the Dubai ruler, Said Al Maktoum, his opinion that instead of a more popular *majlis*, the ruler should "associate his people with himself in his government according to *immemorial Arab custom* by formation of a Council" (Davidson 2008, 36, emphasis added). Popular participation and "progressive tendencies" (35) were certainly not part of "immemorial custom," according to this logic. To his credit, the ruler refused and acquiesced in his people's demand for a more participatory government. In turn, the (albeit short-lived) majlis left a significant modernizing legacy from which Dubai citizens still benefit today (see discussion in chapter 1). The articulation between conservative politics and reified constructions of culture, however, would become a more permanent feature of the political and cultural milieu of modern Dubai and other parts of the UAE. The framing of local culture as an essence residing in a supposedly autochthonous "Bedouin" society, as a mystery which can only be articulated, oracle-like, by selected representatives of the ruling family, and, not least, as ethnically Arab, would become useful in the post-independence period. This is a period in which the ruler and his allies would attempt to negotiate the contradictory claims made by different constituencies—critics of the modernizing trajectory, on the one side, and, on the other, proponents of the path chosen by the post-independence rulers Rashid and Muhammad. The latter constituency would appropriate the family-state's Westernized, market absolutism (Kanna 2010a) and reframe it as an apolitical, Arabized neoliberalism (see chapter 4). The former, the critics, would appropriate the regime's representations of Arab authenticity and, like their compatriots in the neoliberal camp, reproduce apolitical constructions of culture. In an earlier time, their critiques might have taken a different shape; these critics might have been anti-colonial reformist nationalists. It is a testament to the triumph of the ruling bargain ideology that criticism of Dubai's version of modernity today tends to take, instead, an ethnocratic and religiously conservative form. It is to this tendency, what I call the "neoorthodox" persuasion, that I now turn.

CHAPTER 3

THE VANISHED VILLAGE

Nostalgic and Nationalist Critiques of the New Dubai

> In an ethnocratic system, especially one where the privileged ethne is in a minority, the perception of external threat is constant.
>
> —Anh Nga Longva, "Neither Autocracy nor Democracy but Ethnocracy"

> My optimism in ending the crisis, and confidence in Dubai's ability to restore its strong growth rate soon, is . . . linked to my bedouin roots which my nation and I are proud of. . . . Bedouins are strong by nature with strong will in combating crisis. They only know determination to achieve the goal and walk towards that end.
>
> —Sheikh Muhammad bin Rashid Al Maktoum, late 2009

Among the most important parts of the family-state's and allied firms' development projects during the boom years were well-funded advertising campaigns extolling the glories of the resort, consumption, and spectacular urban enclaves and landscapes these firms were planning or developing. Seemingly everywhere one looked were posters, brochures, models, displays, DVDs, and advertisements masquerading as op-ed or investigative journalism. One of the more elaborate, but not in any way atypical, examples of this was a May 2004 academic conference sponsored by the Maktoum-owned Nakheel Corporation at the architecture department of the American University of Sharjah, a prestigious Western-style university in the United Arab Emirates. One of the largest real estate firms in Dubai, Nakheel specializes in themed entertainment projects, "Disney-style" architecture for the global tourism and real estate investment markets. A public relations official of the firm delivered the keynote address, which was accompanied by a video presentation from which I take the following two vignettes. These vignettes help to illuminate the cultural logic of the family-state's claims on Dubai space and time.

The first part of the video promoted what would eventually become the Ibn Battuta Mall, a "project with a themed concept and historical roots . . . inspired by the travels of Ibn Battuta in the 13th [*sic*] century" (Nakheel). The presenter noted that theming and the incorporation of a story "increase[ed] the lifestyle of the mall" and was therefore part of the project's contribution to "sustainability" (see discussion in chapter 2). The "edutainment" provided to the patrons, including museum-like exhibits on Ibn Battuta and other famous Arab travellers, were other examples of the project's supposed social contributions. The video at this point went from showing a bird's-eye view of a digital mockup of the mall to sensory overload, incorporating images from (what Nakheel understood to be) Arabian travel narratives, before settling into a peaceful scene of an Emirati family of four strolling on a beach at sunset. The husband and wife are young, attractive nationals, their children a boy and girl with a sort of Disney-inspired wholesomeness.

The subject of the next vignette was the so-called Cavern Hotel. It was planned to be an entirely underground ecosystem with mixed-use hotel and entertainment complexes. The narrative begins with an empty desert scene. An Emirati boy in a white *kandūra* (long gown worn by males) is wandering, seemingly aimlessly. Bored by his desert surroundings, he dreams of "the lost city beneath the desert, . . . the city of my dreams." He comes to a cliff. Over the edge, he sees a mysterious city. At this point the scene shifts to the digitally animated model of the projected Cavern Hotel. A roller-coaster perspective takes the audience from hotel rooms "carved out of the very rock of the desert," to diverse ecosystems of marine and earth flora and fauna. Computer-animated kayakers splash down rapids. Multicolored fish and corals appear beneath the kayakers' wake. As we in the audience leave this scene, we fly over to the common-use area of the mall, through a gate, past some camels and *ẓabī* (Arabian gazelles) and swoop into the suq with stalls staffed by Emirati men in local dress. This in-between section of the narrative is characterized by sensory overload and figuratively represents uncertainty. The sequence ends the same way that the other one did, with a local family of four strolling along a beach at dusk.

In chapter 1, I showed how the Maktoum and Nahyan family-states went about their agendas for "total territorial control" (Hazbun) by policing mobility, creating different, fluid regimes of legitimate and illegitimate, protected and unprotected movement for various segments of the population. In the second chapter, the management of space through spatial representation (Lefebvre 1974/1991) was the main theme. By asserting a monopoly on how space is envisioned and developed, the family-state claimed the right to advance its definition of modernity—a vision, in turn, given expert legitimization by various urbanists such as starchitects. In this chapter, narrative and symbolism are central, providing access to the ways the family-state's construction of modernity is appropriated and reproduced by everyday Emiratis. If the politics of protection and the spatial representations of urbanists are important means by which the family-state establishes the conditions for its total territorial control, narrative and symbolism are a means by which everyday Emiratis appropriate and invest these conditions with meaning.

Western writings on the UAE tend to naturalize the development of both the federal and Dubai states as dynastic, authoritarian, and "pro-Western," as well as to assume that the contemporary federal and emirate-level states call forth the popular assent of the overwhelming majority of the Emirati population. However, just as the equation of the identity and interests of the ruling families with those of the peoples they serendipitously came to govern required both expert legitimization and popular demobilization during the time of the British Empire, it requires the same expertise and demobilization today. A main effect of the alignment of the political-cultural vectors I have been calling urbanism has been to depoliticize space and time in the contemporary UAE. Rather than situating the Dubai urbanscape and urbanity, for example, in a history of struggle by various local sociopolitical formations (primarily the dynastic–imperial versus the reformist tendencies) over space and, in turn, over the meaning and trajectory of national development, urbanism frames the urbanscape within narratives of the "authentic cultural identity" of certain building forms and the "visionary leadership" of the ruling family. Time becomes both emptied of social content and de-secularized. For a past, a present, and a future over which a diversity of Emiratis and non-Emiratis have deployed legitimate claims, the depoliticization of space and time substitutes a narrative in which the ruling family is central, with every other social, urban, and political development a footnote to this main narrative. The destiny of Dubai becomes the destiny of the Al Maktoum.

Admitting this into the analysis enables a more complex situation of the scenes from the symposium hall that opened the chapter. How, for example, does the Nakheel presentation, basically a state-produced piece of propaganda, shed light on monopolistic family-state claims on Dubai space and time? How do the claims of the family-state articulate with the everyday cultural milieu in Dubai? A disproportionate weight is given in each vignette to what real estate developers call "theming," which consists of slapping an exotic form on buildings and elevating façade above all other architectural considerations (see Mitchell Forthcoming). This intent to attract potential investors and renters in the tourism and resort markets is neither surprising nor very interesting. More interesting is the way each vignette ends with the image of the idealized Emirati nuclear family, a surprising choice since generally it is not Emiratis that Nakheel wants to persuade to buy properties.[1] Also, each time that this image appears, it follows a part of the video characterized by sensory overload, a clamor of images and sounds that confound any effort to impose narrative on them. A sense of relief, a sort of visual and sensory sigh, accompanies the subsequent resolution of each series of scenes into the pristine image of the family on the beach at dusk. Each vignette appears to follow a Turnerian arc (Turner) in which an undifferentiated, seemingly prelogical initial stage is followed by a chaotic, liminal stage before resolving itself into the structurally integrated figure of the nuclear family, an image that, on the surface, seems extraneous to the rest of the narrative but, I suggest, resonates with hegemonic representations of the meanings of time and space in contemporary Dubai.

If we look at each video as something more complex than simple advertising, as an ideological and symbolic product, we see that the Nakheel presentation emerges in a more elaborate way from the prevailing alignments of cultural politics in Dubai. This seems especially true with respect to the aspects of the presentation, such as the figures of the family and the young boy in the lost city vignette, that resist simple, instrumental explanations. First, the form of the narrative is the same as that of narratives deployed by many everyday Emiratis when explaining the role of the family-state in contemporary Dubai. Figures of uncertainty, aimless wandering, and desert landscapes unyielding to human needs are followed by (again to borrow from Turner) a liminal phase in which structures are overturned, and this in turn becomes resolved into figures of stability. As in the ritual process, there is an implicit message—by showing the chaos resulting from destructuration, powerful actors legitimize the specific, contingent alignment of structured relations from which they most benefit. Such a framing of structure becomes naturalized. Second, in terms of content, idealized images of the family will resonate with the ways Emiratis invest time with meaning in the postindependence period. In a meticulous study of political culture in the UAE, anthropologist Andrea Rugh shows how an Emirati cultural model of the family has been one of the main sources of stability for Emirati society as it has undergone the economic and demographic convulsions of the past four decades (14). This model complements a second more "egalitarian" and "communitarian" worldview, what Rugh calls the "tribal model." While the tribal model emphasizes consultation, generosity, and accessibility to leaders (18–19), the family model is hierarchical and entails a system of obligations connected to gender, age, and social role. Obligations to others rather than entitlements, argues Rugh, are so central because they rest on divine authority—to perform one's duties to the other is to fulfill God's will (25–26).

While I remain agnostic about whether notions of "family" signify deep cultural structures (let alone about Emirati perceptions of their "divine" provenance or lack thereof), or are, as I suspect, historically and politically contingent, it is undeniable that the idealized family plays a prominent symbolic role in Emirati discourses about change, identity, and social values. Indeed, it is the very aspects cited by Rugh, hierarchy, obligation, and the interests of the collective over the individual, that Emiratis point to as central to their identity and to the family's role in preserving that identity. Moreover, in the context of Dubai's emerging neoliberal regime since the 1990s, two features of discourse about identity have become salient. First, a particular construction of the family—patriarchal and hierarchical—seems to be in the ascendant over notions of "tribe." Second, the family has come to be understood to play a central, if not *the* central, role in preserving what many Emiratis consider authentic national culture. Perceived lapses of "authenticity," such as an insufficient fluency in Arabic, lack of Muslim piety, or improper sexual behavior, are attributed to failures of family socialization or deficient family organization. I call discourses and spatializations that draw upon such idealized family images, and related imaginaries of "traditional" village life, marriage, and labor, "neoorthodox." In so doing, I differentiate these discourses and identity symbolizations from other tendencies in contemporary Dubai (see chapter 4), and I point to their modernity and processuality. There is nothing simply and monolithically traditional or orthodox about neoorthodoxy. It is not a perfect reflection of a supposedly authentic, transhistorical Emirati identity. Rather, it emerges from modern, especially postindependence cultural politics in Dubai. It is a symbolic response to what is perceived to be a rapidly changing society, as well as an active, determinate, sociopolitically structured appropriation of hegemonic framings of the meaning of these changes.

By naturalizing the patriarchal family and connecting it so inti- mately with the preservation of national cultural identity, modern Emiratis construct time and space in specific, situated ways. The spatialization of inside and outside, what belongs to "us" and what does not, is analogized as a family affair. The integrity of the family house stands in for politics. Political and social issues, such as immigration, shifting gender roles and aspirations, and cultural or linguistic change, get framed as issues of threat and survival. The polity is imagined as ethno-linguistically pure, patriar- chal, and autochthonous, emerging whole cloth from a time and place in which these qualities are thought to have prevailed. The contemporary city by implication becomes a time and place in which these qualities are be- ing lost.

This may be called an Emirati version of modernist nostalgia. Per- haps most influentially theorized in the Western context by Georg Lukacs and elaborated upon by more recent scholarship (Bach; Boym; Smith), modernist nostalgia narratives are ones in which the past is represented as a fulfilled time in which experience was immediate and authentic and people were generally noble, and in which material deprivation was accompanied by, and perhaps even underpinned, solidarity, self-sacrifice, and courage. The present, by implication, perhaps is a time of material contentment, but also of levelled values and egotism. Nostalgia, as Jonathan Bach has put it, is therefore a longing for a kind of longing that is no longer possible (547). My intention here is not so much to revisit the theme of modernist nostalgia (a well-trodden area of scholarship) in everyday Emirati laments for a lost place and time, but rather to focus on the ways in which these and related discourses resonate with, and help to secure the monopolistic claims of, family-state representations of Dubai space and time.

As I showed in the first chapter, the symbolism and politics of na- tional identity in Dubai since the period of the reformist struggle have not been simply reflections of the cultural values of tribalism or Arabian desert democracy. Discourses of authentic national identity and related practices (such as the famous local Arab "national dress") are part of a larger family- state–centered hegemonic project to marginalize reformist tendencies and to replace them with the politics of paternalism, dependency, and popular deactivation. The ruling bargain, or family-state paternalism, ideology was favored over other definitions of citizenship, often based on logics of na- tional self-determination and popular participation.

With this came an increasingly naturalized, ethno-national or ethno-cratic spatialization of inside and outside, local and foreign. An observation from Akhil Gupta and James Ferguson is apposite here. They write that anthropologists must begin to interrogate the seeming naturalness of territorializing concepts of culture and identity (1997a, 45, see introduction). Identity is not simply a symbolic process, the success of hegemony not just a matter of intellectual persuasion based on effective manipulation of symbols. As the case of neoorthodoxy in Dubai shows, the production of identity and the securing of state hegemony is a spatial–imaginative, or spatializing, process. It depends on the effective persuasion of subjects to appropriate hegemonic constructions of *inside* and *outside, self* and *other,* as well as the making of this spatialization part of the given order of things. This takes our analysis from the institutional, often state-centered contexts of spatial representation (chapters 1 and 2) to the everyday contexts of the appropriation, reimagination, and cultural reproduction of hegemonic spatial representations.

On Sources of Data

In a society in which family name carries a great deal of weight and where citizens are not unlikely to personally know each other, Emiratis are understandably reluctant to speak frankly about issues of national identity, their feelings about the changes Dubai is undergoing, and what role the family-state has played in this process. Nor, in general, did I push them to delve into uncomfortable subjects in interviews and conversations. There are, however, less intrusive ways to gain a deeper understanding of the social anxieties and collective framings of controversial issues, employing methods that are, perhaps, also more revealing than interview data or notes from conversations. Indeed, there is a provocative literature in critical theory (Benjamin 2002; Jameson 1991; Kracauer) which has argued that the explicit utterances within discourse and relatively self-conscious products of cultural life (a society's "judgments about itself," as Siegfried Kracauer has put it) are inadequate if not deceptive guides to the alignment of powerful forces shaping daily life and the finer-grained textures of experience. This literature has been a corrective to the superficial equation of cultures of officialdom and power with culture tout court. There is a strong argument to be made for applying these insights, as well, to the Gulf context, where scholars and journalists have tended to treat everyday life as a mere footnote to the utterances and self-representations of state power.

Siegfried Kracauer and Walter Benjamin have both argued that it was the inadvertent, marginal "side effects" of cultural process, the trivia and "debris" of everyday life, that opened a more direct aperture into the structures of social power and the constructedness of everyday experience. As Kracauer explains,

> The position that an epoch occupies in the historical process can be determined more strikingly from an analysis of its inconspicuous surface-level expressions than from that epoch's judgments about itself. . . . The surface-level expressions . . . by virtue of their unconscious nature, provide unmediated access to the fundamental substance of the state of things. (75)

While we naturally have to be critical of such broad claims about "unmediated access" to "fundamental" substances and the implication in this passage that society is static, Kracauer's formulation about the surface-level products of culture is useful in trying to interpret cultural process in a society, such as the UAE, in which public culture usually occludes rather than facilitates our access to social reality. In this chapter, my data are often the unstated or secondary meanings of utterances or products of popular culture. In this vein, I have not confined myself to Emiratis' speech, but have tried to collect and draw upon materials, such as newspaper comics, letters to the editor, and (as noted in the chapter opening), data from visual and popular culture, which although intended for very different explicit purposes and usually seen by Emiratis as trivial, reveal the shape of important dimensions of Emirati social experience. Unlike in the United States or Europe, op-ed pages of Arabic-language UAE newspapers are "loose baggy monsters," as Henry James once said of Russian novels.[2] Along with what Westerners would recognize as the normal contents of such pages (academic and intellectual opinions, editorial reflections on major current events, and so on) they are forums for what would seem to Western readers as materials with a tenuous claim on serious editorial attention. Examples include poems submitted by readers, essays reflecting on the nature of parenthood, odes to the supposedly wise and visionary rulers, short stories written by readers, and jokes and comics, usually mocking the petty foibles of society at large or of stock characters, such as the neglectful father or the wayward wife, which are understood by Emiratis as objects of mirth and metaphors for social ills. Because these pages are heavily censored, they would never dare to discuss openly serious political issues, at least not ones directly relating to the UAE. They therefore tend to overemphasize the cultural and social spheres and to deal only in abstractions, never "naming names." I suggest, however, that it is because of this seeming triviality that these materials reveal significant things about Emirati daily life and experience. Perceived triviality can be liberating, opening spaces for the safe, indirect expression of sentiments that, expressed more openly or in more serious venues (venues of power), can be dangerous. These materials, often seen as mere amusements, can illuminate specific Emirati views on the meaning of nostalgia and identity and anxieties over the rule of the family-state. Most importantly, these data are well situated to provide insight into how Emiratis unconsciously deploy specific discursive and imaginative devices to depoliticize and culturalize time and space, thereby reaffirming family-state and neoliberal claims on the Dubai polity and society. These materials, in other words, tell us a great deal about the spatialization of national identity, collective memory, and the contemporary urban landscape.

In Search of the Vanished Village: Depoliticizing Time and Space in Dubai's History

As already discussed (see introduction) Dubai during the years before the crisis of 2008 was expanding out from its core and putting up skyscrapers, shopping malls, and resorts at a furious pace. In conversations, newspaper articles, and human-interest stories in the media, Emiratis often debated the theme of change and the meaning of the transformations the city was undergoing. Idyllic images of village and family life were central to these debates and often had a depoliticizing effect, removing traces of struggle or diversity from the story of Dubai's past and that of its present. The family in the pre-oil boom Dubai is often represented as the repository of the best values in Emirati society, a place where each member unambiguously knew his or her role and stayed within the boundaries of that role. Family life was characterized (we are told) by a simple, unspoken *'aṣabiyya* (esprit de corps, solidarity), untouched by the decadent ways of *al-ḥadātha* or *al-tamaddun* (modernity, urbanization).[3] Marriage, in turn, is also thought to have been simpler and more humane. "Marriage," begins a typical newspaper piece, "is a sacred institution, a union of minds, a life of sharing and raising a family. The focus [in the past] was on simplicity, innocence, tradition and heritage, with the bride and groom occupying centre stage, and the others on the periphery, as it were. That was then" (Menon). While the subjects of the piece are men who often complain that marriage today, unlike in their grandfathers' time, requires massive outlays of money for dowries and entertaining guests, women too critique aspects of the present by recourse to romanticized images of the past.

This sense of lapsed esprit de corps cuts across class, gender, and generational divisions; although for me, it is especially clear in the reflections of two young women, Raghad and Naila, corporate managers at a large Dubai firm.

> RAGHAD: Everything is becoming modern. We used to complain that Dubai was too small, everyone knows you. Now, you're more free and anonymous. But it's no longer as cozy.
>
> NAILA: They say "We want to open up to tourists," but they never talk about the bad things that tourists bring, the alcohol, the prostitution, and drugs.
>
> RAGHAD: The divorce rate is increasing. Because of modernity. Before, a woman would know her place in society. Now, the woman is more independent, she can work. But this is causing *tafakkuk al-'ā'ila* [the breaking apart of the family]. The family is not as close as before. The father is off on business trips, the woman says, "why do I need my husband?" Before, the wife [i.e., the fiancée] was not allowed to see her [arranged] husband before the [wedding day]. You saw a photo and you spoke on the phone. This still exists, especially with the Arabs,[4] but now it is different.
>
> NAILA: Before, marriage was much better. There was no *ighrā'* [temptation]. Now, with [things like phone number] papering,[5] things have become easy for the men. Men used to stalk women when they saw them on the street walking. Now it's the men who are being hunted.[6]

Maktoum Jassim, a Dubayyan in his late fifties, met me one day at his office in the Shindagha neighborhood of Dubai. I asked him what his opinions were of *madaniyya* (urbanization, urban civilization), a concept Emiratis often used, in conversations with me, as a description of urban and social change. During our interviews, he drew on a familiar, almost stock, juxtaposition deployed by Emiratis:

MAKTOUM: In spite of madaniyya and the refined life [*al'aysh al raqīq*], [in the past there was] *tafāhum ijtimā'iyy dhātī* [literally, a deeply engrained sense of social harmony].

AHMED: So there has been some *tafakkuk* [social disintegration] today?

MAKTOUM: I mean, in those days, it was impossible for you to sleep with a full belly while your neighbor was going hungry. Impossible. The second thing is, say even if you had a small meal, or one type of food on your table, if you sat on the table, you would find many types of food. Why? Because this person would come with something and another with something else, and the third with another dish, and so on. Why? Because there was *takāful ijtimā'i* [social solidarity]. [People's] hearts were pure, there was no hatred or malice. There was collective compassion [*mā fī hiqd, wa mā fī daghāyin 'ala baadl fī tarāḥum*] [7]

Abdullah Al Muṭair, a septuagenarian, put it this way.

We worked to live. We worked in the sea. You would work and work and maybe you wouldn't even earn 1000 rupees in a whole year. But if you got 200 rupees you'd be comfortable. Everything was cheap. . . . In the past, the body was tired, but the heart was peaceful. Now [it's the opposite]. Now there is comfort, but the heart is tired [*kān il-jisim ta'bān bas il-galb mirtāḥ. Bas il-ḥīn al-jisim mirtāḥ lakin il-galb ta'bān*]. . . . People were comfortable [*kānat al-nās mirtāḥa*]. [8]

I have drawn examples from as wide a range of Emirati sources as possible a state-sanctioned newspaper; young, self-styled "modern" women; a middle-aged government employee; and a retired former fisherman—to show that a sort of modernist, perhaps "structural" (Herzfeld 1991), nostalgia is a fairly common means by which Emiratis invest the transformations of their society with meaning. While clearly reflecting deeply held social values—solidarity, egalitarianism, respect for status superiors (see Rugh)—these recollections are selective. They romanticize the past while implying that in the present the Emiratis are losing their way of life, values, and so on. Such recollections also homogenize the past (and, implicitly, the present) by suggesting that all Emiratis shared the same values and viewed the world the same way before some temporal break disjointed society (often, that moment is said to be the oil-fueled boom of the 1970s).

Such narratives, in short, assume the primeval autonomy of the imagined community, to adapt a phrase from James Ferguson and Akhil Gupta (1997a, 35). My ethnographic objective is to interrogate how that community is made in the first place, how it is imagined, and how this imaginative process emerges from specific political and social alignments. What Ferguson and Gupta have claimed for the modern social sciences can, in this case, be applied to the imagined community—notions of rupture or radical break, they argue, constitute a central organizing metaphor in the social sciences, and yet these notions are so naturalized that they virtually disappear (33–34). In naturalizing the construction of Dubai as a once self-contained, hierarchically structured village community characterized by social solidarity, the politics and diversity of the historical process by which the city and its social and political institutions have taken their modern form are erased. Moreover, this spatialization of Dubai Emirati culture sets up a dilemma. If in the past we were whole and in the present we are fragmented, how do we navigate the present? The response to this dilemma becomes a tautology, re-spatializing the imagined community as autochthonous, primeval, and in need of defense against further incursions into its qualitatively unique way of life. Moreover, in the following discourses, which I summarize with the term neoorthodox, it is the figure of the hierarchically structured community governed by a unitary sovereign, that is spatialized as the ideal. In short, this imagined community is, implicitly, the one envisioned by the family-state and the ruling bargain ideology.

Naturalizing Ethnonational Identity

One of the legacies of the British imperial period in the UAE has been a unitary, hierarchical, and centralized conception of state sovereignty (Bose). After crushing the Qasimi state in the early nineteenth century, Britain sought both to fragment the so-called Trucial Coast and to formalize and centralize its constituent states. This would serve to promote an imperial order in which threats to Britain's control of trade and communications routes, such as the one posed by the Qasimi state, would never re-emerge. To maintain this order, writes Sugata Bose, the British elevated ("invented" may not be too strong a word) pliable local potentates, enveloping them in the trappings of tradition and legitimacy. As they were doing in the Malay Straits Settlement, the British established in the Gulf a system of sovereignty underpinned by a logic of unitary, indivisible governance, "a major break from ideas of good governance and legitimacy that had been widespread in the Ottoman, Safavid, and Mughal domains and their regional successor states." In the latter "precolonial" empires, what might be called a "galactic" type of sovereignty had prevailed, an umbrella of imperial centralization overlaying multiple, legitimate, regionalized and localized claims to territory, the seas, and communications routes (25).

In other words, state sovereignty in the nineteenth-century Gulf was forced to transition into a precursor variant of what James Scott has called the high modernist state (1998). This entailed a spatialization of the state as governing an indivisible territory and a homogeneous citizenry. This shift goes a long way to explaining the transformation of the mode of national imagination in the Gulf, from what has been called an "anational," arguably culturally pluralistic imagining (Anscombe) or a "hybrid," pan–Indian Ocean cultural type of identity (Onley 2005), to a mode of identity formation (in the latter half of the twentieth century) resembling European ethnonationalism. This spatialization of national culture has been reaffirmed by institutional state practices and ideologies, such as the ruling bargain and the post-1970s official reorientation of the Emirati people and history toward the Arab cultural arena and away from the Indian Ocean and Persian arenas.

This state spatialization of culture articulates with everyday popular constructions of Emirati space in which the state, territory, subjects, and culture of the Arab rulers are equated with each other. Issa Khalil, an Emirati architect in his early thirties, was a helpful guide to local culture during my fieldwork. During one of our conversations, he reflected on Dubai's transformations by comparing the older Al Ghurair neighborhood of Deira (in the eastern part of Dubai) with the wealthier and much newer Jumeirah section of western Dubai. His brother had recently moved to Al Ghurair, which would have bemused his compatriots as this neighborhood is now regarded as lacking in prestige. But his brother's family likes it, said Issa, in spite of some unexpected problems.[9]

> ISSA: They walk everyday, they go out, everything is close to them. But, you have dangerous things like thieves and things.

AHMED: Really?

ISSA: Yes. Actually, one Chinese guy jumped into their house. . . .
I think Dubai is changing a little bit. You used to keep your
car open and you go and nothing will happen. But now, you
feel like you should lock it and you should have, maybe, an
alarm. So, it's changing. Actually my dad, his age is maybe
seventy, he got [robbed] maybe three weeks ago, for the
first time in his life. He got robbed by an African guy. I
shouldn't generalize, I don't know where he is from, but
he's from Africa.

AHMED: And [as you said in an earlier conversation], you had your
mobile [phone] stolen.

ISSA: Yes, my mobile. So it's changing. But, I think, when you
have a city which is growing and [is getting] a lot of foreigners, [things] happen.

Although far from a xenophobic person, Issa nevertheless suggested
(albeit somewhat reluctantly) that negative changes in the city were connected with an increase in the presence of foreigners. In chapter 1, we
saw in the example of Abdallah Humaid's letter to the editor a similar, if
more outwardly xenophobic, association between foreigners and danger,
specifically a connection between foreign laborers' bodies and public hygiene. "The Department of Health," Humaid demanded, "must punish the
careless Asians and introduce them to the concept that health is the most
precious thing in existence, and that the Emirates are not India." Another
Emirati, a middle-aged real estate developer, was as explicit, in a conversation with me, as Humaid was, and he elaborated upon this sense of ethnonationalism. He offered his thoughts on identity in the context of a conversation about architectural form. Explaining that his company's projects
included some of the more important and aesthetically distinguished resorts and gated communities in Dubai, he reflected on the values that guide
his conceptualization of new projects. Much to my surprise, he said that he
dislikes the notion of "Islamic architecture." "I try to develop the desert.
You cannot build Islamic architecture there. The rule in the desert is *simplicity*. Simple buildings. The desert is about feelings of space. . . . Good
design has to have spirit." When you have a great site, "you don't have to
build anything, because God gave you everything."[10]

This feeling for simplicity, he said, is connected with the fact that
"I am a Bedouin." "We don't have a [house], we have a tent." While

Europeans, he said, are partly responsible for imposing their notions of "Islamic" and "authentic local" architecture on the Emiratis, the lion's share of the blame for what he considers the generally execrable architecture in the UAE falls on two groups in particular, the Iranians and the Indians. The Iranians are responsible for the ubiquitous wind-tower structure (*barjīl*) seen on many pre-independence buildings and referenced in postmodern ones in the UAE. But such buildings are not Emirati, he says. The original windtower houses were built by Iranians, "not by us." Worse are the Indians. Abu Dhabi, he said, is the worst example of the influence of Indians on Emirati architecture. It is filled with so-called Islamic buildings, but they are artificial and expensive. In Abu Dhabi, he said, you always see Indians designing arches. These are not "Islamic; [they are] Indian."

When this developer says that he is a "Bedouin," he is referring to the main ethnic divide in the UAE, that between Emiratis who consider themselves "pure" Arabs (sometimes called *bedu* or "Bedouin") and those who are of Iranian descent (*'ajam* or *'ayam*). Dubai, the developer's home city, is also implicitly referenced, since its population of Emirati natives is overwhelmingly Iranian in extraction. (Approximately 80 percent of Emiratis from Dubai are *'ayam,* according to many locals to whom I spoke.) A third important group, from this developer's perspective, is the expatriates, who constitute a majority of the UAE population and among whom South Asians are disproportionately represented. (South Asians are often grouped under the catchall phrase "Indians," as seen in the developer's case.)

When the Gulf states started absorbing greater numbers of immigrants as oil wealth increased, they initiated cultural nationalist projects to assert or maintain what their rulers saw as their authentic Arab (i.e., *bedu*) identity (Khalaf 1999; 2000). The story is complex and also is connected with the rise of Nasserism and other nationalisms of the left in the Arab world, ideologies that were confrontational in relation to the Gulf monarchies and sought to paint the latter as spear-carriers for British and American imperialism (see chapter 1). The process was also more pronounced in Abu Dhabi than in Dubai. In the latter, the rulers' assertions of Arabness, through the aforementioned invention of national dress and immigration and naturalization policies favoring ethnic Arab immigrants over Indians and Iranians, were checked by their attempts to cultivate those very Indian and Iranian merchants as part of their power base as well as to maintain an openness to Western, especially British, connections. The Gulf national dress, consisting of traditional gowns and headdress—the Emirati *kandūra* and *ghuṭra,* the Bahraini *thawb,* or the Saudi *disdāsha* and *shimāgh,* for example—each derive from Najdi, i.e., "Bedouin," roots and are the most visible example of this "Arabization" of countries that are, and to a great extent have always been, multinational or even "anational" (Anscombe; Onley). The Arab/Bedu-'Ayam distinction and the feeling of anxiety about a potential flood of Indians remain unresolved legacies of the Gulf economic boom and state-building projects.

It would, however, be a mistake to see Issa's connection between foreigners and urban danger as an example of simple xenophobia (although it is probably not possible to be so charitable in either Humaid's or the "Bedouin" developer's case). Another framing would have to take seriously the depth of the historical memory among many Emiratis of the privileged status given Persian and Indian capitalists during the British Empire period. We should remember in this connection that the reform movement of the 1930s drew its social base from an emerging ethnic-Arab capitalist class who were chafing under the exclusionary regime put in place by the British, primarily benefiting (as the Arab merchants saw it) the protected Indian and Persian intermediary capitalists (Al-Sayegh, 95–96). This was a system, moreover, maintained and defended by the ruler (Abdulla 1984, 90). The Dubai National Front, at least before expanding its platform to a multiethnic anticolonialism in the latter half of the 1950s, leveled similar critiques at the ruler (Davidson 2008, 43–44). Moreover, as I showed in chapter 1, because the articulation of British and royal interests have tended to marginalize projects of self-determination and participatory citizenship, conceptions of politics and citizenship in the unitary, dynastic UAE have become equated with ethnically purist, exclusionary modes of self-identification. Discourses of self-determination have therefore been eclipsed by discourses of autochthony and exclusion. It is indeed perhaps the most pernicious legacy of British imperialism and the system of unitary, centralized sovereignty that it put in place to have permanently thwarted the possibility of Arabs, Persians, and South Asians fashioning an alternative modernity in which the claims of all three communities on the Emirati society and polity would receive equal legitimacy and respect or, if not this, then to revive in some form pre-colonial Indian Ocean and Middle Eastern traditions of galactic sovereignty in which a flexible state centralization coexists with and overlays multiple claims to territory and political recognition (Bose).

A more sensitive framing would also acknowledge that Humaid and the "Bedouin" developer represent one of several tendencies in contemporary Dubai. While a purist, ethnocratic construction of identity is hegemonic, there is considerable negotiation within its terms among Emiratis. It is not uncommon, for example, to hear locals speaking Arabic, Persian, and Urdu or Hindi, a linguistic diversity not atypical of older Emiratis and something signaling that the purist framing of identity overlays a deeper transnationalism in Dubai. An ethnically plural, multi-linguistic society remains part of local imaginings as well, even in the memories of younger nationals such as Issa Khalil. He, along with other informants, both Emirati and Indian, spoke of cultural referents and a lingua franca shared by the two communities. For example, they remembered frequenting the Bollywood films at Dubai's movie theater in the 1980s where, Issa claimed, the Emiratis could easily follow the subtitle-free dialogue. There are other, even more contemporary examples: Indian TV series set in Dubai narrating Dubai Indian love triangles and conspicuous consumption; popular Arabic-language shows depicting Emirati and Indian protagonists communicating in Hindi; a radio dial on which Emirati Arabic, pan-Arab, Hindi, and Malayalam, along with English, are represented; and at least five major daily newspapers, the Abu Dhabi based *al Ittihad*, which focuses on pan-UAE issues, the Sharjah-based *al-Khaleej*, more pan-Arab in its orientation, the Dubaibased *al-Bayan*, a sort of Arabic-language *Financial Times*, as well as the South Asian–oriented English language *Gulf News* and *Khaleej Times* (not to mention dailies in various other South Asian languages, along with those in Persian and, increasingly, Russian and Chinese). A thirty-ish Emirati businessman's joke, made in a conversation with me some years ago, suggests the flexibility and segmentary logic of self-identification among both Emiratis and South Asians. He said, "the Emirati and Indian merchants understand each other; they are of the same mindset. Not like the Chinese [a newcomer to the Dubai merchant scene]. The Emiratis and Indians say about the Chinese, 'They eat the green and the dry (*yāklūn al-akhḍar wi'l-yābis*).' That is, they eat everything, which, my interlocutor explained, means that they are equally inscrutable to Indian and Emirati. Among other things, the comment signals a now less visible deep history of Indian Ocean interconnection between Emiratis and Indians, which seems to entail a segmentary approach to identity—in opposition to each other when only locals and South Asians are concerned; in alliance with each other in relation to "outsiders" from further afield in the Asian–Indian Ocean arena.

Nevertheless, the general assumption is that the nation is under threat of being overwhelmed by foreigners, especially those from Iran and South Asia. The terms *"khalal sukkānī"* (demographic distortion or imbalance) and "threats to national identity" are the most often recurring slogans in the media and the *majālis* (receptions or salons) of the more cultivated locals (Habboush; Hussein). These anxieties continue to exercise Emirati officialdom and the elite today. It was recently reported, for example, that the UAE president Khalifa bin Zayed Al Nahyan nominated 2008 as the "Year of National Identity" and suggested renewed, federal-level vigilance over the issue, initiating a committee to study the cultural and linguistic effects of "the introduction of habits and social manners foreign to Emirati society" (Habboush). "Officials and social experts alike have identified cultural and economic globalisation as a major threat to Emirati identity," according to the article. The central problem, the committee suggested, is the "population imbalance, . . . one of the gravest threats to identity." Of particular interest was the testimony of one Dr. Obaid Al Muhairi, a deputy from the emirate of Ajman, "We [the parents] are responsible for marginalising the Arabic language. . . . I sent my children to English schools because I want them to learn English while I talk here about national identity, that's why I say we are the problem." Another testimonial came from Bilal Al Budoor, head of the so-called Arabic Language Protection Association, who "said in evidence to the committee that his sons spoke English at home and they could not read Arabic properly."

Wayward Youth, "Wild" Women: Naturalizing the Patriarchal Family

Salim Al Ubeidi, who, in his late thirties, is a few years older than Issa Khalil, works in administration at a local university. He was one of the Emiratis that, during my fieldwork in Dubai, I got to know fairly intimately (or, as intimately as a *wāfid,* or expatriate, can get to know a national). One day, Salim told me his father's story. Before he began the story, he went to a bookshelf in his office and retrieved a glossy photo book of the old Emirates, before the oil boom of the 1970s. He flipped through the pages as he spoke. His father, he began, was from a well-known Bedouin tribe that has branches all over the Arabian peninsula. His father's family was *nizih,* "immigrants," who settled in the emirate of Ras al-Khaimah, to the east of Dubai. As a boy, Abu Salim woke early in the morning, and every day walked five or six kilometers to school, Salim said. He returned home in the afternoon, helped with the work of the house, and ate dinner with the family. At this point, Salim paused, as a new idea seemed to occur to him. He flipped around in the book and finally came to the page he was looking for. There was a black-and-white photo, taken sometime in the 1950s, of several bearded men in ʿabāyas (external gowns covering the upper and lower bodies, usually brown or gray) and ghuṭras (white head scarves worn by Gulf Arab men, usually in the warmer seasons). The men were sitting on the ground around a large circular metal dish of rice. This, according to Salim, is an accurate representation of a communal tribal meal "fi ayyām al-ajdād," literally, in the time of the grandfathers. Electricity, he continues, had not yet reached his father's village, so he did his homework by the light of a gas lamp when the sun went down. Socializing was open and neighborly. If a neighbor stopped in, he would be warmly received and food and coffee shared with no hesitation. Reciprocity was an unwritten rule. Indeed, the village's survival depended on it, as, for example, when a house was damaged by a storm. The entire village was expected to help with fixing the damaged house. But with madaniyya, things have changed. Salim acknowledged the benefits of "civilization" and "urbanization" (taḥaḍḍur, madaniyya), such as material well-being. But with it comes a weakening of the old communal bonds. Drawing on the familiar discourse of "threatened national culture," Salim made the conventional argument that "the introduction of habits and social manners foreign to Emirati society" (Habboush) was causing Emiratis to lose their sense of identity. To clarify, Salim made an analogy with horse training. You take a wild horse and you must domesticate it through meticulous riʿāya (custody, care). But today, families get Filipino and Sri Lankan maids to look after their children. How can children be brought up with the values of ayyām al-ajdād? (One woman's solution to the problem, added Salim, parenthetically, was to set aside a part of her house as an "Arab" section with "Arab" objects, which were intended to educate the children about their roots). Social interactions today, among his generation, are frivolous, he says. Whereas in the past, friends would talk for a long time over a cup of coffee about "real social things" (his words), life and family problems, experiences, and sufferings, today interactions are more superficial. Now, mostly it's two friends who will set up a time to meet at a café, and talk about "cell phones and cars and the women's phone numbers that they got."

Numerous Emiratis of Salim's generation and, especially, of his father's generation, recounted stories with a similar message: today's youth are feckless; they waste their best years at the shopping malls hanging out, smoking and drinking tea, and this is an unintended side effect of the Emirati welfare state and of careless family upbringing. By the mid-1990s,

Figure 8. "Car Accidents." Source: al-Khaleej June 8, 2004. Reprinted with permission of Dar al-Khaleej.

writes Christopher Davidson, even Emirati officialdom had begun to publicly voice concern (Davidson 2008, 178–79, see chapter 1).

The cartoon above, from the Arabic-language daily *al-Khaleej,* dramatizes some of these sentiments. The scene consists of the typical surroundings of today's Emirati youth (at least from the perspective the image represents, that of an older, perhaps male, generation): the shopping mall café, cups of tea, a water pipe. The boy on the right is saying to the other boy, "I was sitting with Khalid, God rest his soul (*allah yirḥama),* we were chatting with Rashid, God rest his soul. A couple of our friends whom we hadn't seen since high school came up, God rest their souls, and they reminded me of the time when we won the school championship, God rest the souls of the whole team!"

The contrast between the image of reciprocity and solidarity in Salim's narrative and that of the suicidally reckless youth in the *al-Khaleej* cartoon cannot be starker. Such discourse is nostalgic in a structural way (Herzfeld 1991), selecting out or inventing aspects of the past and fashioning them into stories not about what society was actually like in the past, but about what society should be in the present. Moreover, because the implication is that the youth are solely responsible for social problems, the older generation, it is suggested, are the sole authorities on questions of social values. "Generation" here is a term that shifts in meaning. It can as easily be deployed to distinguish a thirty-something Emirati from a twenty-something or a teenager, as well as distinguish a seventy-something grandfather from all three. The key is the social work done by the term, whose function is to reassert the authority of the elder over the younger and to equate the perspective of the former with the social ideal or norm.

Nostalgia's generational assumptions are also shot through with gendered ones. Ali al-Rafidayn, a septuagenarian former mechanic, expressed this well in a conversation we had.[11]

> It used to be that women weren't allowed to leave the house. She was head of the family, she was respectable (*rabbat al 'ā'ila, muḥtarama*). Now, it is a scandal (*muṣība*). Now, children don't know their own mother. They only know the Filipina that raises them. It's become something else now.

"*Dunia ṣār ḥilu,bas ma'īsha murr* (earthly things have become sweet, but life has become bitter)." He did not mean "bitter" in a wholly figurative sense, either.

> In the past, [all we had to eat] was tea and Paratha. There was no '*ashā* [dinner, or main meal]. There was no '*ashā* but there was *ṭa'ām* (i.e., the food had flavor, it tasted good, life had flavor). Because the *ḥarīm* [the women] cooked back then. Now, we have '*ashā* but there is no *ṭa'ām*, there is no *lidhdha* [we have plentiful food, but it has no flavor, it is not delicious anymore]. *Al insān mā yishtihī* [one is not even tempted to eat]. The women of the house no longer cook. Now it is the Filipina.

Echoing Salim Al Ubeidi, Ali's story is about how Emirati women's abdication of their responsibilities has invited the aforementioned foreign influence, in turn threatening Emirati identity. The following cartoon dramatizes this association of threat to the family with women's supposed weakness of will. The woman on the right tells her friend that when she talks about her husband's position as a general manager, the husband yells at her, saying that she publicizes his secrets. The woman on the left

Figure 9. "Husband's Secrets" from *al-Ittihad,* June 19, 2004.

responds ironically, saying "no, *indeed*, you protect his secrets."[12] The woman on the right stands in for an abstraction, the "woman" behaving unconsciously, the "woman" left to her own devices and who has no shame. The woman on the left, by contrast, is the "cultured woman," whose essential nature has been mediated by culture. She is the woman as superego of the patriarchal family, carrying out her proper duty as defender against the intrusions and gazes of outsiders.

Another version is the "woman as manipulator of men." "The thought pattern of some wives" is the caption of the following comic. Inside the thought-bubble, under the word "husband," is an image of a man in local dress, out of whose head sprouts a key. The implication is that some wives trap men into being tools. Women, it is suggested, are naturally manipulative and, when not civilized by *ri'āya* (the protection and guidance of their husbands), remain materialistic, governed by their appetites.

The contributor of a polemical essay, *"Ainahum min al-ta'addud?"* ("Where are the polygamists?"), to the Arabic language daily *al-Ittihad,* took a slightly different angle on the problem of women's supposed immorality.

Figure 10. "The thought pattern of some wives" from *al-Ittihad,* July 6, 2004.

Yes! Indeed, some of them are not respectable. But they would never have reached this point of immorality [*in'idām al-akhlāq*] if not for the men of society neglecting their role in caring (*ri'āya*) for and protecting [women] and [their] dignity (*karāmatha*). Were these women to find a husband who cared for her (*ra'aha*) . . . and responded (*yulabbī*) to her needs as a female (*untha*), she would not be found displaying herself to every random person. In the shopping centers and such places. (Kalbani)

Another editorial contribution contains the narrative arc and characters which we now can see as conventional—the ungoverned wife abandoning the husband, in turn inviting corruption, familial and cultural, by way of the foreign domestic.

In my experience, I've learned that there is a large and dangerous question, and that is the question of the mother. What was she like before, what has become of her? . . . She was once aware of her love and tenderness, her compassion. Today, she is no longer interested in her children and devotes herself [only] to her desires.

There's now a new way of doing things, and that is that the maid does everything around the house, takes care of the kids, and is even the one taking care of the husband! We should not be surprised that such a mother would abandon her children to the influence of a woman from another culture. (al-Kiwari)

This comment contains the essence of the patriarchal-familial political model—the equation of the ungoverned woman with an opening in the edifice of the national culture to the habits and manners supposedly corrupting Emirati society with foreign influence.

It is important to note that such discourses do not only indicate an aesthetic distaste or a cultural antipathy towards certain unorthodox types of gender identity and behavior, as salient as these are. Calls for gender orthodoxy, as we might call it, tend to be closely connected with discourses about rights and obligations (in Arabic, "*ḥuqūq*," sing. "*ḥaqq*"). In other words, they presuppose not only cultural-behavioral norms but also a normative polity. They are political discourses, taking for granted a basic structure of how power is distributed in society and what the individual's place is within this distribution of power. Here is one of our polemicists again.

To put it more clearly, it is the mother who has the right and the duty (*'alayha ḥuqūq*) to raise the children, not the maid. We should not be surprised that [such a mother] ignores her husband from time to time. For it's now the case that modern mothers are most interested in getting new friends and spending their best time with them, leaving behind their responsibilities. They have also become obsessed with buying name brands so that they can show off how advanced and cultured they are. . . . I have learned that not every woman who gives birth becomes a mother. . . . Motherhood is not an easy thing. Because of the mother's immense struggle (*juhūdaha al-kabīra*) to raise the children, Islam gave the mother expansive rights and duties (*ḥuqūqan kabīra*) and favored her over the father. But, if this mother is too busy to raise her children, who will do so?. . . I will conclude by saying that the future of our children rests on the mother. If it improves, then the children's future will be bright. If not, then she will be the main reason behind the children's ruination (*ḍayā'uhum wa halākuhum*). Mothers would do well to look at the mothers in Islam. . . . (al-Kiwari)

A third contribution elaborates on *huqūq,* connecting them to issues of beauty (physical and, more importantly, intellectual, spiritual, and social).

> There is nothing more beautiful in this world than a virtuous and pious (*sāliha*) wife who raises children in a virtuous, Islamic way to build a civilized, attentive and heedful (*wā'iya*) nation. . . . In turn, in order for the family to achieve the stability for which every family strives, it is required of the wife to obey the husband. For just as the wife claims certain rights and obligations (*huqūq*) from the husband, so too does the husband claim certain rights and obligations from the wife. Obedience is the paramount duty, specifically with respect to those things pertaining to obedience, for example, treating money, allowing strangers entry (*idkhāl al-ghuraba*), etc. Not blind obedience, which contradicts Islam and its laws. . . . For God has required the wife to obey her husband because men are the guardians (*qawwāmūn*) of women. . . . Because, in general, women are guided by their emotions, whereas men are more rational. . . . Among the husband's rights is that the wife should raise the children and undertake domestic affairs (*shu'ūn al-bayt*). This does not of course mean that the husband has no role in these affairs. He is required to assist his wife in raising the children. He also has ultimate authority (*al-sulta al-'ulyā*) over them. (Al-Zawja al-Mithalia)

In these essays, and neoorthodox discourses more generally, women's supposed nature as reproducers of the family is directly related with their ascribed role of reproducing the polity. The irony here is that this view of gender relations sees itself as pro-women, exemplifying the ironic insight from Western feminism that such talk about "elevating" women or women's supposedly higher spiritual calling always conceals a patriarchal politics. Anh Nga Longva came to a conclusion very similar to my own from her work on Kuwait. For Logyva, there is a connection between Kuwaiti ethnocracy and Kuwaiti patriarchy—ethnic stratification was connected to a "devaluation of work, an activity associated with expatriates," which led Kuwaiti women to opt out of the labor market unless they could secure one of the "mostly symbolic" jobs in the public sector (Longva, 130). This quasi-voluntary turning away from the workforce, in turn, reaffirmed patriarchal notions about women's supposed physical and intellectual or spiritual weakness and created the "need" for protection from men (130–31). This exacerbated the relegation of women to the domestic sphere, further strengthening the association between them and the roles of childrearing and keeping up the home (*ri'āya wa tarbiyya*).

The domestication, so to say, of women is, in turn, dialectically connected to the status of migrant workers, especially domestics, in Gulf societies. As we see above, the "Filipina" domestic, or a variation on this figure, reoccurs frequently in neoorthodox discourses of cultural anxiety. In Kuwait, writes Longva, expatriates in general are a source of anxiety for nationals, but it is South and Southeast Asians in particular that are perceived to be a source of "moral threat," i.e., a threat to cultural values and identity (122). This is because Asian expatriates have a "unique access to Kuwaitis' private worlds and, paradoxically, develop an intimate knowledge of this aspect of citizens' lives. . . because they are part of the household, they partake of the private world of their employers, which is also the locus for the reproduction of the most important part of the society's moral system, namely family relations and relations between men and women" (124–25). In particular, the possibility of "adultery" is an enormous source of anxiety. Adultery here is defined more broadly than in the West; it includes any sexual relations outside of marriage, whether or not any of the partners involved is married. Moreover, it is common, according to Longva, for an employer to define as adulterous any situation in which the domestic is alone behind closed doors with a person of the opposite sex. "Their structural position at the bottom of the social hierarchy, combined with their status as unaccompanied women, and the inevitable cultural and linguistic miscommunication render foreign maids vulnerable to all sorts of accusations against which they are incapable of defending themselves" (125). The presence of foreigners helps to produce Gulf national identity and, as I have been showing (and will show in more detail in the chapter 5), Gulf ethnocracy produces the identities of foreigners.

Conclusion

The voices captured in this chapter—those of Salim al-Ubeidi, Ali al-Rafidayn, the comics artists and their presumed audiences, and essayists for the Arabic-language dailies—made a number of assumptions about change, social values, and political order in contemporary Dubai and the broader UAE. They all share a certain quasi-modernist nostalgia for the supposedly vanished village. There was more solidarity in the past, they said.

People worked harder and were more honorable. The youth of today are feckless. Most dangerously, the women are morally suspect. These women and youth could use much more patriarchal *ri'āya*. In short, these were discourses of social and cultural chaos. The vignettes at the Nakheel symposium that opened the chapter are structurally identical, following the narrative arc of the ritual process outlined by Turner. Figures of destructuration and chaos are followed by a liminal interregnum figurative of wandering and searching. These are then resolved in figures of restructuration. Such discourses and figurations are not, however, simply ways in which Emiratis invest the profound changes of the past few decades with meaning. There is a cultural politics at work here, in which the contemporary city is spatialized in a particular way. The ethnically homogeneous, autochthonous, and patriarchal society assumed to be the ideal in these discourses reproduces an important ideological pillar of the family-state, an ethnocratic, paternal politics of exclusion. Society and social process become analogous to (patriarchal) family order, politics becomes a relation of *ri'āya* and deference to authority, and history becomes (the ruling family's) hagiography.

Consider a couple of examples. When Ali al-Rafidayn first came to United Arab Emirates in the 1960s (having been born in another Arab country), his first jobs in Abu Dhabi and Dubai were as a mechanic. This was physically demanding, dangerous work, and he eventually had a serious accident that hospitalized him for several weeks. Having very little money at the time, he came to the attention of the ruler of Abu Dhabi, Sheikh Zayed, for whom he had done some work. The Sheikh, Ali said, unhesitatingly intervened and helped pay for the expenses. Eventually, the then ruler of Dubai, Sheikh Rashid, granted him citizenship papers. Juxtaposed to the *shuyūkh* (rulers) in Ali's story are the figures of the uncaring Indian hospital workers and the incompetent and indifferent *mas'ūlin* (functionaries, bureaucrats) at the hospital. Again, *ri'āya,* caring and custody, explicitly connected here, significantly, to paternalism, is the individual's defense against a world of chaos. The latter, also significantly, is represented by a foreigner and by the state bureaucracy. The ruler, by contrast, stands for intimacy, caring, a sense of home and belonging.

The second example will at first seem to have little connection with Ali's anecdote. "Dubai transforms itself from a village on the banks of the creek to a global city" runs the headline of a typical newspaper piece (*Al Khaleej*). An official in the Dubai Executive Office is quoted: "In the seventies, eighties, and nineties, a lot of people were content and wanted us to stay (at the same level of development). The recent prosperity, however, has surprised them, and convinced them that, had we stopped where we were back then, we would remain to this day merely a small fishing village."[13] The article goes on to attribute such farsightedness to Sheikh Muhammad bin Rashid. The message here hinges on the implicit figure of the *qarya,* the village, which is represented as lacking in the attributes of modern civilization. By contrast, the *madīna 'ālamīyya,* the "global" or "world" city, today's Dubai, appears to be the product of ruler's *ri'āya.* This may seem a reversal of the general denigration of the modern city in relation to the supposedly noble village in evidence in much of the discussion in this chapter. The constant, however, remains paternalist guidance and custody, seen to be an inherent quality of the patriarchal figure of the ruler.

During my fieldwork, I was struck by the ways in which many of my Emirati interlocutors personalized the legitimacy of the UAE ruling families. There was a distinct conception, among the Emiratis to whom I spoke, of the *shuyūkh* as accessible, caring, almost avuncular figures. One interlocutor, a young architect, echoed Ali al-Rafidayn, telling me how the UAE education minister personally interceded on his, the architect's, behalf, to provide a scholarship to go to the United States for graduate school. A marketing professional in her twenties who worked for Sheikh Muhammad's technology and media free zone told me how touched she was to see the Sheikh at the funeral of a fellow employee's mother. A third summarized this personalized system in a description of government in the UAE, where unlike in the West, even the humblest citizen has direct access to the ruler in the *majlis,* the ruler's reception hall. This understanding of the nature of the ruler, it should be added, is distinct from the local conception of the state. The ruler's *amr* (command) can override the laws of the state. As Ali suggested, whereas the state is run by *mas'ūlīn* (officials), impersonal and anonymous, the ruler is no mere official, but a guardian of the people, someone to whom access is both equal and immediate.

As these pages go to press, Dubai is going through one of the darker moments in its memory. As recently as early 2008, the city was being referred to as a "utopia" by global actors, such as starchitects. In this, starchitects reflect their background as Western cultural actors with a generally uncritical neoliberal worldview. Even as late as November 2008, no less a figure than Executive Council member Muhammad Al Abbar was minimizing the effects of the crisis on Dubai (*Sky News*). By late 2009, however, it became impossible to deny that Dubai had become a nearly perfect example of the disastrous consequences of casino capitalism. Witnessing the city's collapse is analogous to experiencing vertigo. Whether rising with breakneck speed or spinning down in a nosedive, Dubai always seems to do things in a dizzying way. All the more striking, therefore, was Muhammad Al Maktoum's sober tone in a November 2009 comment in which he attempted to reassure observers about Dubai's resiliency.

> My optimism in ending the crisis, and confidence in Dubai's ability to restore its strong growth rate soon, is . . . linked to my bedouin roots which my nation and I are proud of. . . . Bedouins are strong by nature with strong will in combating crisis. They only know determination to achieve the goal and walk towards that end. (Bowers)

Not a reassuringly detailed plan, admittedly, but the reference to "culture" does, arguably, invest the turbulent present with a modicum of stability. Since the struggles over self-determination in the early and midtwentieth century, the family-state has always had to negotiate a volatile terrain, attempting to establish simultaneously two kinds of hegemony, whose respective logics were often in tension with each other. The first was to monopolize the discourse of identity and to readapt it for the purposes of popular depoliticization. The hegemonic success of this project depended on popular appropriation of idealized representations, such as those discussed in this chapter, of village, family, and "Bedouin" identity. The second is the subject of the next chapter, readapting a market absolutism and Western-dependent economic trajectory to local lived experiences. The neoliberal tendency in Dubai is a set of discourses and representations through which many contemporary Dubayyans would critique what I have been calling the neoorthodox discourses. For a time, this tendency, which had seemed to bring together successfully a radical depoliticization with Western-oriented visions of entrepreneurial merit and consumer polity, appeared to be in the ascendant. Dispensing with what they considered to be old-fashioned notions of tradition and family, the Dubai neoliberals were making bold claims about Dubai being historically unconstrained, future-oriented, creative place (Shehab). The neoliberals were members of a newly empowered social group, "non-pedigreed" (in the words of one of my interlocutors) "flexible citizens" (Kanna 2010a; Ong 1999) whose outlook was global, consumerist, individualistic, and entrepreneurial. Figures such as Al Abbar, Muhammad Al Gergawi, and Ahmad bin Bayyat were for them symbols summarizing and embodying Dubai's future. In late 2009, Al Maktoum removed Al Abbar, Al Gergawi, and Bin Sulaym from their posts on the Investment Corporation of Dubai, a major subsidiary of the Maktoum organization. This triumvirate had until then seemed unassailable in its position as the advance guard of a supposedly new, more neoliberal Dubai. Al Maktoum's rhetoric of Bedouin roots and implicit identification of Bedouin identity with that of the whole nation (i.e., Dubai) would suggest that this drive to the neoliberal future is now, at least, in abeyance. Before the crisis, however, this did not seem conceivable. Neoliberalism was de rigueur, Bedouin symbols unfashionable. In the next chapter, I look at how some critics of neoorthodoxy attempted to reconcile neoliberalism with national cultural expectations.

CHAPTER 4

THE CITY-CORPORATION

Young Professionals and the Limits of the Neoliberal Response

Hādhī hādhī D'bai, hādhī dār-il-ḥayy, illī trajji' al-shāyib ṣbayy.
[This is Dubai, this is Dubai. This is the fountain of youth that turns the old man into a young boy.]

—Poem related by locally-based social scientist

If you don't keep up with the times, you're considered not to exist.

—Emirati manager at Majid Al Futtaim Corporation

While they represent an influential tendency in UAE cultural criticism, the nostalgic, or what I have called neoorthodox, voices in the previous chapter are regarded as stifling and rigid by many other Emiratis.[1] It is not uncommon for younger Emiratis, especially from among the neoliberal managerial class, to orient themselves towards a perceived multinational modernity beyond the confines staked out by these voices. This is not to suggest that these more neoliberal Emiratis simply reject Emirati ways of identification and investing their lives with meaning, nor to imply that the neoliberal modernity with which they identify is a wholly foreign set of values imposed from outside. These managerial types, what I call (after Ong 1999 and Wilson) Dubai's "flexible citizens," certainly would reject the types of nostalgia voiced in the previous chapter. They do not, however, reject Emirati and Muslim identities. They read them and attempt to live them in a different way. A facile rejection of the ascendant, state-led neoliberal modernity of the past two decades is not a possibility for them. Rather, they engage in an active, often creative alignment of Emirati and neoliberal values.

It is in the context of the most recent, 2008–9 world economic crisis that I began to more fully appreciate how intimately connected neoliberal ways of imagining the community and identifying oneself are among these flexible citizens. The crisis badly bruised Dubai, knocking it from the perch on which it had been set by many admirers during the past decade and even turning it, for many, into a reflection of the rot in the contemporary global financial and real estate economies (Kanna Forthcoming). As one friend, an expatriate now based in North America but who has lived for decades in Dubai, noted after a recent trip back, "I'm actually curious to see what will happen post-recession. I was there in February [2009] and 90 percent of the people I know there . . . lost their jobs. At least traffic is now bearable!" Some of what is in store in the near future is anticipated by the UAE federal state, which has recently taken more interventionist measures, such as passing laws making it effectively impossible to fire nationals from the private sector. More ominously, foreigners applying for work visas must now demonstrate knowledge of "UAE culture" (*Gulf News* 2009; Issa).

A recent blog entry by a friend, an educated, multilingual Emirati currently studying for an MBA in the United States, is therefore striking. In an entry from June 2009, responding to questions posed by expatriates about Dubai's current economic challenges, he admitted that "our giddy property bubble popped, we're super-over-leveraged and a severe globally synchronized slowdown is going down taking our trade and tourism with it. How do you put a positive spin on all that?" (Shehab). His suggestion for a Dubai recovery—Sharpening "Brand Dubai." (The headline of the webpage is a logo of indeterminate origin, in which the Arabic word "*mārka*" (brand), is juxtaposed to the English word "Dubai." Responding to an interlocutor, the blogger added, "I agree that '*trust*' (of investors, expatriates, tourists etc.) will be an important pillar. Though I would love to see Dubai champion not its '*rich heritage,*' but rather its postnational, tabula rasa nature, unburdened by tradition, determinedly future-looking" (Shehab, emphasis in the original).

Over the course of my fieldwork, many Emiratis, especially from the generation and occupational (if not social) background of the blogger Shehab, spoke in similar ways about their city. One Emirati, an academic, reacted (in a slightly menacing way) to a construction worker uprising in fall 2005 by saying that the image of Dubai must not be allowed to be tarnished by unruly workers. Several other interlocutors expressed pride in the *image* of the city, in both a literal (representational, pictorial) sense and a figurative sense (how the city reflects the informants' values). Moreover, as I showed in chapters 1 and 2, the landscape and urbanscape of the contemporary Emirati city is envisioned by rulers and urbanists, first and perhaps most importantly, as a visualized and imagistic city. This is also meant in at least two senses—the city must look a certain way (starchitecture, monuments, eye-catching buildings), and it must represent certain values (free-market globalization, a neoliberal kind of cosmopolitanism, family-state power).

One of late capitalism's most elegant tools for synthesizing imagistic representation and (a reified version of) cultural values is, of course, the brand. City branding is not a new phenomenon, and in several important ways, Dubai borrows much from the repertoire of deindustrializing Western and developing Asian cities whose pro-business leaders have attempted to reimagine urban identities and urbanscapes by branding these cities as places of spectacle, a "powerful growth rhetoric," and an intense "cultural boosterism" (Short, 115). In Dubai, this logic is often taken to extremes, especially among the neoliberal class I describe below. The Emirati political theorist Abdul Khaleq Abdulla (whose early, critical study of UAE political dependency has already been discussed), writes, somewhat ironically, in his recent essay "Dubai: The Journey of an Arab City from Localism to Cosmopolitanism" that,

> The state as brand and the city as brand, just as with the branded commodity and the branded corporation, is a natural phenomenon, and does not diminish the standing of cities, the dignity of states, or the depth of civilizations and cultures. . . . There is no difference in the age of globalization between the commodity, the state, merchandising, the city, cultures, and services. All are equivalent . . . for the surface, in this day and age, is as important as content itself. (12–13)[2]

For the neoliberal class of flexible Dubai citizens who have become a main social basis for the legitimacy of the Maktoum regime over the past two decades, Abdulla's formulation is common sense, and in spite of the author's critical intentions, an example of the success of family-state hegemony. Moreover, the blogger, Shehab, makes Abdulla's thesis more explicit. For him, the city's heritage is less important than an almost utopian post-national futurism. My argument is that when Shehab and people of a similar outlook speak about Dubai's futurism and its post-national orientation, they are not rejecting local identities and traditions per se. They are reappropriating them and implicitly responding to the neoorthodox position. How did this understanding of the relationship between society, politics, and urban space emerge in the first place? How is it embedded in contemporary local structures of meaning, and how is it related to transnational historical and cultural processes? And what are the implications for contemporary Dubai urban space?

A key to addressing these questions is an understanding of the emergence over the past two decades of neoliberalism in Dubai, as well as its connection to the subjectivity of the young professional citizens of the city-state who reached adulthood in the 1990s and who form the social basis of the emerging, if now significantly damaged, corporate-dominated order of the early twenty-first century. While the neoorthodox tendency described in chapter 3 claims the mantle of cultural authenticity, it is the neoliberal tendency, in the person of Maktoum, the figure of his holding corporation, as well as in the self-understanding of self-styled modernizing groups such as Dubai flexible citizens, that has been in the ascendant in recent decades (hence the feeling of alienation among many neoorthodox voices). Yet this ascendancy would have been less secure had neoliberal values, much as a prior incarnation of free-market values, not been successfully aligned with local cultural attitudes and dispositions.

Crucial to the implementation of neoliberal governance, according to the more insightful current thinking on the issue (Cahn; Freeman; Ong 2007; Wilson), are its productive interconnections with everyday lived experiences in local contexts. The ways neoliberal discourses resonate with and are made persuasive within local contexts of identity, conceptions of selfhood, and idioms of citizenship are essential to their appropriation by the subjects targeted by neoliberal modes of governance. The principles of neoliberalism (for example, the emancipation of capital from the oversight of the state, the commodification or marketization of realms of life that were previously the prerogative of the state, the apotheosis of the entrepreneur as a creative genius, and the analogization of society as a corporation) must be translated by powerful influential institutions and actors, such as Maktoum, Majid Al Futtaim, and the corporations they run, as well as within privileged sectors of the state. These ideologies must then be taught to and internalized by privileged segments of the population, individuals who are taught to think of themselves as a cadre, a vanguard, an exceptional fellowship carrying the neoliberal and family-state vision of the future.

This cadre must negotiate a tricky symbolic field. Cognizant of the neoorthodox suspicion of "over-Westernizing" or "inviting foreign influence," the neoliberals must embrace global and multinational identities while remaining patently authentically Emirati. Their dilemma, as I show below, is very much that of the Rashid bin Said branch of the Maktoum, to which the ruler belongs. Following Ong (1999) and Wilson, I call the young Dubai professionals engaged in fashioning a locally inflected neoliberalism "flexible citizens." This term captures their shifting between different scales and cultural worlds in constructing their identities. In aligning neoliberal ways of self-fashioning and self-identification with local meanings and values, Dubai's flexible citizens attempt to negotiate the often-contradictory demands of neoorthodoxy and neoliberalism.

The Emergence of Neoliberalism in Dubai

Neoliberalism in Dubai: A Political Genealogy

As has often been noted, Muhammad Al Maktoum calls himself the "CEO of Dubai," something reflected in the way many Emiratis make an analogy between the city and a corporation. This is especially true of Dubai's flexible citizens, who not only make this analogy but also tend to regard Muhammad as its visionary, paternalistic chief executive.[3] The emergence of this way of seeing the city and its ruling regime is connected both to the ascent of neoliberalism as an orientation of the family-state and also to a deeper history of colonialism in the southern Arab Gulf.

The historian Fernand Braudel has shown how the rise of European capitalism as a global phenomenon was based on a network of trading and

Figure 11. Dubai Media City, part of "Tecom," late 2006.

port cities governed by intensely concentrated institutions of power, such as the Venetian Signoria or the Counts of Flanders in the medieval Low Countries. Such towns, ruled (in Braudel's words) by "colluding [capitalist] social hierarchies," have historically been geographical and sociopolitical "entry points" for capitalism. Through them "the connection is made, the current transmitted" (65), the town integrated into global networks of trade and power. In Dubai, the Executive Council, headed by the ruler and consisting of twelve appointed notables, closely resembles previous mercantile–urban "colluding social hierarchies." While neoliberal in its orientation today, it must be situated in Dubai's colonial and neocolonial contexts.

Between their entry into the Gulf in the early 1820s and their withdrawal in the late 1960s and early 1970s, the British were mainly concerned with two threats, piracy in the first half of the nineteenth century and, a century later, nationalism. To combat both, the British recruited and maintained local potentates, whom they provided with protection and rent. In the process, they elevated these monarchs to absolute dominion over newly invented territories. These dynasts, such as the Al Nahyan of Abu Dhabi and the Al Maktoum of Dubai, were remarkably efficient in securing British hegemony. In dealing with their Gulf protégés, moreover, the British commonly made a distinction between these supposedly modernizing and forward-looking rulers, on the one side, and their *primitive* and *tribal* people, on the other. Even as late as 1971, at the founding conference of the newly independent UAE, the British lobbied (with eventual success) for a loose, federated independent state. According to the British Political Resident, this was because "the Trucial states [i.e., the future UAE] . . . were relatively 'primitive and needed to be kept under a more colonial character'" (Davidson 2008, 59). Generally, as Christopher Davidson has convincingly argued, the British saw the dynastic, absolutist state as closely reflecting the "immemorial Arab custom" of governance (36).[4]

The emergence of a neoliberal Dubai, effectively governed by the ruler's Executive Council, is marked both by paths not taken (those of nationalism and a participatory political system carrying a lively public culture) and paths taken. In the mid-1980s, Abdul Khaleq Abdulla brilliantly pointed to the articulation of the respective Emirati family-states' authoritarian agendas with a reductive politics of culture, both tribal and Western (see chapter 1). For the lively, more participatory society envisioned by the reformists, hierarchical governance based on political dependency and paternalism was substituted. By the time he wrote his Georgetown dissertation analyzing this situation, the "political deactivation of the [Emirati] populace" was nearly complete (Abdulla 1984, 182). Thus, it is not surprising that by 2006, Abdulla would write that because of Dubai's, or as he puts it "the city–corporation's," radical free-market policies and official orientation, "politics are inconceivable" (2006, 14). The functions of politics—the negotiation by the populace of questions of governance, the ideal distribution of social resources, the cultural cast of public life, etc.—have been made obsolete by the market's ineffable wisdom and the fact (from the neoliberal perspective) that Maktoum can preternaturally divine this wisdom.

"A Country Is like a Company"

In the post-independence period in Dubai, both the ruler and important merchants, such as the Al Futtaim and the Al Ghurair, either founded or consolidated large holding corporations that would, in effect, control Dubai's economic trajectory, public space, and public culture. These corporations espouse the ideologies outlined by Abdulla (1984, 2006), representing today's Dubai as an inevitable outcome of a teleology from which politics have been erased and in which, for example, modernity is equated with consumerism, authoritarian capitalism, and free-trade ideology. These companies have also become the milieus in which Dubai's flexible citizens reframe cultural values in neoliberal terms.

At the top of the hierarchy is Muhammad Al Maktoum who owns a complex network of subsidiary companies. The Maktoum organization is an elaborate version of the traditional Dubai family corporation (Field) with its massive portfolio of diverse interests and subsidiaries. Examples of such subsidiaries are Dubai Holding, headed by Muhammad Al Gergawi, of which the Technology and Media Free Zone (Tecom), whose employees are an important subject of this chapter, is itself a subsidiary; real estate behemoth EMAAR, headed by Muhammad Al Abbar and specializing in resort and high-rise developments across the globe; and Dubai World, chaired by Sultan Ahmad bin Sulaym. Nakheel, which specializes in themed retail and resort developments, is a major part of Dubai World.[5] All of these corporate chiefs are members of the previously mentioned Executive Council, headed by Al Maktoum, a body that is the eminence grise behind the official Dubai state. Although Maktoum recently removed these "big three" (Abbar, Gergawi, and Sulaym) from their posts on the Maktoum holding company Investment Corporation of Dubai (ICD), during the period of my fieldwork (2002–early 2007) they were, as anthropologists say, "summarizing symbols" for the Dubai flexible citizens, embodying the future-oriented, driving, progressive Dubai of their aspirations (Shehab).

By the late twentieth century, the Executive Council began envisioning the imminent end of the oil economy. As an alternative to the mineral extraction–rentier state, there was an increasing emphasis on foreign private investment, the real estate sector, and the development of free-trade zones. Established on a relatively modest scale during the reign of Rashid bin Said Al Maktoum, free-trade zones had become immense in size and a common feature of the Dubai landscape by the turn of the twenty-first century. Free-trade zones such as Tecom do not conform either to Dubai or to UAE laws in areas such as employment and visa requirements, labor market nationalization policies, or media infrastructure and censorship. Multinational companies enjoy full ownership and profit repatriation within the confines of the free-trade zones, as opposed to stringent profit-and-ownership-sharing laws in the "outside" economy.

Abdulla's recent essay (2006) is also highly suggestive in this connection. Indeed, it can be usefully read as a variation on the theory of "graduated sovereignty" (Ong 2000). Freely borrowing from recent urban theory, Abdulla sees in Dubai the manifestation of the central principles neoliberal and postmodern urbanism, such as commodified and spectacular landscapes, the marketing of city image, and the centrality of foreign investment (see also Short, 111–25). Mainly a consideration and critique of a negative conception of emancipation (he reflects, for example, on the "noninterference" by the wider society in "all aspects of [the] life" of the city-corporation [15]), Abdulla's essay provides a good summary of the ideology of the Maktoum and other well-connected and politically powerful family corporations, such as Majid Al Futtaim (MAF). The chiefs of these corporations subscribe to the city-corporation principles of commodification, labor exploitation, and the withering of the state, and their employees are trained to internalize these values.[6]

The flexible citizens to whom I spoke generally viewed Abdulla's thesis about the city-corporation quite favorably. Muhammad, a young management-level employee at MAF, for example, scoffed at me during one of our many friendly arguments, in which I would try to puncture his highly optimistic view that Dubai was a model of modern capitalism by pointing to the city's labor regime. "A country is like a company. If it doesn't make a profit, it doesn't succeed," he said. "Show me a single society that doesn't exploit somebody."

Linguistically, culturally, and often physically mobile, but often socially marginal, the flexible citizens of Dubai see their city and themselves as a genuinely progressive force in their country and in the wider Arab world. They constitute a committed cadre of the city-corporation state and Sheikh Muhammad's future vision for a polity in which capital is dominant. There are objective reasons that they are among the most committed to the Sheikh's project. Among other things, flexible citizens consist of disproportionate numbers of nonelites (individuals whose extraction is considered, locally, to be non-noble, nonpedigreed, or even "foreign") as well as women. For these groups, the generation that reached adulthood in the mid-to late-1990s is the first to have such a prominent public and responsible role in the fortunes of top Dubai firms. Moreover, there is the socialization that these subjects undergo in the process of working for (and, prior to that, gaining the proper training to be able to work for) firms such as the various Maktoum subsidiaries. Following E. P. Thompson's classic work on the processes of identity-and class-formation among the English proletariat, Ara Wilson has noted the educative character of work at the Thaksin Shinawatra firm among the aspiring Bangkok middle class (141). Work in the Maktoum and comparable firms in Dubai is similarly educative in the sense of shaping new social and class identities, desires, and visions of the future among middle-class Dubayyans.

Yet in less obvious ways, there are factors, gender being most significant among them, that make the relationship of the flexible citizens to the city-corporation model much more complex and ambivalent. By looking at these flexible citizens and situating them in Dubai contexts of identity, we can begin to appreciate how they draw on city-corporation ideology to cultivate themselves, in turn refashioning the meanings of being culturally and ethically Dubayyan. A sensitivity to the ambivalences and tensions that arise in these cultural processes, moreover, clarifies the prevailing structures of meaning that shape contemporary Dubai urban experience. Finally, because the modes of self-cultivation and identification among Dubai flexible citizens align with and are useful to the family-state, they illuminate the structures of hegemony that may persist for some time in spite of the gravity of the current toxic, credit-driven mess.

Ethos of the City-Corporation

The Social Context

The neoliberal ethos of Dubai's major holding corporations and of the flexible citizens recruited to management positions within these corporations is ambivalently situated between notions of authentic Arab identity, a variation on the neoorthodox ideology, and an explicit ethnic pluralism, which

I call a "post-purist" orientation. This is because of the ways that neoliberal ideology aligns with specific local historical legacies. Because many Gulf ruling dynasts, such as the Rashid bin Said branch of the Al Maktoum of Dubai, were uniquely dependent on British (and now American) protection, they became targets of Arab nationalist attacks. In the 1950s, for example, Dubai Nasserists accused the Rashid Al Maktoum branch, in spite of its Arab extraction, of excessive deference to the British imperial and South Asian and Persian merchant interests.

Many Persians (and some South Asians) have since become Dubai citizens, officially Arab and patriotically Emirati. Indeed, the majority of Dubai citizens today are ethnically Iranian. While the Dubai rulers, enabled by oil wealth and imperial protection, have largely co-opted or otherwise marginalized nationalist and reformist aspirations, they remain sensitive to representations of their Arab authenticity, or lack thereof. Like their counterparts in Abu Dhabi and Qatar, they devote considerable resources to staging their authentic Arabness. Poetry competitions, camel races (Khalaf 2000), heritage museums, the local media, and diplomatic and material support of "Arab" causes, such as aid to the Palestinians, are among the attempts to maintain this image.[7]

A countervailing pressure, felt especially strongly in largely post-oil Dubai, is the regime's perceived need to present an image of being open to Western investment and tourism. This has led the city-state in the past two decades to embark much more aggressively than its neighbors on a trajectory guided by the development of urban landscapes of "bourgeois gratification" (Ghirardo, 15), such as resorts, spaces both of commodity and cultural consumption, and other leisure-oriented projects. This has, in turn, triggered renewed critiques, especially from among Dubayyans of a more neoorthodox orientation, of the supposed cultural "inauthenticity" of Dubai's modern path, a resentment that can often bleed over in informal conversations to veiled criticism of the regime (Habboush). It therefore makes sense for effectively ruling-family–owned corporations and allied merchant houses to present as a vanguard a generation of managers for whom ethnic and national boundaries are (at least ostensibly) of secondary importance. By doing so, the Maktoum and allied powerful corporations seem to be responding to implicit attacks on cultural "inauthenticity" by equating a nonpurist (even arguably a post-Arab) identity with neoliberalism, and therefore, in their view, both with progress and modernity.

The Dubai flexible citizens to whom I spoke were ethnically diverse. Among them were both "pure" Arabs, members of families tracing their origins to the Arabian peninsula, and "pure" Iranians (*Khodmoni* or *'Ayam,* in local parlance), who traced their origins to the predominantly Sunni Iranian Gulf coast. These two groups are considered the elite of Dubai. At the very top is the so-called patrimonial, administrative stratum, those most closely allied to the ruling family. They have been drawn almost exclusively from the "pure" Arabs, and more specifically, from the Al Bu Falasah section of the Bani Yas tribe, to which the Al Maktoum belongs (Davidson 2008, 153–58). Iranian families, while excluded from this stratum, nevertheless number among the most powerful trading houses in the emirate. Two older men of Arab background gave me a sense of how this ethnic division continues to shape Emirati social hierarchies. Both told me on different occasions that up until the 1950s, most Arabs regarded trade as "beneath" them, preferring to rely instead on such occupations as fishing and pearling for subsistence. The *'Ayam,* by contrast, are seen to be avid and capable traders by nature. My *'Ayami* Emirati interlocutor Naila al-Musawi,[8] for example, told me that in the 1930s, "when my grandmother first came here, the [*'Ayam*] said the lifestyle of the Arabs was inferior. They considered it *qarawi* [provincial, backward]. The *'Ayam* brought most of the trade, they were more advanced, more well-traveled." This broad division can be seen throughout Dubai's history, and has been attested in various sources.[9] (Admittedly, this division seems to have become more rigid since the discovery of oil and the parallel process of the consolidation of the Emirati, ethnically Arab, nation-state. See Onley's well-supported treatment of this [2005]). Another fairly stable division is that of gender. As my interlocutor Maryama bint Rashid Al Thani[10] once told me, women in the UAE don't participate in politics (unlike in Bahrain and Kuwait) "because that is something we just don't do."

Urban settlement patterns have historically reinforced ethnic identities and continue to do so to some extent today. Before locals moved out of the original core of the city and into settlements on the outskirts of Dubai, they tended to live in "identifiable groups" in recognizable neighborhoods (Heard-Bey). This meant that people lived primarily in self-contained family compounds tending to be located in neighborhoods predominated by one ethnicity. (These neighborhoods were not, however, homogeneous.) For example, the Shindagha area north and west of the creek around which the old core of Dubai is centered, was traditionally known as the Arab area; whereas, Deira, to the east of the creek, was known as the *'Ayami* area. This process of geographic–ethnic boundary making was reinforced by settlement patterns in which individuals and groups moving into the town from the hinterland would settle in the compounds of their extended family.

The majority of the flexible citizens I met, however, came from a third group, Emiratis whose families each had at least one parent who was a naturalized Arab from non-Gulf countries.[11] Unlike the "pure" Gulf Arabs and the *'Ayam,* this group is not considered to have *aṣl,* "pedigree," as one of my interlocutors, himself the son of naturalized non-Gulf Arabs, put it. Often, this means that they cannot marry either Arabs or *'Ayam,* and, as we see below, are regarded as a "second class" by Emiratis more invested in the pedigree system.[12] It is, however, significant, that the Dubai ruler Muhammad Al Maktoum has appointed (and recently reshuffled) two individuals from among this "nonpedigree" group, Muhammad Ali Al Abbar and Muhammad Abdullah Al Gergawi, to Dubai's Executive Council. Not coincidentally, the companies headed by Al Abbar and Al Gergawi, EMAAR and Dubai Holding, respectively, are also two of the companies most invested in the postpurist framing of identity. Regardless of their background, the employees of such companies repeatedly emphasized their own uniqueness among Emiratis, citing as a main example their recognition that for Dubai to be truly global and modern, Dubayyans should reduce their evaluation of family background (how they fit within the system of pedigree) and begin to frame value in terms of individual merit, entrepreneurialism, work ethic, and willingness to self-improve. In short, to be a "valuable" citizen should be an active, locally-situated, subject of neoliberal governmentality.

Exceptional Identities in the "Zone of Exception": Individuality and Community in the City-Corporation

The so-called ruling bargain in Dubai and other parts of the UAE is a social contract in which the state provides all citizens with jobs, education, housing, and welfare. It is a commonplace belief among analysts, both foreign and Emirati, that the majority of Emirati adults of working age are incapable of productive work. Davidson claims that over half of working-age UAE citizens receive social security, that only 20 percent of Dubai's young adults are "worthwhile" (with respect to productive work), and that 60 percent lack sufficient training or discipline for any private sector work (2008, 178–82). This view is not only characteristic of Western academics or corporate analysts; it is shared by many Dubai nationals as well as South Asian middle-class Dubai residents (the latter are discussed in chapter 5). Indeed, Davidson's figure of only 20 percent of UAE youth being "worthwhile" is from a prominent Dubai national, the merchant and diplomat Easa Saleh Al Gurg. An Emirati friend, a shopping mall manager with the Majid Al Futtaim (MAF) company, made a statement almost exactly the same as Al Gurg's. Most of his compatriots, he said, would never be able to work for MAF. There are too many rewards ("fancy cars" and "high salaries," he said) that could be attained in public sector jobs or highly state-controlled and effectively subsidized private sector jobs with short hours and in which the functions these workers were supposed to be performing were actually done by foreigners.[13] Another Emirati friend, an artist who made ends meet by working with the Dubai municipality, expressed his annoyance at his municipality co-workers' absenteeism and non-work-related activities in the office. It is within this context that major Dubai parastatals and private firms have apotheosized an ideology of individual merit and entrepreneurship over the past decade. When Dubai flexible citizens sermonize about their individual merit and temperamental uniqueness among UAE citizens, they are rejecting an association between themselves and the (not entirely) stereotypical characterization of UAE youth as "unfit for meaningful employment" (Davidson 2008, 178). In turn, the discourse of merit and entrepreneurialism is connected to framings of identity that shift national belonging beyond the equation of Emirati-ness with ethnic purity, traditional patriarchy, and fears of threats to national culture.

No organizations better represent Dubayyan post-purist and neoliberal modernity than the aforementioned Maktoum parastatals and MAF firms. To both their management and their employees these organizations embody the values sketched in theories such as that of the city-corporation—they reflect neoliberalism both in the negative sense, the alleged liberation of the market from state intervention and from politics, and in the positive and active sense, as a space of individual creativity and the creation of novel identities as well as of progress beyond the rentier mentality assumed to be characteristic of most other Emiratis.

When I interviewed him, Ahmad bin Bayyat, member of the Executive Council and head of the Maktoum subsidiary Tecom, theorized that Dubai's national identity was indissociable from the new neoliberal regime. For example, in Dubai people have "a completely different mindset" from their neighbors both in the UAE and in the region. "We are not laid-back and relaxed. There is a hunger here for new ideas and different ways of thinking." Unlike in other parts of the Arab world and the UAE, according to bin Bayyat, the people of Dubai do not depend on the government to subsidize services. This in turn reinforces the practices of the government, which has to have "a commercial mindset." This has made Dubai natives less dependent, according to bin Bayyat, on the welfare state. Unlike in the "government sector," at Tecom,

> We treated everyone the same. . . . Once you bracket off [a certain part of the population] you treat them as a number, not based on their merit. Locals [i.e., Dubayyans, Emiratis] are not simply numbers to us. A majority of the locals we hire are young, with two to three years' experience. . . . Here, you work from 8:00 a.m. to 5:00 p.m., [in the public sector] you work from 8:00 to 2:00. So, they are serious, not frivolous. We only get the serious ones. But the situation is different in most GCC [Gulf Cooperation Council] countries, including the UAE. They think that their way is normal. No, we are normal! We think they're being abnormal! [14]

Three employees of Tecom, Tanya, an Iraqi expatriate, Marcus, an American expatriate, and Nadia, an Emirati whose father was a diplomat and had lived abroad for many years, elaborated on bin Bayyat's themes over lunch at a restaurant in the Tecom complex one day, giving me a flavor of what it is like, subjectively, to work for what they called the "mother company." Tanya praised the caliber of her coworkers: "People are so conscientious. They don't have to [work overtime] but they want to. This is a continuously evolving place. Recruitment is selective. And every individual is unique." She added that she particularly valued the emphasis on the "betterment of the individual" and the "sense of camaraderie."

> NADIA: The sense of community is part of the reason I decided to join Tecom.
> TANYA: I don't know, maybe I'm romanticizing things. But I definitely think that people care about each other here.
> MARCUS: The purpose of [the enclave] is to promote interaction. It is to encourage creativity. . . . A good question to ask is how has this community helped [employees] transcend national boundaries. [He indicates Nadia.] Among locals, it's taboo for a woman to sit with men, like we are doing now.
> NADIA: I lived abroad most of my life, so I don't see things that way. You can't avoid socialization with men, with others

[i.e., foreigners]. I don't think there's anything wrong with this, as long as girls don't abuse it.

MARCUS: What this community is about is liberalism, liberalizing oneself. It teaches you the necessity of crosscultural interaction. You can't isolate yourself, you have to communicate.

In the interview, bin Bayyat repeated many of the central concepts of the neoliberal city-corporation theory—the superiority of the market model over the statist national model; the view that Dubai is exceptional in its national and regional contexts; the assumption that free market policies will modernize the UAE and its people's mindset; and that for Tecom and organizations like it to pull the rest of Dubai and the UAE into the modern age, these companies must first carve zones of governmental exception from the larger state. There is also the Tecom self-image of an organization that values individuality and creativity, unlike the surrounding national and regional contexts where states allegedly treat their people like numbers.

Tecom employees to whom I spoke, both the ones already mentioned and numerous others, reiterated and elaborated on many of these themes. The values of Tecom, as the employees see them, are a care for the individual, creativity, and a sense of community. Moreover, when Nadia refers to the sense of community at Tecom, she is not talking about this vaguely. She is typical of her generation. In the past two decades, Emirati women have gradually surpassed men in their level of education, accounting for a majority of nationals with university degrees. According to a recent official estimate, there are 24 percent more Emirati women than men in UAE institutions of higher education, and nearly eight out of ten UAE women move on to higher education after high school.[15] Of course, these figures must be approached with care, as one of the reasons there are so many more women than men in UAE colleges and universities is that Emirati men tend to go the United States or Great Britain for higher education, while women are disproportionately prevented from doing so because of family pressure. Yet almost to a person, female managers at firms such as Tecom, MAF, and others claimed that women are energetically seizing the opening of the labor market under Sheikh Muhammad's reign for increased, and increasingly influential, participation.[16] These developments are, however, countered by demographic pressures and the national state's response to them. A law promulgated in 2002, called the Sheikh Zayed Marriage Fund, while incentivizing UAE men to marry compatriot women, is especially restrictive in relation to women—those who marry foreign men "effectively have to give up their nationality, as their children will not be entitled to a UAE passport and therefore neither they nor [the husbands] will be entitled to the benefits of the welfare state" (Davidson 2008, 152). A common theme of conversation among female flexible citizens was the contradiction between women's new educational and professional attainments and ambitions, on the one side, and the difficulty of fulfilling their families' informal, and the state's formal, expectations of conventional marriage, on the other. Adding to the complexity of their situation, as we will see in the following section, is the increasing social and sexual libertinism of Dubai. Not unjustifiably, these women (and probably many others) see the availability of alcohol, prostitution, and drugs, which have been part of the greater emphasis on tourism, as increasing the "temptations" (*ighrā'*), as one of my interlocutors put it, pulling men away from committed relationships.[17] Thus Nadia's comments about the Tecom "community,"—the employees' claims about their sense of camaraderie, along with descriptions of the long working hours, the "campus feel" of the Tecom complex, and the frequent social events and commensality—emerge from the increasing feeling among more educated women of distance from the modes of social integration taken for granted by their mothers and grandmothers.

The Tecom employees argued that working for the mother company was a progressive mission or calling. The process of working for Tecom is a process of enlightenment, they suggested. Moreover, especially for women, neoliberal and local ethical worlds align with particular resonance. The simultaneous emphases on individual responsibility and commitment to something like a modernizing, national struggle offers a resolution of the conflict between Dubai's particular contemporary economic trajectory, on the one side, and the temptations for libertinism and anti-social behaviors, on the other side. This subjective sense of participating in a greater calling, something that may be unpalatable to the masses outside the enclave, as well as of being, as Nadia suggests, temperamentally unique and therefore capable of being so educated, are traits shared by Dubai's flexible citizens.

The Cultural Self-Fashioning of Dubai Flexible Citizens

In Dubai, corporations such as Maktoum and MAF actively recruit individuals with backgrounds that favor a flexibility in some of the ways that anthropologist Aihwa Ong and others have described—an ability to negotiate Arabic and English linguistic milieus and Middle Eastern, Western, (and often South Asian) cultural worlds (Ong 1999, 6; Wilson, 133–62). In turn, it is through working in and participating in the social worlds of companies such as Maktoum and MAF that these Emiratis negotiate local structures of meaning, fashioning emergent identities that are rooted in local social contexts, but which these actors perceive to be somehow exceptional or transcending those contexts. Specifically, for these flexible citizens, being a good neoliberal and national subject means seeing oneself as a sort of creative artist of identity, extracting useful and (allegedly) progressive aspects of ascriptive identity and reframing them through neoliberal values of entrepreneurialism, individualism, and cultural flexibility.

Among the relevant structures of meaning are generation, gender, and ethnicity. The generation of people that came of age during the 1990s and were in their mid-twenties at the turn the twenty-first century happened to enter the workforce at the same time that the Maktoum, MAF, and similar firms began ambitious initiatives and projects, such as Maktoum's Tecom, EMAAR, and Nakheel, and the large MAF retail outfits. These companies became known for hiring and especially promoting disproportionate numbers of women and ethnically mixed or naturalized (i.e., non-Arab, non-'Ayam) Emirati employees, as well as expatriates, especially South Asians.

Dubai's flexible citizens are usually fluent in English, often as a result of their having done higher education in the United States or Great Britain. Although travel is much easier for men, women are compensating for this by enrolling in various English-language higher education institutions in Dubai and nearby Sharjah (if they have not already enrolled in one of the Dubai's prestigious English or American primary–high schools). Either way, young professionals in Dubai now master at least two languages, Arabic and English, and often Persian as well.

Language, Ethnicity

Linguistically, flexible citizens often prefer to converse in English. Most, if not all, connect with friends, family members, and colleagues using English text messages on cell phones, and many maintain English language Facebook pages. A few blog in English, including my friend Fuad and the blogger Shehab, an emerging celebrity among young, globalized Dubayyans. Talal, an employee in his mid-twenties at the Executive Office, headquarters of the Executive Council, said that because of his schooling at secondary level in the UAE and at university in both Great Britain and the United States, he was actually more comfortable using English. Hiba,

Talal's coeval and colleague in the office, said that although she was educated only in Dubai, she too preferred English. She said, "I think in English. [In school] English was our first language. We took Arabic in a class
called 'Religion and Arabic.'" (She also spoke about the influence of the
Western media, which has a strong presence in Dubai.)

Social factors, especially ethnicity, are also significant in shaping
the identity of flexible citizens. Maryam, who is in her mid-twenties and
the oldest of three siblings, is a management-level employee at the Executive Office. Her family is, by her description, typically Emirati in its
social outlook (if not in its social location). Her father is a businessman
who subscribes to both a strongly entrepreneurial worldview and a traditionally patriarchal set of family values and who, according to Maryam's
description, would likely find much of the neoorthodox worldview (chapter 3) to be simple common sense. Her mother, although equally devout,
was often an advocate for Maryam and her sister's more unconventional
desires, such as traveling abroad for school. Maryam's case shows how
ethnicity and gender complexly influence physical mobility, and thus the
ability to accumulate the symbolic capital (language, specialized training,
etc.) that shapes flexible citizenship. Although her family is Emirati by
nationality and therefore considered national or local (*muwāṭin*), they are
also seen, informally, as foreign because both parents are of non-Emirati
extraction. That is, they fall into neither of the broad categories, Arab or
'Ayam. "My being half 'foreign' is sometimes used to excuse things. When
I went abroad, people said 'She went abroad because her mother is [for-
eign]. They do things like that.' If I don't stick to the traditional rules,
they say, 'Oh, it doesn't matter, she's [foreign].'" Unlike pure Arab or pure
'Ayam unmarried women, for example, Maryam's traveling abroad without a male guardian (*miḥrim*) was not seen as problematic by her compatriots. (Her father was less easy to convince. Maryam told me later that her
mother's perceived foreignness is more salient when such conflicts arise
because the mother is a more recent immigrant to the UAE than the father.
Hence Maryam's description of herself as "half foreign.")

While her parents, according to Maryam, are concerned with family
reputation, a responsibility that falls more heavily on females, they were
not rigid in this regard. Maryam talked about the playful arguments with
her father about her parents' unconventional marriage, in which her father
had directly proposed to her mother (a practice not typical among their generation where arranged marriages were the norm). Maryam also described

the firm, yet reasoned and ultimately flexible, resistance of her father to her studying in the United States. While it was her "foreign-ness" that "excused" many of her behaviors and attitudes in her compatriots' view, it was her non-threatening alignment of her family's values with the aims of her education that enabled her to persuade her father to permit foreign travel. Like most other female flexible citizens to whom I spoke, Maryam's goal was to be "modern in a respectful way," to get a good job and attain financial independence, as well as to find a life partner and to raise a good, devout family. As Nadia, the Tecom employee, noted, socializing with men and foreigners are routine facts of life and should not be avoided, "as long as girls don't abuse it." Maryam similarly cultivated an orientation that drew on a neoliberal sense of modernity, in which an American business education played a central role, and aligned it with an Emirati sense of social and family responsibility.

Rana is a market analyst in her late twenties who works at Tecom. Rana is the daughter of an Arab Emirati father and a Levantine mother. By her own account, her father's travels and experiences with different cultures from India to Africa to Europe gave him a cosmopolitan worldview that deeply influenced her. He met Rana's mother while on a business trip and proposed to her through her father. Both of these factors, her father's *riḥla* or *Bildungsreise,* and her mother's Levantine background, helped Rana develop what she calls her open-mindedness. During one of our interviews, I asked her to comment on a peculiar remark that one of her colleagues at Tecom, an expatriate, had made.

AHMED: Tanya said that you are a second class citizen. Is that true?

RANA: [Laughs] Some people think this way. Not on a daily basis, but when it comes to marriages and when it comes to talking about traditions. They always prefer pure Arabs whose mother and father are from the region [i.e., the Gulf]. So for example if there is a guy whose mother and father are from Dubai, he will think twice before proposing to me because my mother is not local.

AHMED: Why is that?

RANA: They think they're very pure. People from here look down on people from other countries, and they think [that roots are everything], although, I used to think that only British white people used to have this *tafriqa 'unṣurīyya* [racial discrimination] you know, but here you can find it only when it comes to big decisions, like marriage, like all life-related things, I would say marriages and relations and . . . like, "don't trust him, he's *'Ayami* and he must be very *bakhīl* [stingy]" or like "don't trust him, he's Bedu [i.e., Arab], he must be very stubborn." . . . But I think that the changing trend has started, because we started talking about it openly. We're opening up, we're discussing it. Because we used to just [say] "this is the rule. *'Ayam* is *'Ayam* and Arab is Arab."[18]

Ahmad, an artist and intellectual in his mid-30s, does not precisely fit the ethnic schematic that I sketched above. Both his parents are so-called pure *'Ayami*. Nevertheless, owing to factors of education, travel, linguistic ability in and sometime preference of English, a flamboyant sartorial style, and his marriage to a Western woman, he is considered both by himself and by many other Emiratis to have willed himself, as it were, into a novel identity category. Another Emirati, who also knew Ahmad, has said of him that he does not have a definite *risāla* or *uslūb*. Roughly translated, this means that Ahmad lacks both an aim and a manner that would be recognized, by this speaker and by many other Emiratis, as appropriate and respectable. The speaker's position was generally neoorthodox, in other words. When I asked this mutual acquaintance to elaborate on his comment, he said that Ahmad seems still to be at a stage in his life where he is playing around with lots of incoherent ideas and identities. "There comes a point when you have to ask yourself, 'will I follow my parents?, . . . Even if you don't choose, you have chosen."[19]

As for Ahmad himself, he would likely agree that his identity is unorthodox by the speaker's standards, but he would obviously give this situation the opposite moral valence. A self-proclaimed "outsider" to Emirati society, who claims not to have many *muwāṭin* (nor, for that matter, many expatriate) friends, Ahmad traveled in his late teens to Western Europe. Ironically, when he graduated secondary school, the "outsider" Ahmad undertook a typical and thoroughly (male) Emirati rite of passage, the *riḥla,* or *Bildungsreise*. After his *riḥla* he applied to college abroad and graduated with honors. Following this stint, he traveled to another part of the continent and got himself accepted into a prestigious graduate school, in the city where he met the woman who would become his wife. After these adventures, he returned to the UAE in the late 1990s ready to pursue a career. In all, he felt that he benefited a great deal from this trip abroad, where he learned, by his account, the values of modernity and tolerance necessary for contemporary, cosmopolitan life. (This is, again, ironic, for Ahmad's estimation of the value of the *riḥla* as a process of enlightenment closely parallels that of many other Emiratis). Expanding on the theme one evening over coffee and Gauloise "reds," Ahmad made the distinction between Emiratis who traveled abroad and those who stayed at home their entire lives. The former tend to be much more progressive and open-minded, they assimilate the benefits of globalization, he said. Those who never leave the UAE lead intellectually impoverished lives. For example, in relation to his compatriots, he was more skeptical and even disdainful of the reified images of national tradition applied to the built environment (a field in which he was more than superficially interested) and evidenced by such aspects of cultural life as the Emirati national dress. Like Shehab, the blogger, Ahmad values not Dubai's "'*rich heritage*,' but rather its post-national, tabula rasa nature, unburdened by tradition, determinedly future-looking" (Shehab, emphasis in the original).

For Ahmad, a skepticism of tradition, however, does not necessarily mean a jettisoning of it. Rather, it entails a playful attitude towards it. For example, the local dress of Emirati men, which consists of a *kandūra,* or long, flowing gown, usually white, and either a *ghuṭra,* or headscarf, usually white, or a red-check *shimāgh,* is considered by most Emiratis to be a sign of exclusive, authentic national identity. It is a floating signifier, to which national, pan-Arab, and regal signifieds are variously attached. It is, for most Emirati men, a serious matter, a boundary-maintenance mechanism that is a response to uncertain demographic times, in which (as we saw in the previous chapter) national identity is perceived to be under threat. Ahmad himself wears the national dress, but usually only when on official business. In other contexts he wears a Western jacket, trousers, and shirt. I asked him how he decides when to wear one or the other outfit. "It's a matter of taste," was his response. Sometimes he just feels like wearing the national dress, sometimes he doesn't. Here, tradition is qualified as a matter of taste. For Ahmad, it is neither a deeply engrained disposition, a matter of tacit cultural knowledge (in which case, it would likely not be explicated in the way Ahmad has done) nor an example of a more explicit cultural knowledge and behavior, such as an active display of personal veneration of or identification with national identity.

I asked Ahmad whether he was religious. He said that, while not exactly religious, he does consider himself a "spiritual person." This phrase, which I cite verbatim, struck me as a particularly American inflection of the question. Perhaps, I thought at the time, he picked it up during his *riḥla* to America. It makes little difference, he continued, whether you are Muslim or Christian or Jewish. "They are all basically the same," he continued, in English. "If you are going to convert then converting from one to the other is pointless. You should become an atheist if you really want to convert." Here, Ahmad plays on an ambiguity inherent in a high Muslim tradition that both values "the religions of the Book" as almost equal in stature to Islam itself, and which, at the same time, values extremely highly, as approved in the eyes of God, the conversion of those same peoples to Islam. Compare this almost playful attitude to the religious tradition with Ahmad's image of the arid, dogmatic religious person.

There was a friend of the family, a certain Muhammad from Saudi Arabia, who used to come by Ahmad's father's house. "His stomach was out to here" he defines a sphere over his rather more modest belly. "His beard was down to here," he pulls down an imaginary beard. Muhammad has always dominated the conversation; he was always talking about religion, and "it [was] always in this narrow-minded, extreme way. I normally ignore him, but one day, I had just returned from the States, *kinit ḥār* [literally, "I was hot," i.e., I had a short temper]. I'd had enough. So I went and started arguing with him. I said, 'if someone had a time-machine and flew back to the times of the Prophet [Muhammad] or Jesus, people would regard him as a prophet too. They would probably even think that he was God or something!" It is all "time-specific. . . . A ten-year old today, with the knowledge and information that he has, if he has a time-machine and goes back to those times, people would probably think he's God too."

"So, anyway, this Muhammad with the belly and the beard, he's been scared of me ever since. Whenever he sees me, he just goes the other way." Ahmad laughed. "I've never been convinced by people who wear their religion for everyone to see, who wear beards, and pull up their kanduras to show their ankles."[20]

As I reread my interview and field notes of my encounters with Rana, Maryam, and Ahmad, I realize how frustrating it was to get finally to a point in our relationship where these generally quite generous and engaging interlocutors were comfortable enough even to broach issues of family, subjectivity, and their daily experiences. Whereas I did earn a minimal trust among some interlocutors, especially with Rana and, oddly, other women, many people to whom I spoke seemed to present aspects of themselves that they thought that I, as a so-called expert, should hear. Reviewing my field experience, it becomes clearer to me that Ahmad and others, whether consciously or unconsciously, were never going to allow me to broach topics about contemporary Emirati society and culture that they perceived to be trivial, controversial, or perhaps shameful. For example, at the time of this writing, I had known Ahmad for nearly seven years, and our conversations always took the same direction—Dubai's modernity, its futuristic orientation, and so on. For Maryam, Dubai society is always more generous and communally supportive than other societies. To attempt to discuss more controversial issues, such as Dubai's political economy, labor regime, and so on, would, I sensed early in my relationship with them, have been inappropriate.

I write this because I think it is necessary to be explicit about the fact that my position as an ethnographer, and therefore (supposedly) an expert, of Emirati culture likely influenced what interlocutors were willing to teach me about their culture and their lives, and therefore shaped what kinds of data I was allowed to collect. An awareness of this in my anthropological thinking and writing is fundamentally important, because it determines what claims I am permitted to make about the data. While I cannot say much about what many interlocutors "really" felt about, for example, the Maktoum family-state or whether, after conversations with me about how great and splendid everything was in Dubai, they went home and wrote Winston Smith–like diaries blasting "Big Brother," the utterances of interlocutors did have an intrinsic structure that is accessible to an anthropologist in my situation, whose access to participant-observation, my discipline's primary means by which to distinguish between what people say they do and what they actually do, was significantly restricted in interactions with Emiratis. In turn, this linguistic structure is tied to an ideal type of self, a kind of ethnically post-purist Emirati neoliberal self. Since flexible citizens likely perceived the neoliberal discursive field to be one that I shared, in spite of my own anti-neoliberal politics, which I tended not to discuss with interlocutors, these interlocutors felt comfortable enough to present one version of what I believe to be a self with which they strongly identified. However, although the flexible citizen identity is likely performative (as are the other identities discussed in this book) and only one part of self-fashioning among these interlocutors, it is not insincere or neatly distinguishable from what interlocutors might really feel. For these flexible citizens, the Maktoum-centered image of futuristic, global Dubai of the turn of the twenty-first century was (and seems to remain) a powerful summarizing symbol of aspiration and modernity (Shehab).

Rana, Ahmad, and Maryam are saying important things about how Emirati Dubayyan society stratifies and internally organizes itself. What is more interesting, for our purposes, however, are the ways in which all three use discourse in the process of exploring and presenting a kind of entrepreneurial self characterized by a figurative, unencumbered mobility between tradition and the new, the future, and so on.

The literary critic Mikhail Bakhtin has drawn attention to the sociopolitical implications of (written, literary) language, insights useful to anthropologists studying the interconnections between the social and the pragmatic-linguistic. For example, Bakhtin argues that language is not only stratified into dialects, but that it is also stratified into socio-ideological tendencies connected to professions, generations, subcultures, and so on (259–422). Moreover, this stratification is a source of heteroglossia; it draws on the centrifugal character of language, its almost intrinsic resistance to the centralizing projects of institutions of power. Juxtaposed to the neoorthodox position and neoorthodox discourse, the essence of what Bakhtin calls the centripetal force of high traditions and institutions of power, flexible citizens' discourse can seem heteroglossic and therefore anti-authoritarian. Rana's, Maryam's, and Ahmad's utterances each exhibit aspects of heteroglossia. Each, fluent in English, chose to speak to me in both English and Arabic, a linguistic hybridity, as I have been suggesting, characteristic of the neoliberal flexible citizens of Dubai. Secondly, each speaker made skillful use of reported speech, another source of heteroglossia, according to Bakhtin. Here is Maryam, for example, on traditional marriage practices.

> For traditional Emiratis, the name of the family is very important. They stress very heavily on the purity of the lineage. "Is this family [consistent] with our old Arab *'ādāt* and *taqālīd* [customs and practices]?" [Some 'Ayam] don't want a traditional Emirati; they'll say "*hādha Badawī*" [he is a Bedu]. See, whereas the Bedu [i.e., "pure" Arabs] say it with pride, the other guys will say, "No, we don't want someone backward. We don't want somebody who does this and who does that."

In the same way, Rana evoked a type of Emirati who would talk about "stingy *'Ayam*" or "stubborn Bedu," or who would inflexibly distinguish between the two ethnicities. The reported speech abstracts aspects of experience or memory and distances them from the speaker, positioning the experience in such a way that it becomes boiled down to its essence, or rather, to that part of its essence that emotionally interests the speaker. In this way, the speaker can more concretely imagine her identity and position herself in an ideal way, aligning the contingent presentation of her self at the given moment with the demands of the speaking context.

Bakhtin also sees an important role for irony, parody, and jokes, which consist of using the word "not in its primary sense" (237).

> In all these approaches, the *point of view* contained within the word is subject to a reinterpretation, as is the modality of language and the very *relationship of language to the object* and *to the speaker*. A relocation of the levels of language occurs—the making contiguous of what is normally not associated and the distancing of what normally is, a destruction of the familiar and the creation of new matrices, a destruction of linguistic norms for language and thought. (237, emphasis in the original)

Ahmad's discourse combines dialogism with humor. He discursively constructed a type, the religious Saudi, a type that became the target for Ahmad's sarcasm. This construction exhibited a skillful, informed juxtaposition of two, as it were, centripetalizing traditions, that of a neoorthodox interpretation of Islam against that of a self-imagined Anglophone cosmopolitanism, tactically deployed to (arguably) amusing effect. Elsewhere, Ahmad intensified the logics of high Muslim traditions (of *ahl alkitāb,* or "peoples of the Book," on the one hand, and, on the other, of conversion), and juxtaposed them to generate an amusing hypothetical situation involving a time-traveling prophet-child. In these ways, institutions and traditions of power, along with their "centripetalizing" discourses, are "purged through laughter" (Bakhtin, 240).

Or so Ahmad would see it. As I have been arguing, a chief conceit of Dubai's flexible citizens is that they are exceptional, unlike any other group of Emiratis. They tend to see themselves as temperamentally more inclined to modern ways of thinking, by which is meant a logic that is a hybrid of Maktoum family-state ideology and a sanguine neoliberalism. Flexible citizens, according to this logic, are creative artists of identity, moving easily between tradition and modernity, unencumbered by the constraints of either. However, as I showed earlier, our mutual acquaintance dismissed Ahmad as someone without a coherent sense of identity. This speaker clearly meant that Ahmad did not conform to an appropriately neoorthodox identity. But not all potential disagreements with Ahmad's position can be easily dismissed as neoorthodox. One such position, neither neoliberal nor neoorthodox, is reflected in Abdul Khaleq Abdulla's dissertation on UAE political dependency (1984). This work emerged from now largely forgotten but once influential political currents in Dubai, what we might characterize as the reformist *tiers-mondisme* and Arab nationalism of the 1950s

Dubai National Front. Ahmad's discourse would likely be regarded, from this point of view, as too dismissive of local traditions and even as classist. Abdulla highlighted a limitation of neoliberalism's precursor when he wrote about how the free-market class masks its essentially feudal politics with the façade of Westernization, how it conflates a free-market ideology with modernity (1984, 175–76). As I show below, there is a tendency among flexible citizens (especially male flexible citizens) to conflate neoliberal values, such as individualism and consumerism, with modernity and progress tout court. In Bakhtinian terms, the tendency is to conflate essentially safe types of seditious speech and behavior (because, while culturally rebellious, such acts are essentially in agreement with neoliberal governance) with anti-authoritarian, heteroglossic speech.

In short, Dubai flexible citizenship is shaped by the state's project of class formation. Essential to the state's hegemonic project is the management of individual subjectivity by inculcating an ability in flexible citizens to speak and enact creative, entrepreneurial, and even rebellious identities in ways unthreatening to the state's essentially neoliberal commitments. According to this logic, it is unnecessary and even perhaps inefficient to be culturally rigid or monochromatic. Cultural exclusivism is bad capitalism (Michaels). Going against the neoorthodox grain in Dubai is a project largely aligned with neoliberal governance. Being culturally unorthodox and fashioning and presenting oneself as unique usually goes along with a tacit agreement with the family-state monopoly of politics.

Along with being shaped by class, flexible citizenship is an identity shaped by gender. Consider the identification some flexible citizens make between sexual libertinism and modernity. Fuad, a former employee of the Executive Office, is another mid-twenties Emirati of "foreign" extraction. His parents emigrated from a non-Gulf Arab country before he was born. Like Maryam's father, Fuad's father became close to the former Dubai ruler, Rashid, via business dealings, and like many other non-Gulf Arab immigrants in the 1960s and 1970s, was eventually granted naturalization papers by the ruler. Like Maryam's family, Fuad's family was considered *muwāṭin,* "national," in the official sense, but ethnic outsiders. Fuad elaborated upon the connection between ethnicity and life chances and implied that the order being implemented by Sheikh Muhammad heralded new things. Growing up in Dubai, "I guess I sort of inhabited this gap. I wasn't really an expat, but I wasn't a typical *muwāṭin* either. . . . There isn't a category [i.e., Arab or *'Ayam*] that I fit into. But like an *'Ayam,* I would be problematic in marriage issues."

"You mean, [Arabs] would have a problem if you wanted to marry their daughter?" I asked. "Yes. I wouldn't have pedigree. The *'Ayam* too, they're not considered [by the Arabs] to have pedigree either. There was a lot of discrimination against them by [the Arabs], but Sheikh Muhammad is trying to change that. He nominated [Muhammad] Gergawi to head Dubai Holding. He was the first Iranian (i.e., *'Ayami*) to hold that high and prominent a position in the Dubai government." Perhaps inferring a critical edge to my question, or to his reading of it, he paused thoughtfully. Then he began again, "Everyone very easily challenges your attachment to this place if you criticize it. In fact, I am very attached to this place. It's where I grew up; it's where all my best friends are from." Another pause. "Sometimes, you're pleasantly surprised, though. The other night I was at the [Dubai] Jazz Festival, and they were handing out condoms. Can you believe that? Here, in Dubai."

Ahmad similarly connected the issue of sexuality to Dubai's modernity in the "Muhammedan era" (Abdulla 2006). In the same conversation where he linked the experience of travel with personal growth, he made an analogy between the travel experience and crossing boundaries, both literal and mental. One became seasoned, he said, less governed by taboos, perhaps even blasé, in one's approach to everyday life. At a gathering that he and I attended one evening, the hosts were playing the film *Clockwork Orange* (Kubrick). The scene where the main character is forced to watch nude women caused a reaction in the audience, which prompted Ahmad to reminisce in the following way. Some years before this gathering, he and some friends had organized a semi-public screening of the same film. Against Ahmad's resistance, the fellow organizers cut out the nude scenes, fearing the police turning up. "But things are changing in Dubai," he said. "Pretty soon, pictures of nude women will be no problem." He clearly meant that this was a sign of progress.

The ways in which Fuad and Ahmad linked sexual openness with modernity suggest that the discourse of modernity in contemporary Dubai may be gendered in ways of which male flexible citizens may be unaware. In her work on Bangkok middle-class flexible citizens, Ara Wilson observes how the seemingly apolitical nature of consumer culture turned out to be, in fact, a mode of the redeployment of the state's power through invisible controls of which middle class subjects were largely unconscious or about which they were not skeptical (Wilson, 141). In this chapter's section on the emergence of neoliberalism in Dubai, I discussed a similar collusion between capital and the state in demobilizing the citizenry by identifying consumer capitalism with progress and modernity. Fuad and Ahmad both envision the city-corporation period in Dubai's history as an advance in emancipation, an overcoming of tradition. The MAF employee Muhammad had connected this theme to the emancipation of business from politics. For Fuad and Ahmad, this emancipation is more spiritual, an evolution of Dubai into a place less governed by taboos and artificial social distinctions. For all three of these male flexible citizens, politics somehow disappear. In the discourses of female flexile citizens, however, politics reenter through the door of gender.

Gendered Ambivalences

My discussions over the span of a year with four female employees of MAF and Tecom show that although Dubai, as a space for the expression of novel identities, has been reconfigured and perhaps expanded in the Muhammedan era, this reconfiguration remains regulated by patriarchy, which is in turn enabled by the city-corporation's increasing governance by market fundamentalism. Fuad, Ahmad, and Muhammad's liberatory Dubai becomes a much more ambiguous place in the renderings of Raghad and Naila (first introduced in the previous chapter) and Randa and Rana, who perceive complex connections between gender, generation, aspiration, identity, and the city-corporation. Raghad and Rana, incidentally, are both,

Figure 12. "National Identity" on display, MAF's Deira City Center, 2004.

like Maryam, Muhammad, and Fuad, Emiratis of foreign extraction (Naila is an Ayami, while Randa is of Arab background). Each had a more complex reading, for example, of the increasing sexual openness of the past few years. Each, like Maryam, expressed a generally positive attitude towards the changes characterizing contemporary Dubai. Furthermore, each expressed relief that modernity, as Raghad, using the English, put it, was being guided by what they considered to be wise men such as Sheikh Muhammad and Majid Al Futtaim. Each found the companies they worked for to be progressive and supportive of women's advancement and, thus, strong evidence in support of the appeal of the city-corporation model. In any case, Randa said, there was no use complaining about these changes, because they are part of trade (*tijāra*), which is in the interest of all Dubay-yans (*li-ṣāliḥ kull-ḥadd*).

Nevertheless, they were also more likely than their male compatriots and coevals to emphasize the importance of balancing the desire for the new with a respect for the "traditions" (*taqālīd*), maintaining that openness to the modern or the foreign without "respect" (*iḥtirām*) for the past and the local was meaningless. A good example of this was the exchange, discussed in the previous chapter, in which Raghad and Naila talked about modernity and *tafakkuk al-'ā'ila* (the breakup of the family). There was less "temptation" (*ighrā'*) before modernity, according to Naila. Now there is more sexual libertinism—drugs, prostitution, alcohol. In the same conversation, Raghad continued (speaking to Naila),

> There is a hush-hush mentality here. There are websites, for example, that are only available outside the UAE, that advertise rates for prostitutes in Dubai. You can't access those sites here. It's enough! There is no respect for religion. It is too open. We have to have balance. There are also double standards. There is no democracy. I can't discuss sensitive issues [like these] with locals, especially with the Arabs [i.e., Bedu]. But it's a general problem with the Arabs [i.e., people from the wider Arab region]. Everything is a sensitive issue with us. There is lots of segregation. The man does his own thing. The woman just spends money and is bored.

The ambiguities of flexible citizenship, and the complexities of its mediation by gender and ethnic background, are most vivid in the case of the Tecom market analyst Rana, who was discussed above. Like Fuad, she pointed out how most Emiratis would not permit their sons to marry her. In one of our conversations, Rana connected the issue of marriage to her own sense of uniqueness in relation to other Emiratis, who, she claims, marry because of family pressure or the desire to conform to social norms (implicitly, the Emiratis who abide by the ethnic purity rules).

> RANA: I'm a very complicated person. My understanding of marriage is not like anybody's understanding of marriage. Like any woman, I want to be a mother, but I want to be a useful mother. I don't want to harm my kids, and I don't want to raise kids who will have no future. So, then the beginning should be right. I should get married when I'm ready for it, and I should get married to someone who is [of] the same mind, who understands where I'm coming from, and who will not get married for the sake of getting married, who wants to get married because he wants a life partner, somebody who will support him and back him and be there whenever he is needed and the other way around. Kids are not the core objective. Kids come out of a relation[ship]. [If] the relation[ship] is there, then we can think of bringing the fruit of the good relation[ship]. But if it's not good then why [bring kids into it]? The kids will not be happy because the parents don't understand each other. And even with my kids I would love to have a very open-minded kid, I would love to give them their space. Different than this society. I want them to be themselves, I want them to be very independent. But my mentality is very different.
>
> AHMED: Independent of what?
>
> RANA: To give them their free space, without any control of tradition, or people's perceptions.
>
> AHMED: What do you mean by "tradition" and "people's perceptions?"
>
> RANA: I don't know if you've noticed, but most people here restrict their kids from doing certain things. Like, for example, a boy will grow in a way that "you shouldn't cry because you're a man," and, for a girl, "you shouldn't go horse-riding, because this is a man's thing, you shouldn't wear this color.". . . And you're really restricting your kids, you're not giving them space to find out what are their tastes like. They should figure it out. This society controls them in

a way that they don't have enough space to try things and to have their own lifestyles and tastes. They're either partially or fully directed by other people.

During various conversations, Rana and her co-workers, such as Tanya, emphasized Rana's creativity. Tanya, for example, extolled Rana's mastery at preparing sushi, asserting that "maybe it has something to do with the creativity of the people who tend to work at Tecom." At the time of my fieldwork, Rana had been for some years a serious artist as well. Rana attributed this creativity to two sources, her family and her workplace. Like Ahmad, she pointed to the influence her father had on her. His wanderlust and ability to do business in many languages made her more aware, she said, both of the smallness of the UAE and the complexity of the larger world. He was of the generation of Emirati businessmen, she said, who could not rely on capital to come to the UAE, but had to travel abroad, to Europe, South and East Asia, and Africa, to make contacts. Because both of his parents were teachers, he also knew the value of education.

Like Tanya, Rana also made the connection between uniqueness, creativity, and the experience of working at Tecom. When she was recruited to work at Tecom, what appealed to her was the sense of being involved in something both different and vital in the context of her home city: "I liked the idea of [working in] a free zone, where people will have 100% ownership, in so and so industries, so and so areas, and it's going to shape the new economy of Dubai."[21] She added that Tecom was exciting because "it's new, a start-up, and I'm very open to new ideas, I'm very adventurous, and I don't mind trying a new job." But the stakes were more than personal, "This is a country adventure, it's a Dubai adventure. So, if we get through life, if we are adventurous, and if the whole country is doing the same, let's try, and if we fail, we fail together, and if we win, we win together."

> AHMED: In what ways then would you say that [working at Tecom] is different from the common, everyday experience?
> RANA: The image that Dubai is trying to build is "Dubai is different." Different in terms of lifestyle, different in terms of the number of nationalities that we have here, different in terms of concept. How many media, technology, and education free zones do you have around the world? So it's the uniqueness of it. That's why it's a trial, it's in the future.

"I think Sheikh Muhammad is trying to add more value to our social life," she added.

> Be traditional, but be modern. I can manage to be both. I don't know how. A few days ago, one of the ladies in my group, [an Emirati], was wondering how I could, for example, walk into press conference, ask questions, where I become very forward, go take pictures of people that I don't know. Speak to anyone, help anybody. And she was wondering, why am I doing this, what is there in my personality that gives me the power to be so natural. And actually it's nothing, it's just that I am very natural, if I don't harm anyone and it'll help me learn, whether it's in a modern way or a traditional way. It's very simple, it's not complicated.

Here Rana is drawing on the main themes outlined by technocrats such as bin Bayyat. Dubai is exceptional; the ruler is wise and forward-looking, acting in the interests of all Dubayyans and making it possible to balance the traditions with modernity. Like these elites and the company employees, Rana also focuses on how a special class of people are drawn to companies like Tecom. They are true individuals, they stand out from the herd, they are not culturally monochromatic; rather, they are "complicated," creative, and committed to the progressive vision of the Sheikh.

Promises and Limitations of the Neoliberal Response

It is difficult to imagine that the neoliberal ideology that has characterized Dubai over the past decade or so, and is evident in the voices of the Dubayyans discussed here, will be maintained with quite the same optimism in the near future. At the time of this writing, things in Dubai appear to be in chaotic flux, with seemingly contradictory assertions regularly emanating from the realms of officialdom. In late 2008, Muhammad Al Abbar denied that Dubai was in trouble; a few months later, he was removed from the ICD. Shortly thereafter, in late 2009, the Burj Dubai (later named the Burj Khalifa) was finally completed. Depending on one's perspective, the Burj will either be a rebuke to Dubai doubters or a gesture not without some pathos, a monument to an already receding historical era of faith in urban imagineering and the wisdom of place wars. At the same time, Dubai officials have started to frequently revisit claims of cultural authenticity, with no less a personage than Sheikh Muhammad asserting, in late 2009, that Dubai's bedouin roots will be a source of regeneration in the future (see discussion in previous chapter). The juxtaposition of the Burj, perhaps the most powerful symbol of "New Dubai," with reified notions of local culture might indicate a new alignment of cultural politics, in which neither neoorthodoxy nor flexible citizenship are in the ascendant, but in which these two tendencies coexist and may in fact reinforce each other.

Whatever the case may be (and, unlike my flexible citizen interlocutors, I hesitate to make any confident assertions about such a moving target as Dubai), one can at least say that the current alignment of faith in the free market and reductive official constructions of national culture is not surprising. The Dubai ruling elite have long been allied with global interests over local ones and have accordingly espoused a radical version of free trade ideology. Economic crises threaten this order, pressuring an essentially reactive welfare state by pitting its distributive commitments against the demands of private sector profit. Vocal critique of this situation is predictable, and is often expressed indirectly, targeting elites' stewardship (or lack thereof) of national cultural identity. Neoliberalism, with its valorization of the individual entrepreneur, its provocation to question tradition, and its commodification of culture, has in the Dubai context strongly resonated with elites' interest in fashioning a usable, post-purist sense of identity. It has been useful in making more palatable what is seen by many Emiratis as the elites' modus vivendi with global capital (see chapter 1). In the near future at least, Dubai flexible citizens will likely remain an important social base for the Maktoum and allied interests and continue to appropriate vestigial elements of neoliberal ideology into their identity.

My argument in this chapter emerges from recent developments in the anthropological analysis of neoliberalism. The complex ways in which different parts of the global economy have responded to the global economic pressures of the past few decades have confounded theories of neoliberalism as a "package of policies, ideologies, and political interests" (Hoffman et al., 9; see discussion in introduction). Instead of assuming the meaning of neoliberalism, as such theories tend to do, it is more productive to shift the focus towards two areas—to the ways in which local structures of meaning and symbolic contexts inflect neoliberal policies and ideologies, and to the ways in which everyday people actively cultivate selves and subjectivities in relation to emergent neoliberal governmental regimes. Although I have drawn much from Aihwa Ong's insightful work on neoliberalism, I have also suggested that the Arab Gulf context presents unexpected data that require reformulating parts of her theoretical apparatus.

For Ong, what is particularly salient about the Southeast Asian neoliberal state is its highly mobilized, elaborate regime for creating or engineering economically "valuable" citizens (2007, 4, 185, 189, 219–39). In an Arab Gulf state such as Dubai, the citizen population is too small to be productive on a national scale, and thus issues of productive and worthy citizenship are not framed in terms of economic value. Rather, they are formulated in terms of national ethics and the modes of proper and authentic citizenship. Unlike in much of Southeast Asia, especially Singapore, Dubai flexible citizens attempt to align non-neoliberal social expectations, such as those pertaining to gender, with neoliberal notions of selfhood.

Such dynamics of cultural process should be contextualized within the specific historical situation of Dubai. The emphasis on cultural authenticity and proper, ethical citizenship carries particular significance in a polity where the ruling elite have historically struggled to legitimize themselves as representatives of the populace. Because the Al Maktoum were historically very close to their imperial protectors, they became the targets of nationalist attacks on their legitimacy. Although such criticism has its origins in the anticolonial movements of the mid-twentieth century, it continues today in the everyday discourses of many Emiratis, where there is an often unstated but unsubtle assumption that modernity has been somehow disjointed and that nationals are losing their identity to foreign influence (Habboush). Because of the strong tendency of anti-regime discourses toward a quasi purist ethnic orientation, in which the ethnic Arab identity is assumed to be the authentic Emirati identity (see chapter 3), the regime and its allies have attempted both to present themselves as authentically Arab and to promote a post-purist framing of Emirati identity. The latter seems especially evident in the project by firms such as the Maktoum, MAF, and others to advance a new generation of managers whose social background makes them less likely to esteem ethnic purity, social pedigree, and connections as means for social advancement. This cadre, as it were, of the neoliberal regime fashions an identity based instead on neoliberal notions of business management, self-cultivation and regulation, and individual merit, but which, especially among women, also attempts to observe certain tacit limits perceived as traditional.

In short, the neoliberal emphasis on individual over community identities aligns well with the regime's and its allies' interest in demobilizing potential sources of identification and solidarity not susceptible of state control. For these elites, "social instruments of political dependency" in Abdul Khaleq Abdulla's canny formulation (1984, 124), free trade and Western-style consumerism constitute the limits of the political imagination. And indeed, especially for male flexible citizens, the increasingly libertine cultural and consumerist landscape of neoliberal Dubai tends to be appealing and emancipatory. Females, however, expressed more reservations, and in doing so, seemed to implicitly valorize a more communal vision of Dubai. This is not to say, however, that female flexible citizens were nostalgic for or romanticized a previous age. Rather, they often creatively aligned neoliberal notions of individual merit, education, and aspiration with quasi-traditional notions of familial responsibility, communal belonging, and moderation. This can be seen, for example, when Nadia says that today's Emirati women must mix with men and foreigners but should respect certain tacit boundaries, and is a main theme of other women's interpretations of modernity. It is striking, moreover, that flexible citizens see working for companies such as Tecom and MAF as both a (neo)liberalizing, enlightening process of Bildung, and as a source of community and commensality. The latter is perhaps most pronounced for female flexible citizens because working conditions at these companies appear to constitute a plausible way of resolving the tension between familial and state expectations for traditional marriages, and the increasing openness of Emirati society for women's participation in public life and work outside the home.

Regardless of the complex ways in which they frame identity and participation in the neoliberal context, no flexible citizens would dare to openly question the objective structure of power in Dubai. This is particularly visible in Rana's valorization of Sheikh Muhammad. Such esteem of the ruler and of big businessmen such as Majid Al Futtaim was extremely common in discussions with flexible citizens. Whatever shape their particular fashioning of neoliberal Emirati identity, they simply assumed that Dubai was a prosperous, progressive, and liberal place, and that this was a direct consequence of the magnanimity and wisdom of the *shuyūkh*. In the colonial period, Great Britain's plenipotentiaries routinely asserted, perhaps disingenuously, that it was the "immemorial Arab custom" for the Emiratis to live under an unaccountable, centralized, hierarchical dynastic state. While the now-forgotten Arab nationalist tendency would go on to stiffly resist this interpretation of Emirati culture, today's flexible citizens, more modern, educated (in a fashion), and prosperous than any previous Emirati generation, generally assent without qualm to this notion of immemorial custom. This demobilization is perhaps a not unintended consequence of the emergence of the neoliberal city-corporation.

This is ironic, because flexible citizens often asserted their uniqueness with respect to compatriots, pointing to the latter group's conservatism. The artist Ahmad perhaps best symbolized this sentiment with his self-construction as a rebellious, at times even seditious, young man. Frequently, in conversations with me, he would disparage what he called the "traditional," implying that the term applied to his compatriots. Yet, I have tried to show that while the neoliberal discourses and the self-constructions of flexible citizens indeed appear to be modernizing and progressive, this appearance conceals a more complex reality. Neoliberal discourses and modes of self-cultivation/identification encompass both a critique of orthodoxy (for example, the stifling attitudes towards gender and cultural identity clearly in evidence in neoorthodox discourses) and, for lack of a better term, a reactionary streak of their own, one that is unquestioningly pro-regime. Ironically, in fashioning themselves as flexible citizens, these Emiratis also position themselves as good, docile subjects of city–corporation governance. Whatever critical edge there was to the neoorthodox discourses (for example, the implicit critique of the family-state's monopoly on definitions of modernity) gets sacrificed in neoliberal discourses.

Part of the allure of the neoliberal or New Dubai vision is its promise of emancipation from the strictures of tradition. This is associated both with political and social possibility and with a more individualized promise of anonymity and consumer well-being. Part of why Dubai is so appealing, according to flexible citizens, is that the material comforts it offers as a matter of course are assumed, with some accuracy, to be so rare in other parts of the Middle East. For the MAF manager Muhammad, the fact that he could choose a themed villa from EMAAR and co-design it with the real estate firm was a good thing, evidence of the success of Dubai's consumer promise. Similarly, Ahmad was proud of his elegant clothes and the vintage sports cars with which he liked to tinker during his free time. These consumer goods allowed him to display his style and were intrinsically connected to his sincere belief that Dubai truly was a place of possibility. I discuss the New Dubai in more detail in the next chapter and read it in the context of the image of Dubai as a place of consumer well-being (Vora 2008). The limitations of this version of Dubai's modernity, and the ways in which the New Dubai is not so new but rather an urban image very much shaped by the politics of neoliberalism and the family-state, become especially visible in the experiences of South Asian expatriates.

CHAPTER 5

INDIAN OCEAN DUBAI

The Identity Politics of South Asian Immigrants

Exclusion and Inclusion in Contemporary Dubai: A Pattern of Purity

Lest we are tempted to assume, based on the discussion in the previous two chapters, that there is some neat line dividing the Emirati neo-orthodoxy and neoliberal tendencies on questions of cultural plural-ism, consider the following conversation I had with a young Dubai flexible citizen. Saad is fluent in English and educated in the United States. He is also from the *Khodmoni/Ayami* background and speaks Persian fluently. In short, he knows as much as anyone else that even "authentic Arab" Emi-ratis are very often a mix at least of Arab and Persian, if not also of South Asian and African, roots. Yet he made a revealing comment during one of our conversations. I had asked him and another Emirati mutual friend about the ethnic composition of the UAE and whether it was possible for people to become naturalized. After a short explanation of the technicali-ties, Saad concluded that naturalization is rare, and he added that state de-cisions are often unfair. He knew a Palestinian, he said, who had lived in the UAE "for fifty years or something" and wanted to get naturalized but was not allowed to. "If you have been living here that long, you should be able to get naturalized. Not all nationalities are eligible, obviously. Indi-ans are not eligible. I'm sure that the government has its reasons for this." When I pressed him on why Palestinians but not Indians should be allowed to get naturalized, Saad dismissed my question, implying that I was miss-ing something obvious. For Saad, the notion that a Palestinian could be naturalized was clearly thinkable, whereas the idea that an Indian could be clearly was not. This is a curious development in a society that has had, historically, much closer links with the Indian Ocean than with the Levant.

While eschewing the sorts of cultural reification that individuals deploying more neoorthodox discourses did, the ideologically neoliberal opponents of neoorthodoxy also, it seems, have their limits. Contemporary Emiratis, like most national communities, are both intellectually and politically diverse and, simultaneously, share a set of tacit assumptions about politics, the common good, and national identity, among other issues. A delicate balance must be achieved between social science representations of both the commonalities and differences among Emiratis. A tilt too far in the direction of national consensus risks cultural reductionism or too homogeneous an image of the contemporary UAE, as is the case with much Gulf studies literature. (See Longva, 133–34 for a trenchant critique of this tendency.) Too far in the other direction and the UAE as an imagined community disappears. My view is that a dialectical reading of UAE national identity (and of UAE South Asian identity), in which Emirati identity is seen as a process, made in relation to and through the construction of its others, can best keep this balance (see introduction). The contours of modern Emirati national identity, along with that of its primary other, UAE South Asian identity, should be approached by looking at the patterned inclusions and exclusions discursively constructed and practiced in the UAE.

Dubai is arguably the most "South Asian" of the major Middle Eastern cities. This is both a numerical phenomenon—approximately one in two Dubai residents is a citizen of a South Asian country—and a more complex process of cultural mapping and place-making. Many of my South Asian interlocutors, for example, called Dubai "the westernmost Indian city," an attitude that has been confirmed and explored in greater detail by anthropologist Neha Vora (2008; 2009b). This view is strikingly at odds with that of most Emiratis, who see the large South Asian population more as a threat to national identity and the integrity of Emirati sovereignty. In *Consciousness and the Urban Experience,* writing about another context of rapid, radical urban change (Paris under Haussmann), David Harvey asks,

> How did people view each other, represent themselves and others to themselves and others? How did they picture the contours of . . . society, comprehend their social position and the radical transformations then in progress? (1985, 180)[1]

Harvey's simultaneous focus on the symbolic and political aspects of the urban management of social and cultural difference is wholly germane to contemporary Dubai. So far, in this book I have been making an extended argument about inclusion and exclusion—cultural, spatial, gendered, political, and economic—and how this relates to both Dubai governance and the formation of identity among Dubai Emiratis. In the process, I have identified at least three contexts in which modern Dubai is imaginatively, visually, and physically made—contexts for the spatial representation, spatialization, and incarnation of the contemporary city. They are those of the Maktoum family-state and the urbanists (Lefebvre 2003) enrolled in its project of remaking the city and deploying the regime's total territorial control (Hazbun, 217); that of the neoorthodox orientation with both its nostalgia and its implicit critique of the family-state; and that of the neoliberal orientation, an ideology carried by a kind of committed cadre of the family-state, and which for all its discursive foregrounding of individuality and creativity, signals a more inflexible commitment to and an absence of critique of the family-state.

Although the main actors in these contexts are diverse, they share a set of tacit assumptions about Dubai space and time, assumptions that I suggest constitute a shared and exclusive symbolic economy. Although only individuals who identified with neoorthodox discourse tended to value *aṣl*, ethnic origin or shared descent (Longva, 119), a broader pattern is discernible in which varieties of purity (spatial, temporal, and political) are tacitly advanced within each context, creating an overdetermined milieu in which the city is constructed as a politically and often culturally exclusive space. For example, both urbanists, such as starchitects and urban experts, and neoorthodox actors tended to assume that local culture was homogeneous and autochthonous. They both seized on certain reified images of cultural authenticity (invented traditions, pop cultural icons, myths of prelapsarian village life) as evidence of this authenticity. In turn, this way of imagining the city falsely implies that the city's boundaries (and those of the implicit social group to which it "belongs") are lacking in porosity and that its "authentic culture" and what elites say its culture is are identical. Moreover, all three—urbanism, neoorthodoxy, and neoliberalism—traffic in androcentric imaginings of space, whether these came in the form of the monumental city of the urbanist, the idealized, gendersegregated village of the nostalgic, or the neoliberal, sexually libertine urban space of the male flexible citizen. Also, urbanism, neoorthodoxy, and neoliberal flexible citizenship each tend to view time as a sequence of homogeneous categories, pure in content. Informalized settlements or shantytowns, such as those in Al Ain or Satwa (chapter 1), are represented as quaint, exotic, and "medieval." This is connected with the presence of a certain type of foreigner—working class or informalized and, not coincidentally, South Asian. The implication is that these are pre-modern people, different from modern Emiratis. In an interesting wrinkle on European colonialist discourses of the *mission civilisatrice,* such representations seem to call on state and urbanists to intervene in the space, impose order on it, and modernize it. Neoorthodoxy gives time a different valence, but is no less homogenizing—the past (pre-oil, pre-modernity) is connected with the ideal village, in which (it is asserted) there were few outsiders and they were under control. The present is the opposite. Outsiders are threatening the culture of the UAE.

The family-state's urbanist ideology and practice—its visualization of the monumental city, its spatial politics, its deployment of urbanists—can in fact be seen as ways of managing the potentially competing cultural-political demands of neoorthodoxy and neoliberal flexible citizenship. There are aspects of both tendencies, such as the assumption that politics are unnecessary in a paternalistic political order, that are useful to the family-state, and other aspects, such as the neoorthodox equation of cultural pluralism with inauthenticity, that are not useful and even potentially dangerous. This conflict stems from the attempt by the family-state to do two different things simultaneously—to appear as the legitimate guardian of cultural authenticity and national identity, and to open up certain parts of the higher reaches of the economy to neoliberalism. Through urbanist ideology, the family-state draws on the expertise, uncritical cultural reifications, and political ingenuousness of urbanists to disseminate an image of both cultural authenticity and cultural openness.

An economically and culturally diverse South Asian community straddles the contours of this emergent political-cultural landscape, experiencing both the more diffuse, individualized, and symbolic mode and the more direct and palpable mode of neoliberal governance in Dubai. While working-class South Asians experience the more brutal incarnations of this symbolic economy in the form of constrained living quarters and constrained life chances, worker camps, invasive modes of surveillance, and other direct instrumentalities of ethno-and biopolitics, middle-class South Asians tend to experience this symbolic economy as identity politics. As Vora has put it, middle-class Dubai South Asians simultaneously enact "two contrasting modes of identification . . . as neoliberal participants in a free market economy, and as a systematically oppressed and disenfranchised racial group" (2008, 392).

The urbanist-ideological assumption that spectacular landscapes and monumental architecture embody a progressive vision and futuristic orientation for the city may seem to contrast with neoorthodox laments for an ethnically pure and orderly village of the past. But urbanist practice, in the form of spaces being constructed in the so-called New Dubai (the conurbation first developed during the 1990s outside the old city centered on the creek), betrays a similar if not at times identical exclusionary logic in which class and ethnicity are bound up. The social effects of this logic compromise the veracity of the family-state's claims to cultural openness and distance from nostalgic memories of ethnic purity. This is ironic, because urbanists such as starchitects see themselves as thoroughly global actors. Their radical designs, they believe, are global symbolic capital, highly sought after in the image economy of postmodern urbanism, in the calculations of "urban entrepreneurialism" (Broudehoux). In fact, as I show below, the typical spaces of New Dubai, such as the gated communities of EMAAR and Nakheel and the shopping malls of the giant holding corporations reaffirm highly localized ethnic and class exclusions. This indicates that the relationship between globalized urbanism and local dynamics may be less one-way than starchitects' and other urbanists' self-image suggests Local systems of hierarchy shape and even arguably guide the social effects of neoliberal urbanist spaces.

While the limits of urbanist ideology can be seen in the social contexts through which the city literally takes shape, such as working conditions among migrant laborers and construction camps (Human Rights Watch 2006; chapter 1), and by scrutinizing the politics of cultural and ecological representation working through starchitecture and related practices (chapter 2), it is by incorporating the voices and experiences of South Asian residents of Dubai that the character and limits of neoliberal discourses can be further examined. Like the Emiratis with whom they share some of the spaces of Dubai, South Asians are not a homogeneous group. Coming from different nation-states, regions, and classes, Dubai South Asians constitute a microcosm of their native countries' diversity and they hold different stakes in Dubai life. Many come to Dubai assuming they will remain for a short time, enough to meet specific material goals before returning home. For some, outcomes consistent with their expectations materialize, and they do return after a few years. Others inadvertently find themselves spending longer periods, perhaps even decades, in the Arab Gulf city. Yet others are born in Dubai or raised there. These various conditions shape different experiences and identities.

In her excellent article on Kuwait, "Neither Autocracy nor Democracy but Ethnocracy," Anh Nga Longva argues that widespread capitalist and nationalist assumptions in the global public sphere grant the Arab Gulf states great latitude to exclude foreigners. "The exclusion of foreign workers," writes Longva, "is entirely in line with the . . . widely accepted principle that political rights are a function of national citizenship" (118). Quite correctly, she points out that,

> From the perspective of capitalist and national logic, the political exclusion of expatriates rests on a double rationale which is widely and unquestioningly accepted; . . . some criteria for exclusion are seen internationally as more acceptable than others. For example, following the official demise of the notion of race in international discourse in the wake of the Second World War, exclusion on racial grounds provokes immediate negative reactions: as a result, racial ethnocracies attract attention and condemnation. Civic ethnocracy on the other hand, where exclusion is practiced on the basis of citizenship, strikes most observers as a "normal" state of affairs; . . . it appears rational and justifiable in our world of nation-states. (118–19)

I agree, in general, with Longva's characterization of ethnocracy in the Arab Gulf. Indeed, this book is largely inspired by her critique of much of the Gulf studies literature for ignoring the central role of foreigners in the dialectical process of the construction of the imagined national community in the modern Arab Gulf states. I am curious, however, about a couple of interesting glosses in her argument. Longva seems to read all foreigners through the abstract category of the expatriate, and she suggests that the main conflict between foreigners and Gulf nationals is over *political* rights, that is, over the question of belonging to the polity as subjects bearing political rights. I think that the story is more complicated, one in which different kinds of foreigners, marked both by nationality and by class, are subjected to the governance of the Gulf state in systematically different ways. Rather than reading all foreigners as expatriates, I argue that some are more-privileged actors and some less privileged within the sovereign spaces of Emirati governance. In turn, the foreigners' given situation vis-à-vis Emirati governance strongly conditions whether their structured conflict with Emiratis has to do with political rights/belonging or with economic rights/belonging.

It might therefore seem ironic that middle-class South Asians tend to focus on issues of economic rather than political belonging; whereas, for less elite South Asians, political rights are a more urgent issue.[2] The irony dissolves, however, when the fraught, ambivalent character of the Maktoum state is kept in mind. Janus-faced, "Maktoum, Inc." looks both to the past and to the future, to so-called tradition and to so-called modernity. As shown in previous chapters, values of autochthony and idyllic village life tend to be associated with the former. The latter often comes in the form of neoliberalism with an Arab face. Emiratis who are more sympathetic to the latter tendency view a certain cultural pluralism (governable, safe, culturally rebellious but politically docile) to be a core value and goal to which to aspire. They tend to be impatient with nostalgia and reified notions of tradition. Along with this goes an openness to a certain kind of foreigner, one who self-represents as entrepreneurial, creative, and individualistic. One who above all is politically docile. In return, the middle-class foreigner is rewarded with, and comes to expect, a great degree of economic incorporation, relative to foreigners from non-elite class backgrounds. This in turn explains one of the sources of tension between middle-class South Asians and Emiratis, a difference expressed in discourses from which notions of political rights are significantly absent. It is when ethnocracy (as Longva characterizes it) or ethnonationalism (as I have been putting it) is seen to transgress the tacit expectations of neoliberal consumer belonging that middle-class South Asians voice critiques of Dubai (cf. Vora 2008).

For non-elite foreigners, incorporation, or lack thereof, into the Dubai economy and polity is experienced very differently. Here, often severe material deprivations are countenanced by the state because these foreigners are assumed to be in Dubai voluntarily and "can vote with their feet." In this case, Longva's characterization of the consequences of political marginalization is to the point. Workers get caught in a vicious circle; they lack the political leverage to alter their material situation and their economic marginalization exacerbates their political vulnerability.[3] How South Asians of different classes experience migration to Dubai, and how this experience is inflected by structural factors such as class, are the main themes of this chapter.

Dubai as an Indian Ocean City

In general, Western scholars of the Gulf region have given foreigners scant attention. In the canonical tradition, which one of my colleagues has wryly called the "tribes and oil tankers" tradition of writing about the Gulf, little has changed in the last quarter century. Most of the major works in this tradition have studiously ignored transnational and cultural interconnections between the Gulf and other regions, notably South Asia (Davidson 2005; 2008; Field; Heard-Bey; Herb; Rugh). In this genre, foreigners have usually been represented as, at most, peripheral to the understanding of Gulf societies. Rather, the general implication is that Gulf society should be equated with the national culture of the state. Our knowledge about foreigners, their lives and experiences, and their relationships to the national cultures and states of the Gulf, is, fortunately, slowly expanding. For this we can thank, among others, sociological studies by Indian scholars (e.g., Rahman; Sekher), as well as recent Western scholarship that immensely expands our understanding of cultural diversity and transnationalism in Gulf societies.[4] Following on the seminal insights of Sugata Bose, K. N. Chaudhuri, and Anh Nga Longva there is now an emergent trend in Gulf and South Asian scholarship demonstrating how interconnected the South and Southwest Asian, or Indian Ocean, "arena" (in Bose's words) really is. This chapter cannot do justice to the complexity of interconnections between the two regions, but a close ethnographic analysis of one small part of the Indian Ocean arena—South Asian life in Dubai—will reveal some insights of broader relevance, for example, about the diverse ways that foreigners are included and excluded from parts of Emirati society and about the ambivalences in the symbolic economy of exclusion shaping urban life and experience in contemporary Dubai.

According to T.V. Sekher, labor emigration from pre-Independence India primarily consisted of laborers going to British colonies other than the Gulf, such as South Africa, Sri Lanka, and Jamaica. Most of these laborers were illiterate, unskilled, and poor, and a majority became citizens of the country of immigration. Post-independence India, by contrast, was characterized by two phases, the first of which generally witnessed well-educated professionals migrating to the industrialized countries of North America, Western Europe, and Australia. The second phase, which began with the 1960s–1970s southwest Asian development and construction booms fueled by oil revenues, saw the emigration of mainly unskilled and semiskilled workers to the oil states of the Gulf (33–34). The second postindependence phase, according to Sekher, differs from the first, not only in the occupational background of the migrants, but also because, in the case of the Gulf, migration was considered temporary, workers were hired on a contractual basis, and the host countries categorically refused citizenship to South Asian immigrants (34).

Even before the UAE began exporting oil in the 1960s, Dubai was one of the Gulf's major centers for the South Asian population. Rahman,

Figure 13. Strolling through an alley of Indian shops on Khor Dubai.

Figure 14. Typical street scene, near the Dubai Gold Suq and Fish market.

for example, estimates that there were 3,000 Indian merchant families living in the town before 1970 (16). Other South Asian communities, such as the Baluchis, have been living in Dubai in significant numbers for much longer. Lorimer claims that 200 of the approximately 2,050 houses making up the town of Dubai in the first two decades of the twentieth century were occupied by Baluchis (454).

Thus, migration between the subcontinent and the Gulf is relatively well attested. However, two other phenomena are generally ignored in the literature. First is the more recent migration of skilled, professional South Asians, trained in India or in the West, who go to the Gulf (especially the UAE) for better pay than they would earn in the subcontinent. Second is the generation or more of South Asians who have been born in the Gulf and who consider the Gulf to be, in some way, home. In this chapter, I describe some of the experiences of these three broad types: the classic South Asian immigrant of Sekher's second phase, the transient professional South Asian, and, finally, the South Asian whose emotional attachments are formed in the Gulf. In all three cases, the dilemmas that individuals face are shaped by the much more homogeneous, relative to pre-oil history, state definition of nationality and by the aforementioned symbolic economy of exclusion. However, South Asians in Dubai are a diverse group and their experiences of exclusion are diverse—some focus on issues of economic belonging, some are vulnerable to the dialectic of political and economic exclusion.

In the small, merchant societies of the Gulf and the Arabian Peninsula, such as Bahrain, Dubai, Jeddah, and Kuwait, an outside observer before the oil boom would have been hard-pressed to draw unambiguous distinctions between nationalities. Frederick Anscombe's work, for example, reveals the astonishing diversity of Hasa (the present-day Eastern Province of Saudi Arabia) under Ottoman rule at the end of the nineteenth and beginning of the twentieth centuries. The government bureaucracy in this province was run primarily by Iraqis, for example, but they did not have a monopoly. Afghani and Baluchi gendarmes kept the order as bureaucrats from Anatolia, the Balkans, and the Red Sea region transacted Ottoman business (28). James Onley makes an even clearer case. Analyzing the case of the Safar, a major trading family with branches in Bahrain and Bushehr (on the Iranian Gulf coast), Onley notes the family's "Arab-Persian hybridity" (2005, 65). Between 1778 and 1900, of the thirty-six known Safar spouses, twenty-one were Persian, ten were Arab, four were Abyssinian, and one was Indian (65). Onley analyzes a fascinating photograph of Agha Muhammad Rahim Safar, the head of the family, taken between 1898 and 1899. In the photo, Agha

Muhammad is wearing a Persian-style turban. Onley adds that "virtually all members of the family" spoke Farsi as their mother tongue and went by Persian titles such as *mirza, khan,* and *agha,* which they pronounced, accordingly to Onley, as "au," as only Persians from Bakhtiyar did (64). On the other hand, notes Onley, Agha Muhammad is also wearing an Arab *'abāh* or *bisht* (cloak). Onley's conclusion is that some of the nineteenth-century Safars considered themselves Perianized Arabs, Persians of Arab descent, and some saw themselves as Arabized Persians (65). The family was characterized by great mobility and established businesses in Baghdad, Basra, Muhammarah, Bushehr, Shiraz, Isfahan, Lingah, Bandar 'Abbas, Manamah, Muscat, Aden, Mocha, Hudaydah and Bombay (76). Fluent in several languages, members of the Safar also played intermediary roles between the local rulers and the British Residency. Nineteenth-century Arabia, for Onley, as for Sugata Bose, is best seen as part of a Middle Eastern–Indian Ocean arena that was deeply influenced, linguistically, aesthetically, and culinarily, by its sustained contact with Persia and India.

Since the 1970s, Dubai like other emirates has taken on a more officially Arab cultural cast. The type of cultural nationalism that the UAE federal and Dubai-emirate states have chosen resembles European ethnocultural nationalism, with emphasis on the shared culture of the citizenry, a common language, and even something akin to a racial consciousness—the emergence of so-called ethnocracy (Longva).[5] As briefly discussed (chapter 3) the legacy of the pre-independence sense of linguistic and cultural mixing can still be seen in various areas of Emirati life, especially in Dubai. Older multilingual Dubayyans tell stories of travel, business, and schooling around the rim of the Indian Ocean in ports such as Aden, Mombasa, Zanzibar, Basra, and Bombay. This is attested both by the archival, primary, and secondary sources (British Foreign Office, 371/82047; Fenelon; Lorimer), and by my interlocutors. Rana, in the preceding chapter, gave evidence of this in discussing her father's travels and the importance of these in the formation of her own cosmopolitan personhood. Fuad, Ahmad, Muhammad, and several others told of their own fathers' businesses and travel experiences as well.

It was not only Dubayyans who traveled out into the Indian Ocean arena. As mentioned, under the aegis of the Raj, and also after Indian independence, South Asians came for various reasons to Dubai. During the latter half of the twentieth century, for example, the town was an entrepôt between India and Pakistan, whose traders circumvented the closed borders after 1947 to continue trading links via the Gulf city (British Foreign

Office, 371/82047). Under the Raj, Dubai like other Trucial Emirates along with Bahrain was governed by India, not, as were other Arab territories of Britain, by Cairo.[6] (Well before the First World War, moreover, British influence in the Gulf far outweighed that of the region's major power, the Ottoman Empire.) Therefore, unlike most other parts of the Arab world, Dubai's identity has historically had a strong Perso–South Asian and African cast.

In more recent years, Bollywood films have given Dubai prominent attention, both as a place in itself and as part of South Asian lived experiences (see also chapter 3). Cultural products such as these, along with the strong imprint of South Asian cultures on the contemporary city (Diwali festivals, the Hindu temple next to the Al Maktoum mosque in Bur Dubai, an elaborate and rich South Asian street life with cafes, restaurants, etc.), have dramatized the rich cultural interconnections between the Emirati city and South Asia. The comment of an Emirati businessman (and the segmentary logic it implies) that the Chinese merchants in Dubai "eat the green and the dry (*yāklūn al-akhḍar wi'l—yābis*)," making them equally inscrutable to Indians and Emiratis, has already been discussed (chapter 3).

With oil wealth, however, came a decreasing dependence by rulers on merchant capital as well as a desire by the ruling elites of Gulf states to distinguish themselves from the growing number of expatriates. The 1970s and 1980s are the period of the adoption of "Gulf Arab national dress," when many in the region began discarding their Kashmiri shawls or Iranian turbans (or Western jackets and ties) and began wearing the white Najdi *kandūra* or *thawb* and the traditional head gear, the red-check Najdi *shimāgh* or the white eastern Arabian *ghuṭra* (Onley 2005, 77–78). The predominant foreign influence shifted at this time from the Indian Ocean to the Atlantic, with the United States and Britain exerting greater linguistic, cultural, and economic influence on Emirati culture. In short, the bulk of the Indian Ocean migration to the Gulf came at a time (post–oil boom) when definitions of national identity in the Gulf had hardened.

Patterns of Exclusion in Urbanist Space: Experiences of Ethnic Exclusion in the New Dubai

The "New Dubai" and Economic Belonging

The foregoing discussion will inevitably raise the question of belonging. If a more exclusive construction of national identity emerged as the Gulf family-state became less dependent on merchant capital and more dependent on oil extraction, does this mean that non-nationals felt more excluded from Gulf society? If so, what does this sense of exclusion mean? Does the meaning of exclusion depend on the identity and social background of the nonnational community in question? Briefly, my argument is not that foreigners felt somehow more socially or culturally included in the pre-oil, merchant-capital period and now feel their exclusion to be mainly social. The issue is mainly one of economic belonging. Especially among middle-class South Asians, there is no desire for inclusion into the community of citizens, such as that made available through naturalization (some South Asians born in Dubai would be an exception to this generalization, but working class South Asians probably are not). The desire is for a fair shake in the economic sphere, a feeling that economic inclusion should be based on merit and not on other factors, such as ethnicity or nationality, over which the individual is seen to have less control. To belong to Dubai, moreover, is to partake of greater opportunities for consumer well-being, a kind of "consumer citizenship," in Neha Vora's words (2008, 379). As Vora has shown, however, the privileges given to nationals (and Westerners) by the state are seen by middle-class South Asians as compromising the neoliberal promise of Dubai. Moreover, to be a South Asian expatriate is qualitatively different, is experienced differently, than being an expatriate from most other parts of the world (such as Europe and the United States,

Figure 15. EMAAR's "Street of Dreams" luxury residential development during the early stages of construction.

Figure 16. A completed section of EMAAR's "Street of Dreams."

although there are perhaps similarities to the Iranian experience in Dubai). Because of the feeling that Dubai is both a free-market city in which individual merit and energy should lead to an egalitarian social order, and because of the view that Dubai is in some important way part of the South Asian cultural arena, there is a greater expectation among South Asian expatriates for (economic) inclusion and equality of chances in the migration experience. For middle-class South Asians, especially, Dubai is not just a place simply to travel through, a space of transience. There is a connection deeper than simple economic calculation but arguably less deep than national belonging.

New Dubai is, in theory, the version of Dubai that middle-class South Asians would find in keeping with their free-market hopes for the city. A major conurbation outside the old city core straddling the creek (e.g., the Khor, Bur Dubai, Deira, etc.), this part of Dubai emerged during the late 1990s and early 2000s in the undeveloped hinterland along the approaches to Abu Dhabi. New Dubai is where some of the major starchitectural projects, such as the now-suspended Waterfront City of Rem Koolhaas and most of the large monumental buildings (e.g., the Burj al-Arab), shopping malls, and enclaves were (and are) developed. (Examples of the latter include MAF's Mall of the Emirates, Nakheel's Ibn Battuta Mall, and the Dubailand project.) But New Dubai is more than a technical response to the demographic pressures on the older city. It is a spatial representation in the sense Henri Lefebvre has written about, a space that is both subordinate to a hegemonic logic and that reflects the conceptualizations of experts and elites, or urbanists, as I have been calling them (Lefebvre 1974/1991, 33–41; 2003). Specifically, New Dubai is meant to signal Dubai's future, as seen by Maktoum and allies—a neoliberal Dubai in which, as the blogger, Shehab, put it in a previous chapter, "not its *rich heritage,*" is championed, "but rather its postnational, tabula rasa nature, unburdened by tradition, determinedly futurelooking" (emphasis in the original). With its shopping malls, gated communities, and other urbanscapes of bourgeois gratification (Ghirardo), New Dubai promises to provide everyone with a chance to participate in consumer well-being, to enact a consumer citizenship that reaffirms the freemarket ideal of egalitarianism of opportunities.

Consider the projects of the Maktoum subsidiary EMAAR. Since its founding in 1997, EMAAR has grown into a diversified firm that controls twelve large residential projects in Dubai as well as a marketing and investment arm, EMAAR International, which promotes Dubai as a safe, wholesome and, as the company's website puts it, "visionary" city with world-class projects.[7] EMAAR's mission is, furthermore, to export its model of master-planned communities across the globe.[8] Of the major Dubai development firms, such as Nakheel and MAF, EMAAR's role is central, as attested by Sheikh Muhammad's mandate that it develop the enormous and enormously ambitious mixed-use "Downtown Dubai," the new focal point of the city. The centerpiece of the new downtown is the former Burj Dubai (now the Burj Khalifa), the tallest skyscraper in the world. Along with the skyscraper, the firm is developing what it claims is the world's largest shopping mall.[9] EMAAR thus provides the dominant model of urban development in Dubai—the hegemonic spatial representation of the emerging city—and very likely in other Middle Eastern cities.[10] Several of the residential projects put in the works by EMAAR and proposed for Downtown Dubai were presented in 2003–4 at the "Street of Dreams" showcase villa development, which I researched during my fieldwork. Although I could not access concrete numbers on the demographics of the people who rent these properties, anecdotal evidence that I collected from conversations with Street of Dreams rental office agents suggests that a large proportion of the properties are leased directly by foreign nationals, mostly from Great Britain, South Africa, Australia, New Zealand, and South Asia. The remainder is rented by nationals, who generally turn around and re-rent the properties to expatriates. Most of the residents of these properties seem to be expatriates. The spatial

Figure 17. Pacification by cappuccino? Homes in the "Street of Dreams" development come equipped with computer control systems linked to local shopping malls and to the development's private security force.

interpretation of class and gender here tends to draw on a generalized notion of "Western secular" space rather than on any local traditions. But the effect, a hierarchically-ordered, surveilled, and privatized space, articulates with Emirati (and middle-class expatriate) preoccupations with managing difference.

The villas, which during my longest extended period of fieldwork in 2004 came in four or five different types ranging in price from Dh 250,000 to Dh 5,000,000 (approximately $68,000 to $1,359,000), are relatively affordable to Western middle-class and wealthy South Asian and Iranian consumers, as well as to local investors. Whimsically named such things as "the Lakes," "the Springs," and "the Meadows," these villas can appear to be the embodiment of a certain type of privatized, globally-mobile utopia, an apolitical consumer citizenship promised by Dubai. "The Springs Model Villa 1E" is, aesthetically and spatially, typical. Entering the foyer, one notices an LCD display, with options for air conditioning control and Internet access. It is possible, according to the icons on the screen, to do online shopping of various kinds. "Browse aisle," reads one icon, which links to others labeled "general grocery," "fruits and vegetables," and "meats and chicken." Others are titled "recipes" and "food court." The logos of Pizza

Hut and McDonald's appear in one corner. Other icons are the logos of various brands, or contain brand names within them: UAEfoodmall.com, CNN.com, Spinney's (hypermarket), UAEmall.com, Amazon.com, IKEA. The most interesting feature, however, are the controls for security cameras, which are placed in various corners of the property. The dining room off to the left side is in subdued olive and plum tones. A fondue set is the centerpiece of the table, and a sushi service awaits diners. New Age music, a symphony orchestra playing a version of Pink Floyd's "Breathe," gently pipes in from speakers attached inconspicuously to the walls. In the living room, the coffee table is stacked with books such as *Martha Stewart's Cookbook, The Invention of Chic, Therese Bonney and Paris Moderne, Global Style, New York Interiors, Asian Elements,* and Taschen's *The Lilies.*

Upstairs are the bedrooms, with the master bedroom off to one end and the children's rooms off to another. The respective décor in each of the children's rooms reflects somewhat distinct, perhaps naturalized, gender differences. The boy's desk suggests a connection between maleness and science. There are two faux-antique telescopes, a volume of *Gray's Anatomy,* display boxes with mounted insects and a bat, four globes, an organic chemist's chemical structure toy, and a magnifying glass laid just so over an opened volume of *Great Ideas That Shaped the World.* Einstein, hand on a blackboard with scribbled formulas, looks at us from the cover of *Great Ideas.* The girl's room contains a Phaedon Art Box, an easel with sketching paper, books on painting and drawing, a book on sewing, a box of crayons, and watercolors.

These spaces are clearly drawn from a mail-order catalogue version of modern, secular, Western private space. This type of space is repeated all over the New Dubai, and seems intended to collapse the experiential distance between the prospective inhabitant's home country and their adopted one. Indeed, in conversations with me, several Western expatriates, most of whom thought of Dubai as a vacationland where one happened also to work, mentioned something like this. One of the main reasons they liked Dubai, they said, was that you could have all the benefits of home and even more (driving a nice car; affording a villa which you could never afford in the UK, complete with a maid, again, an impossibility back home; and having access to alcohol and clubs and beaches), without having to bother with the tiresome aspects of life in most foreign countries (adjusting to local customs and worrying about the hygiene issues, etc.) Middle-class South Asian expatriates say similar things, often with more irony. For example, "Dubai is the Bombay where you can drink the tap water" (Vora 2009a).

The maid's room at the model villa is also revealing. It does not have a desk or telescopes or easels or, indeed, any furnishings at all. The room, about four square meters, is thrown into a dark corner just past the refrigerator off the kitchen. Artificial direct lighting would seem to be required all day, because the half-meter by half-meter window does not allow much natural light to get through from outside. Whereas the master bedroom opens onto a large bathroom with a Jacuzzi-style bathtub, the maid will have to do with a simple showerhead. The two types of space, while not literally separate (they are both within the domestic space of the house) are symbolically separate. The space that is intended for the employer family is symbolically multifaceted. It has a utilitarian function, as a space of basic inhabitation, a "roof over the head," but it also has functions that are superfluous to the basic needs of subsistence—luxuries, creature comforts, or, as in the children's rooms, furnishings for a space that stimulates the imagination. The maid's quarters, by contrast, are stripped of all but utilitarian functions. This is fine and well, a critic might say, but is this not also observable in middle-and upper-class houses all over the world? What makes this distinction peculiar to Dubai? I suggest the following connection.

Frequently during our time in Dubai and other emirates, my wife and I witnessed a curious phenomenon. We would walk out of a restaurant and see, sitting outside in the waiting area, a South or Southeast Asian woman watching a stroller with a baby in it; or, we would walk past a children's play area at a mall and notice a group of South Asian women waiting silently by the doorway; or, again, we would be walking at another mall and see a long row of South Asian men sitting on benches in the periphery of the mall, appearing to be waiting for something to happen or someone to meet. What these people were doing was waiting for or with their employers' children, while the employers themselves were off at dinner or shopping or a film. The case of a woman with a stroller outside one restaurant was particularly striking. She was there when we walked into the restaurant, and there again, three hours later, as we walked out. I cannot say whether the employers were expatriates or locals, but, more importantly, all of this does suggest that domestics are both ethnically marked, which is obvious to anyone who has spent time in the Gulf, and that the construction of space that is imposed on them is utterly utilitarian and transitory. Employers seem to assume that it is natural and suitable for domestics and other members of the South or Southeast Asian working class to spend most of their time waiting for, minding, and tending to others, in transitional spaces that are not in any sense their own.

Ironically, far from providing the "answer to modern city living"[11] and "an inspired urban concept,"[12] the Street of Dreams and New Dubai more generally rely on some basic principles of divisive urbanism, such as the privatization of spatial policing and the management of class and gender in ways that attribute danger to class and gender subalterns. The project manager of another New Dubai project, a gated community near the Mall of the Emirates area, made an interesting comment in this connection while giving me a private tour of the project. I had noticed that a tall, approximately seven foot high, metal fence was going up around the grounds, and asked the project manager about this. "It's for security," he said, rather unhelpfully. I pressed him by pointing out that the gated community was in the middle of the desert, miles from any other places where people actually lived, and also that the development was only accessible by pedestrian-unfriendly freeways. He responded that the fences were really meant to prevent wild or escaped camels from entering the grounds, before sheepishly admitting that there was no rational explanation for the fence.

Images and representations of the cultural other as a "threat" are common in Dubai. These representations can be of guest workers absconding, of construction workers rioting, of South Asians bringing disease and public health threats into the country (Humaid), of outsiders breaking into the middle-class or Emirati domestic space, and, perhaps most menacingly (from the perspective of many Emiratis) of outsiders as prostitutes or tempters of locals into moral lapses. As mentioned earlier (chapter 3), this milieu of fear is connected to the specific dialectic of identity in the modern Gulf states. The role of South Asian workers is particularly significant in this context. As discussed in chapter 3, Asian domestic workers have a unique access to the Gulf Arab private sphere, an intimate knowledge of Gulf Arab private lives, and are uniquely vulnerable to accusations of being a "moral threat" or a "threat to local values" (see also Longva, 124).

There is therefore an articulation between local fears of the other and desires for security on the one hand, and middle-class expatriate fears of class disorder and desires for a well-regulated, "climatized" (Baudrillard 1970/2001) consumer polity on the other hand. Transitory, utilitarian spaces in the New Dubai both symbolize and manage this otherness, signaling to Emiratis and middle-class expatriates as well as to working-class foreigners the tacit boundaries governing movement and inhabitation in the city. Taken together, these spatializations and spatial representations of otherness create an overdetermined symbolic milieu in which the city is experienced by less privileged groups as exclusive and highly policed.

The effects are not only felt by working-class foreigners, however. Middle-class South Asians are particularly anxious with respect to such representations, especially as they inflect issues of economic inclusion and equality of opportunity to participate in consumer well-being.

Foreigner as Threat, Foreigner as Servant

For many middle-class South Asians, the experience of New Dubai is a mixture of contentment with its promise of consumer well-being and anxiety over exclusion from the full potential of neoliberal citizenship. Generally, the anxiety is that one of two associations with foreignness might be imposed on middle-class South Asians—identification of the foreigner with "threats" to local culture or of the foreigner with "being a servant" or unskilled labor. The latter is seen in the following comment by an Indian computer professional. She was one of two women my wife and I met at a local mall one day. She and her friend, an American expatriate, were debating the merits of a new shopping mall, when an interesting argument broke out. We were at the Mercato shopping mall, which was new and very popular at the time (November 2003), regarded by many as a sort of spearhead of the New Dubai vision (the mall's aesthetic qualities and urban functions, a blend of high-end shopping and theme park, anticipated the more ambitious projects, such as Mall of the Emirates and Ibn Battuta, which came online in the middle of the first decade of the twenty-first century). The American woman, a teacher, was impressed with the mall, which carried a "Renaissance Venice" theme, but, she said, if she were the landlord, she would turn some of the shops into libraries and well-supervised, educational public spaces where parents could leave their children while they shopped. "You're dreaming!" retorted the Indian woman. "People don't read anymore. All they want is distraction. You know why they come here? Because they can litter! They can litter and expect someone else to pick up after them." By "them," she meant Emiratis. She told me that although she has lived her entire life in Dubai, and has worked very hard to become a computer programmer, she is not, and can never hope to be, regarded as an equal by the nationals. Moreover, she feels like she is a second-class person. "Locals are so arrogant. They look at all Indians and basically everyone but the whites *as servants*."[13] She almost expected "white" people to be racist to her, she says, but for locals, "who are basically just like me," to be racist, that is really puzzling. "It becomes just about money. Indians in the UAE are excluded. They are doctors, engineers. They are very skilled people."

"Other civilizations," she continued, "have had hundreds of years to achieve modernity. Here, it took only thirty years. Other cultures had to gain modernity through struggle. Here, they simply purchased it." Basically, as she saw it, the American woman was uncritically repeating the logic of New Dubai urbanism—that it embodies consumer well-being, openness, and opportunity. My Indian interlocutor rejected this, seeing continuity between what she perceived as an exclusive and closed local culture and the urbanscape of the New Dubai.

The comments of Julian, an Indian businessman and like the computer programmer a longtime resident of Dubai, echo some of her sentiments and also show sensitivity to the "foreigner-as-danger" discourse. Julian's parents moved to Dubai from Southern India in the mid 1960s. (They returned to India in the early 1970s where Julian was born, but they went back to Dubai shortly thereafter.) He has since spent most of his life in Dubai, leaving after high school to go to university in the United States, but returning to take over his father's construction business. Defining his identity is a constant struggle for him, he says, because whereas his passport says that he is Indian, he feels more at home in Dubai. Although quite critical of his parents' adopted home, neither does he fall into the trap of idealizing his ancestral home, as, he claims, his parents do. If it is unthinkable for the Emirati flexible citizen Saad that Indians could ever be naturalized, for Julian this rejection is both irritating and sometimes understandable. Julian's feeling that the Emirati state should permit naturalization of all expatriates who have lived for a certain number of years and have started businesses in the UAE was echoed by a few other middle-class South Asian expatriates I met during my research. Although probably not a majority among the expatriate population, Julian and others' expressed desire for the option of naturalization (while simultaneously maintaining Indian citizenship; basically a desire for being permitted the option of dual citizenship) suggests something remarkable, a wish among some South Asian expatriates to be Emirati citizens. Gulf expatriate experience, already underrepresented in the literature, has to my knowledge never been looked at from this angle. For Julian and like-minded expatriates, dual citizenship would mean more freedom to participate in what he sees as the best of both countries: India's culture ("Bombay is the bomb!" I am told by his close friend, an Indian expatriate named David, upon his return from a visit to the Indian metropolis) and his extended family, along with the relative ease of travel, welfare state generosity, and economic opportunities provided by Emirati citizenship.

Moreover, for Julian, this is not a zero-sum emotional game in which his attachment to India would be emotional, that to the UAE purely material. He feels himself genuinely torn, feeling deep loyalty to both countries. Both, for him, are "home."

Like the computer programmer, however, his attempt to feel fully at home in the UAE is tempered by his awareness that many Emiratis are wary especially of South Asian expatriates. "The locals look at what they have in terms of material wealth and clean and orderly cities," he says in his American-inflected English, "and then they look at cities like Bombay. In Bombay, nothing works. The city is totally chaotic. It takes two and a half hours to travel a distance that . . . should take twenty minutes. The only rule is 'look out for number one.' Locals see that and they don't want it here. . . . They don't want Dubai to turn into Bombay."

"How do you identify yourself?" I asked him during this same conversation. "Indian. Because people here, the Europeans too, always want to put you in a box. They say 'OK, you're Indian, you're Egyptian.'" He is gesturing as he says this, describing with his hands an object that he is putting on an imaginary shelf. "People here also tend to think of Indians as people who do this," he says, swaying his head. "Well, I want to show them that Indians are not all like that."

The anthropologist Neha Vora, in her penetrating recent article on middle-class Indians in Dubai (2008), seems to have people like Julian in mind when she provides the following insight. Admitting that many middle-class Dubai Indians feel compassion for the condition of workers, she nevertheless found that,

> Middle class Indians also attributed some of the racism they experienced in their lives to laborers, arguing that because uneducated and unskilled workers constitute the majority of Indians in the Gulf, people assume that all Indians are uneducated and unskilled. Therefore, my informants' racial consciousness was always qualified by an assertion of middle class status, a status that they used to claim that they deserved less racism than laborers, and a status that made them feel superior to lower-paid Indians. . . . Embedded in this process . . . was also the idea that Indians bring discrimination upon themselves. Many suggested that if only they practiced self-management and greater self-respect, the system might not be so discriminatory. (390–91)

"I'll tell you what happens," Arjun, a leasing manager with a local property developer who came to Dubai from Uttar Pradesh in the late 1990s, told me in one conversation.

> The local kids grow up in an environment where they're surrounded by Asians who work for them, or work for their parents. . . . So when they grow up, that's what the kids have in mind, that "this particular shape and form is going to help me get my groceries, take me to school, whatever." When they grow up, they grow up in a community where everyone is surrounded by that. [When Emiratis become adults] they live in areas which are predominantly local; again they experience the same things, because when they go to shops, they're served by Asians; when they fill up the petrol in their cars, they're served by Asians. So by the time they reach the stage where they're interacting with people who are white collar, it's entrenched in their brains that that's the way the community is, that's what they do, that's what the person from that community is supposed to be doing, because that's what the brain kind of tells them.

In his assertion of middle-class status, Sanjay, an Orissan founder of a technology startup who moved to Dubai in 2001, echoed some of Vora's interlocutors, along with Arjun, but also implied, like the computer programmer ("other cultures had to gain modernity through struggle; here they simply purchased it") that the Indian work ethic and character are superior both to that of Western expatriates and that of Emiratis.

> In general, for the local population [it is people from] the [United Kingdom and the United States] at the top, next would be South Africans and Australians, then [people from the] Arab region, and [finally] South Asian expatriates. What happens with the Indian community in particular is, typically, normally, they feel much cleverer than the local population. It's a feeling that everybody, all Indians have that feeling. And therefore, they [also] feel cleverer than the Brits and the Americans. For instance, there will be one guy who's done his MBA from, say, Leeds University. He will be ranked much higher than me, for instance, where I have done an MBA at what would be

considered [a top school in India]. For me, as an Indian, to get into Leeds, all I would need is money. But to get into the institute that I have got into, it takes serious struggle, serious struggle. Because the competition will kill you.

Although in general he is not unhappy with life as a middle-class professional in Dubai, such discrimination, according to Sanjay, compromises Dubai's neoliberal promise, preventing full equality of opportunity and denying a sense of economic belonging. Such discrimination appears, for example, in the employment packages that local companies offer expatriates.

I mean in India, it's a poorer country, so you're not used to a certain lifestyle [that you would in the West. So if you're coming from the West] you are offered that same lifestyle, you're given a house, you're given a maid allowance, you're given a furniture allowance. If you're Indian-educated and coming from India, it's assumed that you don't expect these things, so you don't get them.

Although the discrimination is based more on the country in which you are educated than on your skin color, it is still "best if you're white-skinned and coming from the West, followed by, followed by, followed by, and pretty much at the bottom of the pyramid is the Indian expatriate."

When I visited Dubai again in early 2007, I reconnected with Julian, the businessman whose parents came from Southern India in the 1960s. We went out to dinner one evening with a few other expatriates, Silpa, Reshma, and David, all from India, but like Julian, brought up in Dubai (David was living in New York City at the time). As we settled into the evening, small talk transitioned into more substantive conversation. It was then that David told a funny yet unsettling anecdote, which although highly stylized and even literary in its structure, opens an aperture into the darker aspects of Indian middle-class experience in Dubai. The setting of the story (or, more accurately, long joke) was the Dubai International Airport, DXB, where David had recently arrived from New York to visit his family. The story assumes a basic knowledge of the arguably singular experience of traveling through DXB, with its juxtaposition of excessive luxury and palpable segregation of nationalities and classes. Specifically, the division between "the West [along with the GCC] and the Rest" is striking, with a much more elaborate system of customs and passport control for the latter (see Kanna 2007). Travelers can circumvent this passport control by paying a fee, a so-called *Marhaba* ("Hello") service geared toward business travelers. It was this division, exacerbated by a bureaucratic mix-up, (which in turn suggested a collapse of all South Asians into one homogeneous racial category, regardless of class), on which David's story hinged.

According to David, DXB had instituted an eye-scan, an apparatus like a camera that electronically corroborates a traveler's authentic passport. This procedure was being applied only to Indian, Pakistani, and other dark-skinned travelers, said David. "I had already paid my [Dh 100] visa fee, so I don't know why I had to do this eye scan." He had just made it to the beginning of a long queue, but passport control asked him to go to another part of the airport to stand in another queue, "with like all these Pathan worker guys," who looked miserable. "I was dressed as if I'd just come from New York City," he said. (He had indeed just come from New York City.) This was an attempt to contrast his appearance with that of the Pathan workers, dressed in *shalwar qameez,* suggesting that he looked, and felt, ridiculous. He continued,

> The queue was huge, and when you thought it was finally over, it looped around a corner and kept going. I was led to this cubicle. At a desk, sitting so high up, I don't even think his feet touched the ground, was this local [i.e., Emirati]. He was . . . swinging this club. He goes "Come." [David flicks his wrist, imitating the passport clerk.] There wasn't a single piece of technology [in the cubicle], they could have done whatever they wanted to me, and no one would have known. It didn't have solid walls, it was one of those open-ceiling cubicles, so I guess [in a worst case scenario] I could have pushed over the walls [and run away]. But on the other side there were all these Pakistani guys, who would have been no help at all, so I'm stuck between this local who's treating me like dog shit and all the Pakistani guys who probably want to jump me because I'm Indian. "Come," the local says, and asks for my passport. He looks it over. "Why you no have eye scan?" They told me the machine was not working. So he flips his leg over the table and brings this huge boot, SLAM down on the passport. I read it. It said, "I scanned."

There was a roar of laughter from the table. He goes on: "I am allowed to return to the [main passport control area]. I head for the *Marhaba* desk. The passport clerk looks at my passport and says 'Why you go [to the other queue]? With Marhaba you get out of here in two minutes!'" Another peal of laughter. "They really treat you like dog shit, if you don't have the right passport," says Silpa.

Aside from the irony and cutting sarcasm of this anecdote (which my retelling does little justice), what is striking about David's story is the worldweariness and sense of déjà vu it almost automatically provokes from the other expatriates at the table. Silpa's comment, "they really treat you like dog shit," is for many Dubai middle-class South Asians a taken-for-granted part of the experience of living in Dubai. Certainly, this phrase does not exhaust the diversity or complexity of the experience. As I show in the next section, there are also modes of belonging (as anthropologist Neha Vora might put it) that middle-class South Asians enact, albeit in ambivalent ways. The context in which these modes of belonging are enacted, however, tend to be market oriented, in corporate jobs and privatized or consumer milieux such as gated communities and shopping malls. Interactions with the state, such as the one dramatized by David, tend to provoke anxiety and to dredge up feelings of being second class. The latter context, in short, collapses middle-class South Asians into the broader and denigrated categories of Asian or Indian. Thus, the dilemma for many middle-class South Asians is that by education, temperament, and worldview, they see themselves as full neoliberal citizens of the global economy. They expect egalitarianism of opportunity in an ostensibly free-market city and the recognition of middle-class distinction that is assumed to go along with this. The Dubai they actually experience is, however, often one of "boxes," as Julian put it. They resent being considered "just Indian," a characterization carrying heavy symbolic baggage in a context in which foreignness is identified primarily with being South Asian and associated with threat or unskilled labor.

Mobility and Immobility: Imbrications of Space and Class

The question now arises of how significant these undeniable barriers are for different South Asians. How determinate of an individual's life conditions and agency are they? It would indeed be misleading to assume that South Asians find little positive about Dubai or see it only as an ethnically exclusive society in which economic opportunity is restricted by social discrimination. Like Dubai flexible citizens, South Asian middle-class expatriates tend to identify with the neoliberal values described earlier (chapter 4). They tend to see the world primarily through the lens of neoliberal self-improvement and advancement, in which economic achievement signifies superiority of work ethic and temperament. For example, in our conversations, I was struck by how Julian idolized the United States. For him, the United States means capitalism. (This was, admittedly, before the financial crisis of 2008.) He saw capitalism, moreover, as a sort of neutral, even utopian space where the individual can emancipate herself or himself from the things that, for an Indian long-time resident of a country like the UAE, tie one down, restrict mobility, and constrain horizons. His version of America is almost a verbatim translation of the American dream myth of perpetual upward and outward mobility.

He told me a story, for example, about his first experience going to a pub in the United States. At the time (mid-1990s), he and his South Asian friends had become used to being turned away at bars in Dubai where bouncers would say that the bar was "members only." This was a euphemism for "if you are Indian (i.e., if you look like you're from South Asia), you were not allowed in," he said. Sometimes, if the bouncer or manager was feeling generous, he would "allow" you to pay a prohibitive bribe and you would be let in. When he first went to the United States, his friend invited him to a pub. "I asked my friend, 'will they let me in, won't they turn me away because I'm Indian?' My friend said, 'What are you talking about? Do you have five bucks [the cover] or don't you?' I was relieved when the bouncer just asked me for the cover and let me in, no other questions asked." This was typical of the United States, according to Julian, and this supposed racial blindness he connected to a capitalist system that valued merit over race or other ascriptive identities. Happily, Julian reports, the Dubai government began prohibiting the racial profiling that used to occur in pubs and restaurants, but this practice does continue informally. (See the discussion in Kanna 2006.)

This identification with the values of capitalism, and more specifically, the values of the entrepreneur and small business owner, add further complexity to Dubai South Asian identity. Whereas middle-class South Asians chafe under the discrimination they often experience in Dubai, the Emirati city is still preferable in many ways to the native country. Emiratis "don't want Dubai to become Bombay," Julian had said, implicitly, if grudgingly, voicing this point of view. This does not mean only that Emiratis want to maintain what they see as a clean, orderly (and, of course, politically demobilized) city with modern infrastructures. It also suggests that Dubai is more purely capitalist than India. There was a strong tendency among middle-class South Asians to denigrate the Third World and Nehruist origins of the Republic of India. Nehru tended to be associated with socialism, and socialism to many middle-class South Asians was inefficient and a corrosive influence on individual enterprise. With Nehru's socialist policies, said Julian, "people got used to taking handouts from the state and giving their votes in return." From this perspective, Dubai is a liberation from the constraints imposed by the Indian state and its social democratic legacy. In this, middle-class South Asians repeat the hegemonic logic of the Dubai family-state, which has systematically attempted to erase the struggle of reformist and nationalist movements from the historical narrative of Dubai. A politically demobilized, class-hierarchical Dubai is appealing both to flexible Dubai citizens and to many middle-class South Asians.

Moreover, South Asian middle-class expatriates, unlike their working-class compatriots, tended to see the neoliberal version of global mobility as liberating, and they often see their temporary stay in Dubai as wholly consistent with the rational choice theory implicit in neoliberalism. The neoliberal version of globalization holds that identity and social-class background, essentially, the historical baggage that one carries, are not very significant. The rationalist economic theory underpinning neoliberal discourse implies that, if you are not satisfied with your current conditions, you should either work harder to change those conditions or, as the saying goes, "vote with your feet." The Gulf version of this free-market ideology, often repeated by Emiratis and middle-class expatriates of various nationalities, is that expatriates ultimately have free choice in coming to Dubai. If they are dissatisfied with their pay, their lack of legal rights, or their lack of state protection, they are free to go back home.

Neoliberal globalization discourse both glamorizes movement and assumes that it is always available in the same way to all individuals. The writings of Thomas Friedman, for example, justify the outsourcing of service and manufacturing jobs from the West to India and China as part of the general technological progress making the playing field of the global economy more and more "flat" (2005). The neoliberal mantra is that the social suffering resulting from neoliberal policies (assuming that such suffering is acknowledged) can be remedied or avoided through market-oriented technological wizardry and through education, retraining, and reorientation of the self away from the social and toward the private—in short, through the market and individual initiative. Just as neoliberalism requires the state to be privatized, so too does it privatize the responsibility for adapting to the social consequences of economic restructuring. For those privileged enough to exercise a great deal of agency over their life conditions, travel and mobility in general can seem exhilarating. "Nonplaces" (Augé) such as airports, duty-free shopping concourses, and trendy clubs, formally indistinguishable from New York to Amsterdam to Kuala Lumpur, can indeed seem breathtaking in the ways in which they seem to compress time and space. Which traveler has not felt at least slightly awed as they are cocooned in the total climatized atmosphere of Heathrow Airport or DXB? Expatriates who profess liking Dubai often mention, as examples of what they specifically like, the feeling that they can have the best parts of home while avoiding the less pleasant parts, thus being everywhere and nowhere at the same time. This positive valence to the experience of being transient, of a kind of inclusion in a social order without the burden of most kinds of social commitment, is another aspect of middle-class South Asian experience in Dubai. Political rights framings of local-foreigner difference in the Gulf and the shochorning of all immigrant experiences into the abstract category of expatriate miss this subtlety. For middle-class expatriates, it is economic inclusion as full neoliberal global subjects that is desired, not political rights in any conventionally understood sense. For middle-class South Asians, the Dubai promise is realized when they feel they are treated as equal, individual market agents, not as rights-carrying subjects of a nation-state or as subjects of transnational regimes and discourses of human rights.

During one of our conversations, Arjun expressed this sensibility when he explained how he and his wife came to Dubai from Uttar Pradesh. I had asked him whether it was mainly economic considerations that took them to Dubai. Not really, he said.

> We were pretty well-off in India. It was more like, at that time [1996–97], the Indian economy was not at its best, and we were getting out of an economic crisis. We didn't really see, in the next five years, any great benefits [to staying there.] . . . And with the offer of triple, four times the money here, then you look at what comes with it. And both of us got a job, and we said, "OK, we'll go check it out, if it works out, great, if not, we can always go back."

Once, over drinks with Julian and his friends, Saleem, a 30-year-old middle-class Indian born in Dubai, and Hugh, a middle-aged professional Briton who had been living in the emirate since the late 1970s, an interesting argument broke out. At the time, I was interested in finding out more about the ways in which people like Julian and Saleem, born or raised in the Gulf but Indian by ascription and family background, identified themselves. Specifically, I mentioned Julian's irritation that people like him and Saleem were ineligible for citizenship. Saleem vehemently disagreed with my suggestion. "Look, it's their [the Emiratis'] country. Why should they be forced to share it with anyone? No one is holding a gun to [the expatriates'] heads. The reason why they come here is because, no matter what it's like here, obviously it's better than what they have at home." Both Julian and Hugh, it should be mentioned, disagreed with Saleem. "Saleem, that's bollocks," said Hugh. "You've lived here for twenty-seven years. I've lived here for twenty-five. This is our home. We've as many rights as any [Emirati]."

Human Resource manager Susan, who was born in the mid-1970s in Dubai to parents from Goa, tells me that in this debate, she sides with Saleem. "I've heard a lot of people grumble about [this issue]. But if you ask me, frankly, I couldn't care less. . . . I know that eventually I'm going to go back [to Goa]. I mean, I'm now twenty-nine years old. I don't care. As long as I've got a good job, as long as everything's fine, I don't really mind." After a short pause, she continues, "I've seen Dubai grow so much. It's unbelievable; . . . if you asked me if I wanted to move to the States, to Canada, I wouldn't." She knows, however, that she will not stay forever; she will move back to Goa where her family already is, but for now "so far, so good. I mean, in some of the other places, you would really have to struggle. Whereas, since I have my in-laws here, they can look after my daughter while I'm working. Otherwise, I would have to stay with her all day, which would drive me crazy. Because I'm not used to staying at home and looking after the kids and that's it."

Arjun, Saleem, and Susan each implicitly affirm the liberation narrative of neoliberalism. In their voices the assumption is clearly that travel and place-making in the global economy can be a matter, more or less, of the rational comparison of different options and the freedom to choose the option that better suits the individual's material, class, and cultural expectations. Susan even vigorously endorsed my use of the term "liberation" to describe her migration experience. This interpretation of mobility becomes problematic, however, when extrapolated to the experiences of differently-situated foreigners. Davidson's generally excellent recent study of Dubai, for example, is at its weakest when asserting that "most [foreign] workers in Dubai are essentially opportunistic Indian and Pakistani expatriates. . . . While such foreigners may have experienced poor working conditions in Dubai, their employment was entirely voluntary, was normally for a short term of two or three years, and was usually paying wages several times greater than could be expected in South Asia" (2008, 187). This book's first chapter is basically an extended engagement with this thesis, but it is useful to reiterate. For many foreign workers, migration can last much longer, and while pay is, in a purely technical sense, higher than can be earned in South Asia, the complexities of dealing with such obstacles as labor recruiters and corrupt employers can significantly reduce real income, increase debt, and, consequently, increase the time spent doing migrant work in Dubai.

Much of the material refuting neoliberal myths of choice in mobility and labor is publicly available, such as reports from local newspapers and the work of NGOs such as Human Rights Watch.[14] The personal stories of two interlocutors with whom my wife and I became friends confirm and dramatize the more general picture outlined in these public documents. These two South Asian domestics, who I call Laura and Rachel here, were particularly generous in helping me gain a less-superficial understanding of their conditions. Laura, in her late fifties, arrived in Dubai in the early 1980s "When I got off the plane I cried and cried." Not, one would venture, a reaction similar in any way to what I imagine was experienced by any of the middle-class South Asians discussed above upon their arrival in Dubai. According to Laura, the terror she experienced was the result of her uncertainty about when she would return home. Her intuition proved correct. In 2004, she was still in Dubai, working until she could save enough to go back home to lead a tolerably dignified life.

Rachel, who comes from southern India, worked in Kuwait before she came to Dubai in the mid-1990s to work as a domestic. She first worked for two expatriate Arab families before ending up with a third expatriate Arab family in the early 2000s. Those who assume that all domestics in the Gulf are mistreated in some way would be surprised to discover that Rachel has formed strong emotional attachments to all three expatriate Arab families. Although the Kuwaiti family she worked for "were decent people, they were *thaqīlīn* [severe, humorless]."[15] The expatriate Arab families, however, she actually came to like. In fact, the first family still telephones her from time to time to ask about her health and her daughters. "The other Arabs [i.e., non-Gulf Arabs] are much better [to work for] than the *khalījīyyīn* [the Gulf Arabs]," who, she says, are too hierarchical and formal. With the current family, "Madam" considers her a "good friend"; yet "Madam," in her mid-50s, nevertheless refers to 40-something Rachel as "*bintī*" (my girl). Also, while "Madam and Sir's" teenage daughter has a casual, avuncular relationship with her, the daughter still sometimes refers to her as "our housegirl."

In comparison to the lives of middle-class South Asians, Laura's and Rachel's experiences in the Gulf are more profoundly shaped by the structural violence of class and ethnic discrimination. While both came to the Gulf because husbands became unemployed back home, Rachel had the added pressure of a marriage in which she and her husband were in profound disagreement on issues of major importance. In Dubai, Rachel's living quarters consist of a small room under the staircase of the "house proper." That is, Rachel's room is not accessible through the interior of the house. To get in and out of her room, she has to go out of the kitchen, and enter the room through a small courtyard. This is sometimes annoying, because, when "Sir" and "Madam" go out, she becomes the babysitter. In the past, she would put the daughter to bed, and then retire to her room, but she cannot do this anymore. One night, when her employers were visiting friends in Abu Dhabi, the daughter woke up during the night, and seeing that the house was "empty," panicked and called her parents at the dinner party they were attending, much to their annoyance. Since then, every time that "Sir" and "Madam" leave the house, Rachel waits in the kitchen until they return, so as to make sure that the daughter does not get frightened if she wakes up.

Rachel recently went home twice on short trips. First, there was the tsunami of late 2004, which luckily seems to have mostly spared her village. Second, soon after returning to Dubai, she heard from her parents in India that her ex-husband was entangling himself in problems, a situation requiring her immediate attention. Rachel is now in her late forties. Her two daughters are in their late teens and early twenties. She has been living and working in the Gulf over a third of her own life and nearly the entire lives of her daughters. At the time of her return trips in 2004–5, she was earning about $245 per month. She had come there not because the Gulf was "the best of many options" but because she had to choose between living with her daughters and sending them to school.

Rachel's mobility, much more than that of the middle-class expatriates discussed above, is structured and constrained by economics, both those local to her native village and the global economic processes connected with neoliberalization, the crisis of agriculture, and the rise of a more uncompromising free-market nationalism in post-1990s India. The role of gender in shaping mobility and the experiences related to it are also different from the case of middle-class South Asians. The labor of Rachel, Laura, and that of the tens of thousands of other domestics in Dubai is commodified in obviously gendered ways. They often come to the Gulf because husbands back home lost jobs, left the marriage, or were otherwise prevented from providing for their families. Working-class South Asian women in turn become the primary breadwinners for their families. As women, they are channeled into particular kinds of work. As domestics, they are channeled into particular kinds of relationships with the state. Unlike male migrant workers, female domestics do not enter into a *kafāla* (sponsorship) relationship with employers; they enter into *mu 'īl* (guardianship) relationships with their employers. The state therefore regards them as wards of the family, into whose affairs the state is much more hesitant to intervene. As South Asian women, they are, moreover, vulnerable to other types of structural violence. The association with threat to national culture, with prostitution, and with adultery, for example, is an association to which they are uniquely vulnerable (Longva).

In 2009, Rachel continues to work, for a different family, in a different Emirati city. In many conversations with my wife and me, she showed us how life in the Gulf was an exercise in constant asceticism and vigilance. She had to guard carefully her everyday conversations and movements from most of the people with whom she came into daily contact, because they could, whether intentionally or inadvertently, harm her.

My partner and I got to know Rachel fairly well because of our contacts with and immersion in Dubai's expatriate Arab community. Nevertheless, because we (and especially I) were so intimately connected with that community (my family was living in Dubai while I was doing fieldwork there), Rachel, understandably, did not wish to confide too much about her daily life. Not that she felt that we would intentionally betray her, but one never knows how closely-guarded information can make its way to the wrong ears. Consequently, the description that I have given above, in spite of being typical of the experience of domestics in Dubai, is clearly (and intentionally) somewhat superficial. The daily life of a working-class person, such as Rachel, is considerably more difficult than my wife and I, immensely privileged in comparison to Rachel, will ever realize. The life of a working-class person is more subject to external and self-imposed control of speech and behavior, more organized by the minute planning of daily expenditures and earnings, more infested with dread and melancholy, and more, probably, boring—Rachel would only really leave the house on Fridays, her day off; on Sundays, to go to church; and when Madam took her on supermarket runs. Fear, anxiety, and boredom, rather than liberation in any sense of the term, are the main features of the experience of mobility in this case.

The feeling of anxiety is not wholly connected to class, however. Early during my fieldwork, I had thought that reticence was a class-related behavior or perhaps linguistic. Very few of the working-class South Asians (from the concierge at my building to the people who ran kiosks at the markets or shops at the malls) seemed at all interested in anything but the necessary verbiage of the transaction at hand. Yet this was not just a class phenomenon as I had initially hypothesized, reasoning that working-class guest workers, having more to lose from unguarded words to people whom they did not know, would be more introverted. My wife and I lived in a new apartment building, and we noticed that our neighbors, who seemed rather well-off, were also distinctly un-neighborly. Very few of them would greet us in the hallways and, particularly galling, were equally unlikely to return our greetings. It was not until one of my friends, a middle-class Keralan expatriate who works in the media department at Sheikh Muhammad's Tecom, noticed the same thing, that I inferred a connection between this rather surly personality of Dubai residents and the nexus of transience and anxiety. Living at the "Greens," another gated EMAAR project for middle-class professionals, my friend noticed that his neighbors were rather un-friendly as well. He connected this with the undercurrent of fear among the South Asian community at large. Whereas in the UAE, "it's not like a totalitarian state, where you're always afraid of the police coming to get you. But here, people are afraid of losing their job." He added that this is because immigrants are not encouraged to assimilate in this society. In the case of immigrants from South Asia, he continued, this leads to the feeling that one is being scrutinized for any sign or behavior that might result in deportation, or, as the current idiom has it, "getting runwayed." This undercurrent of fear, as my friend so aptly put it, seems to me to apply much more broadly, not just to South Asian immigrants, but also to the relationship between Emiratis and expatriates, and between the different expatriate communities—middle-class professionals fearing losing their relatively well-paid jobs, domestics or construction workers fearing deportation and the collapse of the livelihood of their families, Emiratis fearing Dubai turning into Bombay, urbanists building urban enclaves embodying this fear. These seem to be the emblematic phenomena of contemporary, neoliberal Dubai.[16]

CONCLUSION

Politicizing Dubai Space

They just called us to the head office and fired us.

—Alex Wanjohi, cook

What has fascinated me in Dubai is how dominant our [Western] reading is. . . . Dubai happened; we participated in its construction We were complicit in its extravagance. But we were also the first to denounce its absurdity.

—Rem Koolhaas

On September 19, 2005, between 800 and 1,000 Bangladeshi, Indian, and Pakistani construction workers from the Abu Dhabi-based Al-Hamed Company for Development and Projects marched from their worksite on Nakheel's Palm Island Jumeirah onto Sheikh Zayed Road in protest of four-months' non-payment of wages and wretched living conditions at their labor camp.[1] On the face of it, the event was a breakthrough. The workers could not have chosen a better symbol for the protest. Sheikh Zayed Road is, after all, Dubai's main thoroughfare, its two walls of skyscrapers one of the city's more forbidding emblems of the new "Muhammedan era." In the vicinity of an approximately five-mile stretch of Sheikh Zayed Road stand virtually all the monuments of the New Dubai: Sheikh Muhammad's Emirates Towers, the Burj Dubai/Khalifa, the Burj al-Arab, the "Tecom" media free zone, Majid Al Futtaim's Mall of the Emirates, and various luxury residential and resort complexes. With this act, the workers obstructed traffic (until Dubai riot police herded them onto the sandy banks of the road) and, for a moment, unavoidably inserted themselves into the visual field of drivers speeding down the highway.

Yet authorized voices quickly intervened, attempting in revealing ways to contain the significance of the event. Noting that the protesters actually represented about 6,000 others who were being denied wages and decent living conditions by the Al-Hamed company, media depicted the state and the company as separate entities, masking or diverting attention from the interconnection between state and economic actors (see introduction and chapter 1). By doing this, the company could be represented as "a bad apple," and the state as an objective, disembodied, disinterested arbiter of conflicts in the civil sphere. One might also note the swiftness with which local media lost interest in the event, something jarringly out of step with the apparent gravity of such a massive demonstration. Coverage lasted all of two days, virtually disappearing from any public mention by September 22. Another meaningful absence is implicit in how seldom the workers themselves were quoted. Indeed, the only worker voices that emerged in the coverage of the event were confined to the Western press.[2] The only actual people speaking in the major English-language daily, the *Gulf News*, for example, are the Dubai labor minister, Dubai-based legal advisors, professors at local universities, the head of the human rights section at the Dubai police, and representatives of the Al-Hamed company. And *Gulf News* is a relatively pro–guest-worker paper.[3] Finally, it is significant that these authorized voices converge and insist upon a framing of the event as a rights issue. "Construction companies must shoulder their responsibilities and pay workers' wages on time. Otherwise, there will be a 'big problem.'. . . Failing to [pay wages on time] is a violation of labour rights" (Hadid). "Captain Fahd al Awadi, from Dubai police's human rights department . . . said a human rights official would be present 'every day' to ensure salaries were handed over. . . . 'We try to ensure a worker's rights and his dignity [said Awadi].'" As if afraid that the point of the whole containment action might be lost on any stubborn observers, *Gulf News* went on to editorialize that "workers who have contributed to the development of the country must enjoy their *full rights and entitlements*. . . . No company has any justification to stop payment of its workers' salaries. The government should intervene with the *full force of the law* to stop abusing workers' rights" (Salama 2005, emphasis added). And, rather grandiosely, *Gulf News* declared that this was "a victory for all workers" (*Gulf News* 2005).

Far from drawing on the possibility of the event to question the status quo of labor exploitation and the temptations for labor abuse that boom development has created,[4] a predictable cast of experts and state officials was trotted out to set the limits of the debate of the event and to contain its potentially more dangerous implications. No one benefiting from the system needed to fear much more than being forced to pay wages already tacitly agreed upon in terms set by the companies themselves. The labor minister who exacted the fines and promised to visit repercussions on the company "should not be seen as encouraging protests that will disrupt traffic and delay business" (*Gulf News* 2005). The system was in these ways shown to be working. "No conclusions should be drawn by just a few bad eggs in the basket" (*Khaleej Times*). Or, as an expert (as *Gulf News* put it) from the UAE University in Al Ain was quoted as saying: "No one should be allowed to tarnish the bright image of the UAE" (Salama 2005).

The significance of this event does not merely pertain to wages and accommodations, as important as these are. Although the September 2005 strike appeared unprecedented to some (Fattah 2005), labor unrest in fact occurs all the time in the UAE. Just between early September and mid-October 2005, there were at least nine protests in the country, ranging in size from about ten workers, to the (at least) eight hundred already mentioned. Each time, authorized voices assert that the offending company was in violation of supposedly clear labor laws, that the source of the problem was not the structure of the labor regime and local practices of capitalism (let alone capitalism itself), but merely a deviant company. That the protestors in the September 19, 2005, strike were working on one of the Palm Islands, which are projects central to the prestige of Sheikh Muhammad's empire, is significant. It is interesting to compare how little-mentioned the Palm Island was in the context of the strike with how visible it is in contexts, such as marketing seminars, ads, GPS maps, and other official and unofficial representations more under the control of the family-state.

These seemingly forceful interventions by the agents of the state in the name of workers' human rights are in stark contrast to the response a year later of the UAE labor minister Al Kaabi to the Human Rights Watch (HRW) report on the Dubai construction sector (2006). As discussed in the first chapter, foreign workers in UAE, according to the labor minister's reasoning, were not migrant workers and thus were not protected by the United Nations' Migrant Workers' Convention. Because workers in the UAE worked on a "temporary basis," wrote the minister, "the immigration laws applicable in the western countries cannot be applied to these workers" (20).

How does one interpret this seeming contradiction? In fact, there is no contradiction at all. In both the earlier official and quasi-official responses to the worker demonstrations and in the HRW case we see authorized, family-state voices asserting that the state is capable of handling issues of worker welfare and corporate abuse by itself. The labor minister is simply reiterating this by telling HRW that it has no right to interfere in internal Emirati affairs. More interesting are two assumptions that underpin the minister's response. First, the false claim in the teeth of the well-known UN migrant workers convention that western immigration laws do not apply to the UAE. This is a version of the so-called sovereign exception argument often made by states when transgressing international laws, most clearly in the case of the United States since September 11, 2001, (see Agamben). This is an area of convergence between the minister's statement and the earlier worker protests event. In both cases, Dubai or UAE officialdom says, "the state is the final arbiter of ethical and legal issues it considers matters of state interest." The second assumption, bound up with the first, is that the state is a neutral actor; unlike the companies or workers, it is not subject to passions or (as a U.S. constitutional scholar might put it) factional interests. The effect both of the response to the worker protests and of the minister's speech act is to excise the state from the political and economic contexts that shape it.

At this juncture, I want to return to architecture and space. In particular, I want to juxtapose a few instances, respectively, of theory and practice pertaining to what I have been calling Dubai's urbanist ideology. First the theory. In March 2009, Rem Koolhaas addressed the Sharjah Biennial, a highly-regarded arts and architecture congress organized by the government of the emirate of Sharjah. The Koolhaas of the film *The Sand Castle* (*Wide Angle*), poetic, ambitious, a practitioner of the "God's eye" perspective of architectural theory (Scott 1998), appears to have become a more reflective, somewhat chastened version of himself. In particular, Koolhaas is here attempting to see if anything can be salvaged from Dubai's (literal and symbolic) collapse.[6]

> I came here first in 2004. . . . Then, two years ago I became increasingly nervous about the mission of architecture and the uses of architecture. The incredible pressure of the market economy was forcing architecture itself into increasingly extravagant condition. Dubai seemed to be the epicenter of that extravagance.[7] So, I came with deeply ambivalent feelings. It seemed as if the idea of the city and the metropolis itself had turned into a caricature almost, where it's not a coherent entity but maybe a patchwork of theme parks. (Koolhaas 2009)[8]

If the tone is new, however, there are some constants. One recurrent theme, for example is that of finding optimism in the inevitable condition of late capitalist urbanism and of seeing specific cities and societies as instantiations of a quasi-Hegelian process by which architecture seeks its authentic self (see chapter 2): "exactly because of all of this ambivalence, it seemed to me perhaps an ideal opportunity to try to work through the crisis of architecture." The spatialization of Dubai as a blank slate also returns, if, oddly, now utilizing "context" as an alibi.

> We could be liberated from previous obligations and able to start from scratch. My first attempt in Dubai [in a building project proposed in 2005] was to use its expectations of absurdity and to run against them, to propose a very simple, singular, pure building. . . . It was seemingly absurd to think that the age of icon or the age of increasingly bizarre architecture would be over. My theory of expectation was that the building would work best in the context of Dubai, because you could count on the context of contrast to achieve pristine beauty and at the same time eccentricity—perhaps a new declaration at a strange moment in architecture.

My argument in this book has been that in the connection between local agents of urbanism and global experts, such as starchitects, there is a concealed if often unwitting political project that buttresses both the monopolist agenda of local elites on Dubai space and memory and the elitist agendas of global urbanists. A counterargument can be made against this thesis, specifically, that when Koolhaas, Gehry, and others refer to Dubai and other cities as "blank slates," when they refer to "context," they are in fact talking about architectural idiom and not about the society as a whole. These architects' interventions are *architectural,* this counterargument would go, because architecture is concerned with aesthetico-formal, not social and political, questions. It is unfair to critique the political naivety of starchitects, because political and social questions are extrinsic to architecture.

This may be the case, but Rem Koolhaas seems not to agree. In the Sharjah Biennial speech, he goes on to suggest that an analysis of the social and historical contexts of Dubai is intrinsic to his intervention. "As we became increasingly involved in Dubai, it became important for us to understand the place better and to understand how this constellation of buildings and architecture had come about. What were the forces that had changed it? Who were the participants that had generated it?" "Forces" and "participants" would indicate that social and perhaps political, and certainly historical, factors are part of the process of conceptualizing and realizing architectural projects, that architectural space is simultaneously social space. This is something, obviously, with which I agree. Koolhaas continues, thoughtfully, that "rather than judging, we started to look for a more analytical view." Part of this analysis must subject superficial work to critique, again, something that resonates with my argument. Especially troublesome, according to Koolhaas, is Mike Davis's work (2006a; Davis and Monk), which, Koolhaas points out (correctly in my view) is "a superficial reading of the possibility of Dubai. . . . The phenomenon here is immediately ambiguous and multi-faceted, both in the good sense and the bad sense" (see also Koolhaas, Bouman, and Wigley).

Another seemingly positive development is an increasing awareness that Western representations of Dubai, both as a city and as a symbol of something larger and more abstract, say more about Western desires and prejudices than they do about Dubai or the "Middle Eastern city," etc.

> What has fascinated me in Dubai is how dominant our reading is. By "our" I mean the West. Dubai happened; we participated in its construction. We were complicit in its extravagance. But we were also the first to denounce its absurdity. What I fear, now that we have declared the "end-game," is that we will also be the first to tell Dubai not to be itself anymore, to tell Dubai that it's over and to declare prematurely an end, not only to an experiment, but also to a real cultural change that has been taking place in and underneath all of this, and that still deserves to reach its own conclusions. I think that is where it's a little bit strange to quote Anna Wintour, editor of *Vogue,* in this context, as if she's a political thinker. But it is nevertheless significant that New York now looks to Dubai as the definition of what cannot be done anymore. And I really encourage everyone here in the room, do not give too much belief to this kind of material, but instead to what Dubai will eventually have to offer us.[9]

Aside from correctly pointing to the erasure, in Western narratives about Dubai (and perhaps about other cities of the global south), of Western complicity in Dubai's local urban dynamics, Koolhaas is suggesting here that Dubai as a city, a symbol, an allegory, etc., nevertheless remains useful in Western urbanist narratives. This was the case when it was successful and, now, when it has failed. When it was rising, it seemed to confirm the wonders of the Western neoliberal dream (as Mike Davis might put it). When it fell, it did the same thing; it failed, the story goes, because it was not enough like the West; it was reckless, unhinged, "insane" (Parker). Damned if you do, damned if you don't. On this point, I cannot agree more with Koolhaas.

Yet, in spite of these promising developments, other aspects of the speech remain puzzling, and one also senses troublesome conflations and omissions. Koolhaas again, "We simply decided to engage the Arab world, to talk to the Arab world and to comprehend some of the more superficial or some of the more common Western analyses of Dubai." And,

> Perhaps the most interesting things we discovered (for us at least, and at that point it showed our ignorance) is that the number of expats are, for instance, 30 percent in Abu Dhabi and 80 percent in Dubai. How was it that, at the moment when the West is struggling with multiculturalism, in the supposedly intolerant Islamic world, this kind of sharing societies works there? We don't hold any illusions about who those immigrants are, why they are here. It is probably undeniably true that there is an element of exploitation, but we decided to look at these worlds as prototypes of the new Islamic world in which the coexistence of many cultures is an ongoing experiment and probably an ultimately positive experiment.

Contradicting his earlier comment about avoiding judgment and superficiality, Koolhaas returns to clichés about Dubai being symbolic of some larger phenomenon, this time, the so-called Arab or Islamic world (this aside from the genteel evasiveness of phrases such as "an element of exploitation"). What Koolhaas seems to imply here is something like an older anthropological notion of cultural difference, two cultural worlds separated in space and worldview (Crehan, 36–37; Gupta and Ferguson 1997a; 1997b; Malkki). But why spatialize culture in this way? Why not approach Dubai as a product of local-global historical dialectic, or by contextualizing it in the Arab and Middle Eastern regions where there is no dearth of scholarship on cities and urban life? Koolhaas seems unaware that he is engaging in cultural homogenization; in fact, he appears to believe he is doing the opposite. This has pernicious consequences, because for better or worse, Koolhaas and other starchitects have become influential cultural interpreters of the non-West for Western audiences. In turn, cultural homogenization, as I have tried to show in this book, becomes useful to local elites, such as the Maktoum family-state.

Both puzzling and potentially dangerous is the statement about discovering the diversity of Abu Dhabi and Dubai. Koolhaas here is reflecting on events that occurred in 2004 and 2005. It is odd that anyone, let alone a savvy, well-traveled and well-read culture maven such as Koolhaas, should so unexpectedly and belatedly become aware of a fact—the large proportion of foreigners residing in Abu Dhabi and Dubai—so obvious for so long to far less privileged everyday people, most of whom have never traveled to the Gulf. More interesting yet, and perhaps more dangerous, is how close Koolhaas comes to proposing the Gulf as some alternative to Western cosmopolitanism (as ideological and even hypocritical as the latter often is). I do agree, and have tried to show in this book, that the relationship between nationals and foreigners in Dubai is much more complex and nuanced than is readily apparent. But to suggest that Gulf ethnocracies are some sort of vaguely positive experiment in multiculturalism and "sharing societies" is a stretch.

This culturalization of Dubai, its homogenization as one cultural world in which all Dubayyans (citizen or foreign), by implication, equally participate, relates to Koolhaas's retelling of the city's history, a retelling that will now appear familiar from the previous discussion in this book about the struggle and eventual success of the family-state to define Dubai's history and modernity.

> We also looked at the history of Dubai. This is Dubai in 1973, barely more than [a] village on a creek. . . . We discovered there were very serious efforts to plan, very serious involvement of the different kinds of leaderships, real engagement in the small details of infrastructure. . . . What we discovered were actually the remnants of the presence of more serious blueprints that had been put in place by significant coalitions of Arab rulers—Arabs and Western interests. . . . We looked at how we could somehow maintain this kind of Dubai.

This not only repeats the act, up until now only implicit in Koolhaas's lecture, of writing foreigners out of the making of Dubai, it returns to the familiar narrative in which rulers and Western experts are the only actors who warrant representation in the city's story. Of course, there is nothing new in this retelling. Koolhaas simply superimposes the story that the pro-Maktoum camp has been telling (at least since they navigated the tricky period of reformism and nationalism in the middle twentieth century) onto a structure of "tradition versus modernity" that will, if anything, seem uncomfortably close to what I have been calling neoorthodox narratives. Moreover, like Dubai ruler Muhammad Al Maktoum summoning his Bedouin roots and conflating them with Dubai in the November 2009 speech discussed earlier (chapter 3; see also Bowers), Koolhaas here reintroduces a reified notion of local tradition as a critical foil to those who would diminish Dubai's possibility. Strange bedfellows, this cutting-edge Western theorist–architect and the Arabian dynast speaking in a neoorthodox register. Yet this kind of tacit alliance between local elite and global expert was common in Dubai's urbanist moment (and seems to continue to be, in this, post-crisis one).

Far from the towering heights of starchitectural theory and skyscrapers, a few recent incidents can set this theory in relief. By early 2009, reports of mass layoffs in Dubai were being publicized. In February, a construction company sacked 1,300 workers and in early March was still reporting that 50 to 70 workers were being sent home every day (Moussly). Around the same time, a restaurant in Dubai Marina, an upscale resort, fired hundreds of employees, according to one report. Another company sacked 200 gardeners; another was reported to have ordered "workers who had completed at least two years of work to go home on four-month unpaid vacations" (Al Khalil). The unpaid vacations struck the workers as "simply a way of getting rid of people without having to pay them off." In September, a Dubai engineering firm accused 108 Nepali workers of participating in a work stoppage (an accusation the workers said was untrue) and fired them en masse. The workers were summarily deported: "They were not even allowed to collect their belongings from their residences" (*Nepal News*). "They just called us to the head office and fired us," a cook reported about the Dubai Marina mass sacking. One journalist, citing a stereotypical Western media image of "Dubai's collapse," brilliantly captured both the structural vulnerability and discursive invisibility of non-Western, working-class foreigners:

> Reports of hundreds of cars left abandoned at the airport with keys in the ignition and maxed-out credit cards strewn in the glove compartment have become a popular anecdote for the Western

expatriates forced to return home after losing their jobs or being made redundant. But for the thousands of blue-collar workers, going home is not that simple and often means a waste of live [*sic*] savings and the prospect of severe poverty. (Moussly)

"I sold our land and took loans in the village to come here. . . . I paid the agent £2,000 to bring me. . . . When I return, people in the village will want their money but I have none."

Back at the Sharjah Biennial, Koolhaas was pointing to "another very interesting way in which this environment is beginning to function, namely as a secure place for the displaced. Dubai is becoming increasingly an attraction for the children of mixed marriages, who are not at home anymore in the fatherlands of their parents. Only here can they find a real, authentic basis" (Koolhaas 2009). The comment is accompanied by a slide showing clippings from the semi-official English language daily *Gulf News*. Anyone who has looked carefully at *Gulf News* will have noticed a few patterns; for example, it is friendly to the Maktoum regime (not surprising) and it frequently runs stories about expatriates (mostly middle-class or wealthy) who have found refuge in Dubai. Not to recognize these two facts as interconnected is puzzling.

What I want to do, at this point, is to juxtapose these events: the large protest from 2005 and the subsequent identification of the state with human rights protections; the 2006 Human Rights Watch Report and the UAE labor minister's response; the 2009 Koolhaas lecture and the mass sackings that were occurring almost simultaneously. Three framings suggest themselves from a review of these events. We may call them, for lack of better terminology, the frame of the economy, that of the state, and that of culture.

Certain of the events, such as the protests, the sackings, and perhaps the state negotiations of the concept of human rights can be framed as primarily economic phenomena. We can infer, for example, an implicit theory of free labor in the minister's rejection of the Human Rights Watch findings. The workers signed contracts in the UAE, not in the western countries. They must therefore abide by those contracts. The workers did not have to sign those contracts. It is not the fault of the UAE state that UAE contracts differ from those in the West. Or, as one of my Indian middle-class interlocutors put it, no one puts a gun to the heads of foreign workers in Dubai (see chapter 5). The mass sackings can also be placed in the economic frame. Capitalism goes through cycles. Recessions are a natural part of the workings of the market. Economies, states, and individuals must each adapt themselves to these fluctuations. Foreign workers can always go home, reeducate themselves, and make themselves more employable.

The state can also be read in these events, or, as Wendy Brown might put it, the state can seem to be the "it" referred to or signified by them (191). The protesting workers in the 2005 demonstration (like in many other Dubai work stoppages) were, after all, addressing the state. They wanted the state to intervene on their behalf against the construction companies or labor agents. As the construction worker to whom I spoke at Sonapoor labor camp in 2007 put it, "the government is good, the companies are bastards!" Similarly, Human Rights Watch's recommendations in their 2006 report were directed at the state. It was the state that was responsible, according to the report, for enforcing existing labor laws and for setting up commissions of inquiry to investigate companies violating the law. When not rejecting outright the intervention of foreign NGOs, state officials also conformed to this discourse, as can be seen in the example of the labor officials who asserted the intentions of the state to punish violators of workers' human rights. Authorized voices, such as the experts interviewed by newspapers during the 2005 protests, reiterated this state-versus-civil society dichotomy, claiming that offending companies were only "a few bad eggs in the basket." "The state," as Timothy Mitchell has written, therefore "appears to stand apart from society in the unproblematic way in which intentions or ideas are thought to stand apart from the external world to which they refer" (174).

"Culture"—in the sense of habits, worldviews, sentiments, etc.—may also seem like the "it" to which these events refer. Here is Christopher Davidson's interpretation of the September 2005 protest and its aftermath, for example.

> Emboldened by the outcome of [the September 2005] protest, in 2006 an even larger strike was staged at the construction site for the . . . Burj Dubai skyscraper. Incited to violence by a number of ringleaders, over 2,500 workers went on the rampage—security guards were attacked, and several million dollars worth of damage was caused as vehicles were torched, computers destroyed, and machinery broken. By the end of the year nineteen other worker-related incidents had occurred. In early 2007 a stoppage was held on a main road by over 300 workers. . . . They effectively blocked traffic for several hours, with the police being reluctant to clear them from the road, a remarkable development given that

all of the workers were expatriates and only a few years earlier would have been swiftly deported and replaced by a more pliable contingent. (2008, 187–88)

Phrases such as "incited to violence," "rampage," and "a more pliable contingent" displace the significance of these protests from the political and social onto the cultural and sentimental. Such descriptions of worker violence seem disproportionate in a long book that is silent about the much more comprehensive system of structural violence in which workers are entangled. Worker protests are denigrated, represented as the result of worker irrationality, inherent violence, and the generalized menace they pose to Emirati society. There is also a not-too-subtle suggestion that this menace is somehow connected to the workers' foreignness. The ringleaders that turn up here seem to bear more than a passing resemblance to the foreign *agents provocateurs* that were supposedly luring 1950s Dubayyans (those passive objects of whatever larger political currents happen to waft into their midst) to Nasserism and anti-colonialism (40).

"Culture" in a slightly different sense, an anthropological sense (now rather questionable) of "distinct life-ways," coherent, territorialized, and bounded, also emerges from these events. The UAE labor minister rejects the Human Rights Watch findings because, he says, Western labor laws do not apply in the UAE. Along with the aforementioned assertion of sovereign exception, this suggests that Western values do not hold for Emirati circumstances (obviously correct in many cases, but not relevant here). In turn, this seems to entail a spatialization of Emirati culture as distinct from Western culture, whatever that is. Similarly, the Koolhaas lecture territorializes Dubai as both geographically and culturally Arab or Islamic at the same time that it rehearses a kind of historical narrative in which rulers and Western experts meet on the common ground of shared vision and temperamental sympathy (see chapter 2; see also Gjørv). In this way, political and historical encounters are displaced by invocations of "culture."

My argument in this book has been for a different framing altogether, that of the social and the political. This framing, I think, is the most compelling way to both interpret and interconnect such events, events that I take to be typical and reflective of the reality of Dubai in the first decade of the twenty-first century. Taken in isolation, each of the aforementioned frames helps construct a plausible narrative, but they also lead to troublesome consequences. Without context, the state can seem coherent and subjective (in the sense that Foucault, Mitchell, and others have critiqued) and can therefore claim a plausible deniability in involvement with the economic and social spheres; the economy can come to seem a natural phenomenon, following its own laws and therefore disconnected from the social and the political; actions can appear to be motivated solely by intrinsic or cultural attitudes, thereby absolving the powerful from their role in and the structural benefits they derive from the economic and political system. However, when placed in their sociopolitical contexts, those of ethnocracy, family-state power, and the ruling bargain ideology, the events make up an intelligible formation. They create a complex image of state-culture-territory that makes it appear that the state is subjective, coherent, and abstract, that culture inheres in the shared identity of the ruling ethnie and is articulated by powerful men, and that the society's territory is a blank slate awaiting inscription, or a formless clay awaiting molding, by those powerful men. The seeming naturalness with which hundreds of workers can be summoned before their boss, sacked, and swiftly deported; of a Dubai in which Maktoum rule and definitions of modernity look inevitable, and of a city that is a laboratory for architectural experimentation are all effects of this particular spatialization of state and culture in contemporary Dubai. The state, then, deploys a kind of spatial(izing) power. It may or may not possess the monopoly of legitimate violence, as Max Weber said, but (in Dubai at least) it possesses the capacity to regenerate its sovereign territory by making it a blank slate.[10]

This does not, however, imply that its hegemony is complete. The comment of an Emirati friend in late 2004 seemed to indicate an uncertainty about the path Dubai was taking even at the height of the city's boom. We were having lunch outdoors on one of those typical stunning Dubai December afternoons. Our table overlooked the placid waters of an artificial lake and immaculately manicured grounds; behind us were the mirrored-glass office blocks of one of the Maktoum parastatals. In the distance, construction cranes were groaning with activity. It appeared to be another perfect, action-packed day in the Muhammedan era. After a pause following pleasantries, my friend, someone from the social background I have been calling flexible citizenship, picked up a thread from an earlier conversation. "Sometimes," she said, "I feel . . . I feel like our cosmopolitanism has gone too far. Sometimes, you go to places, and you feel like *you're* the stranger. "I feel that, especially with the Dutch and the British, [this cosmopolitanism] is a form of indirect occupation." These expatriates, she said, get preferential treatment when companies are hiring. The government of Dubai is indirectly responsible, she added, because they make deals with corporations so that their own citizens, usually Europeans or North Americans, get three times the salary for the same position that an Emirati would. "[Expatriates] feel as if it's their right [to live and work] in Dubai. They behave as if they're the locals and we're the expats." One time, a Dutch friend really offended her when he said, "we own like half of Dubai."

Some Emiratis, she said, are racist against their own compatriots too. "You know," she said, "the [Emiratis] with the *modern ideas*." Then she paused, before continuing in a resigned tone, "But you don't make too much of it because it could end up offending investors and scaring them away. And Dubai is, first, about business."[11] With this friend, I have since lost touch. I wonder what she would make of Dubai's more recent association with images of "cars left abandoned at the airport with keys in the ignition and maxed-out credit cards strewn in the glove compartment" (Moussly). Would she find them to be exaggerated? Or would she sense some unpleasant truth in them, perhaps that the city has made itself disposable? Maybe both?

ACKNOWLEDGMENTS

This book would have been impossible without the support and engagement of many people. I wish to thank the following individuals and institutions.

The book started as a PhD dissertation at Harvard's Department of Anthropology. I wish to thank my dissertation supervisor, Steve Caton, and my dissertation committee, Ted Bestor, Engseng Ho, and Hashim Sarkis. Not only did they guide me in my early, relatively unsophisticated, attempts to realize this project; they continue to offer support and encouragement. Although Woody Watson and Michael Herzfeld were not on my dissertation committee, they were mentors in graduate school from whom I learned how to be a better, more professional anthropologist and teacher. I owe them a great debt. During the dissertation phase of the project, generous support was provided by the Harvard University Graduate School of Arts and Sciences in the form of various fellowships; the Harvard University Graduate School of Design, which provided a research fellowship, facilities, and intellectual camaraderie during Spring 2006; the United States Department of Education, which conferred a Fulbright-Hays Fellowship for the field research period; and the Harvard University Graduate Society and the Cora Du Bois Charitable Trust of Boston, both of which provided funds for the writing of the dissertation. I am also grateful to the University of Sharjah, UAE, for providing a visa and affiliation during the period of my fieldwork, and to the faculty and students of American University of Sharjah's College of Architecture, Art and Design, who provided a warm, intellectually stimulating environment in which to work and think, both during and after my fieldwork.

At the University of Minnesota Press I thank Pieter Martin, Richard Morrison, and Kristian Tvedten, who worked patiently with me since late 2006 to transform the dissertation into the current book. The external readers Pieter initially recruited, Timothy Luke and Hassanuddin Khan, along with a third, anonymous, reader recruited later to read the nearly final manuscript, were each discerning and immensely helpful in pointing out the manuscript's weaknesses and potential. I am indebted to them. John Kober and Jim Bindas were tireless in polishing the manuscript and helping carry it through the very final stretch of copyediting and layout; my thanks to them for this and for accommodating my endless tinkering.

My thanks to Gary McDonogh and Marina Peterson, and Mike and Kim Fortun, editors, respectively, of the forthcoming volume *Global Downtowns* (University of Pennsylvania Press) and the journal *Cultural Anthropology,* publications in which material from this book will appear or has been published. Thanks to Laura Juk of Models 1 and Dave at www. dave.biz for permitting use of the image in Figure 1. Thanks to the Dar al-Khaleej in Sharjah, UAE, which kindly provided permission to reprint the image in Figure 8, which was first published in *al-Khaleej* on June 8, 2004. My thanks go also to Camilla Hall, who helped with fact checking. There were many interlocutors and colleagues from Dubai and the wider United Arab Emirates who helped in so many ways that it is difficult to summarize. Unfortunately, I cannot name these guides to local cultures and other kinds of teacher, interlocutor, and collaborator. You know who you are; my deepest gratitude and sincere hopes that you enjoy the book and find it useful.

Thank you to Xiangming Chen and Vijay Prashad who generously invited me to be a postdoctoral fellow at the Center for Urban and Global Studies, Trinity College Connecticut, in 2008–9. This was a fellowship without which I would not have had the time or intellectual stimulation to write most of this book. The fellowship also permitted me to meet many dear friends and intellectual comrades. The students of my Trinity College Seminar, "The Making of Modern Dubai," allowed me to see Dubai afresh. Thanks to my former colleagues, friends, students, and haunts at the University of Iowa, especially Virginia Dominguez, Jane Desmond, Denise Filios, Martha Greer, and Downing Thomas. Iowa City and UI were like Trinity, a place of openness and generosity. My two-year postdoctoral fellowship in the UI International Programs was a precious gift of time in which to initiate and do much of the groundwork for this book. My colleagues, friends, and students at the University of the Pacific supported and engaged the project through the final stretch. Laura Bathurst, Annlee Dolan, Arturo Giraldez, Bruce LaBrack, Sarah Mathis, Annie Richard, and Jean-Marie Stratigos were especially generous in providing feedback and intellectual engagement.

I also wish to thank other colleagues with whom this privileged academic life has allowed me to cross paths, and who have intellectually engaged, challenged, and helped me vastly improve the project: Abdul Khaleq Abdulla, Bernard Bate, Amahl Bishara, Michelle Buckley, Mohammad Chakaki, Rodney Collins, Rudi Colloredo-Mansfeld, Gareth Doherty, Liz Faier, Nelida Fuccaro, Andrew Gardner, Farha Ghannam, Susan Harding, Waleed Hazbun, Boris Jensen, Suad Joseph, Arang Keshavarzian, Kevin Mitchell, Sarah Moser, James Onley, Nasser Rabbat, Stephen Ramos, Amal Rassam, Rima Sabban, Smriti Srinivas, Neyran Turan, Melissa Vaughn, Lucia Volk, Neha Vora, Jessica Winegar, and Amy Young.

My family deserves my great thanks: Selwa al-Gailani, Maryam Kanna and Ziad Kanna, for their indulgence of my exotic career choice and, in my mother Selwa's case, the occasional translation of Arabic bureaucratese; Samar, Judy, and Salim al-Gailani; and my father, Ismail, whose memory continues to inspire and guide me. And I thank Anett, Jutta, and Wolfgang Hofmann, for making Germany a second home.

Finally and most importantly, to my partner, best friend, and wife, Ines Hofmann Kanna, this book is dedicated to you.

NOTES

Introduction

1. The first epigraph in this chapter is taken from Parker 2005, 136–37. Parker says that the source is a "white collar expatriate" resident of Dubai. "Raghad" in the second epigraph is a pseudonym. Unless they belong to public figures, all names in this book are pseudonyms. I regret that this is the case, but could not avoid the necessity of protecting my interlocutors as much as possible.

2. This assertion generally holds more for Western journalism than for scholarship, but a lack of theoretical engagement and interest in recent developments in the social sciences also characterizes much scholarship on the region. See Kanna 2010b.

3. Robert Vitalis debunks this, showing how ARAMCO and various Saudi royals, especially Faisal ibn Abd al-Aziz (c. 1904–1975), constructed such a narrative in the case of Saudi Arabia. In this myth, the foreign oil company is represented as altruistic and local elites, the royals and their allies, as forces of modernization, reform, and desert or consultative democracy. Such a narrative has several implications: that neither the oil firm nor the king, for example, are subject to history (simply enacting policies reflecting their altruism) and that the people of the society are voiceless primitives whose interests can only be articulated by the oil firm and the royals (Vitalis). Although differing in important ways from that of Saudi Arabia, the history of the royal families of Abu Dhabi and Dubai is similar in one important sense—the latter, too, were seen, by the colonial regime, as responsible modernizers within their societies.

4. This is obviously not to deny the persistence, and in the age of the so-called Global War on Terror, mutation of the classic stereotypes of Muslims and Arabs as premodern, savage, inclined to terrorism, etc. Such stereotypes, in fact, seem to be a necessary part of the more positive references to selected enclaves of Arab/ Muslim modernity. See Mamdani's discussion of the "good Muslim–bad Muslim" dichotomy in Western imperial discourses.

5. More specifically, Dubai World, until recently headed by Sultan Ahmad bin Sulaym, subsumes the real estate developer Nakheel as a subsidiary; Dubai Holding, headed until recently by Muhammad Al Gergawi, encompasses the real estate developers Dubai Properties, Sama Dubai, and Tatweer (Tatweer's project, "Dubailand," mentioned in this book and recently put on hold, was to be an enclave "three times the size of Manhattan"); and EMAAR, headed by Muhammad Al Abbar and responsible for the Burj Dubai, Street of Dreams (see chapter 5), and other projects. See Hall and Salama for an excellent summary.

6. See Elsheshtawy 2009; Fuccaro forthcoming; Gardner 2008; forthcoming; and Vora 2008. Nelida Fuccaro writes that the history of Gulf immigrant communities is "limited and uneven" (forthcoming, 1). Along with her own important studies (2005; 2009), she cites Al Qasimi 2000 and Khalifa as notable exceptions (forthcoming, 1). Her summary of recent scholarship on a related theme, labor migration in the context of the post–oil boom Gulf city, is very helpful. Among the studies she cites are Bonine; Franklin; Seccombe; and Winckler (see 3).

7. Urban anthropology is itself a young subfield within anthropology. Before the 1970s, under the strong influence of functionalism, the assumption was that anthropological fieldwork was done in rural or other non-urbanized areas. The 1970s, when anthropologists became more interested in urban issues, were, however, a peculiar conjuncture for the Arab world. There were the 1967 and 1973 Arab–Israeli wars, the Lebanese civil war, Ba'thist regimes in Syria and Iraq, not an ideal situation for aspiring urban anthropologists of the Arab world. The Gulf was not regarded as an interesting or, often, feasible place to do fieldwork. (This is still somewhat the case today.) In this connection, the important ethnographic works on pre–civil war Beirut are worth mentioning (Joseph 1977; 1978; Khalaf 1973). I am indebted to Suad Joseph for pointing this out. Personal communication, June 7, 2010.

8. An anthropologist friend doing her research in Morocco said when she visited me in the field that her Moroccan friends referred to Dubai as "the city with the new cars."

9. This perception was confirmed during the so-called Dubai Ports controversy in the United States in early 2006, when the attempted acquisition of some U.S. ports by the Dubai multinational Dubai Ports (DP) triggered a depressing, if predictable, wave of anti-Arab xenophobia among the U.S. political classes. One of my friends, an expatriate professor who teaches in Sharjah, e-mailed to ask me whether Americans had taken leave of their senses and to report the deep sense of offense taken by Emiratis, who are justifiably proud of DP's global reputation as a highly-competent and modern ports management firm.

10. Readers who glance through my bibliography will notice that many sources are listed as electronic documents. Most of the newspaper documents, and nearly all of the ones from Emirati newspapers such as *Gulf News* and *al-Ittihad,* collected before 2008 were originally newspaper clippings, not electronic

documents. These clippings I made at a juncture in this project when I was not as exacting as I am now about recording the page numbers of the clippings. To be as exact as possible in sourcing these documents, and to allow readers to more easily access them, I have listed as many of the Internet sites of these sources as I could find. These sources will appear to have been collected over short periods of time in 2008–10. They usually were not, but were clipped over a much longer period.

11. I do not mean to anthropomorphize Dubai here. The phrasing of this assertion is adapted from Kracauer's statement about a society's "judgments" about "itself," by which he meant the hegemonic ideologies that prevail in a specific society at a certain point in time.

12. Mitchell, for example, points out that a priori notions of the intentional-actor state are unable to cope with the historical question of how that kind of state came about in the first place. Brown makes a similar point, showing how the modern U.S. state has been constructed on the discursive and practical grounds of masculine gender hierarchy. Others, such as Gupta, point to the everyday, grass-roots encounters with agents of the state in rural India. These encounters are mediated by localized technologies, such as newspapers, and by cultural expectations, such repertoires of performance relating to bribes and other interactions with state officials.

13. James Scott's skepticism of recent attempts to deconstruct the agentive state seems to me to be sensible. Responding to critiques of his argument in *Seeing like a State* (1998), which assert that the line between state power and society is far more fluid than he grants, that state power is diffuse and created in complicitous transactions between bureaucrats and everyday people, Scott writes that the difference between "the official and the subaltern is that the former has, when he or she chooses to deploy it, the authority of the official regulations at his or her back and the subaltern does not." Moreover, in relations between state and society, it "may be that in observing any particular skirmish, the battlefield seems all confusion and disorder. From greater distance and with some hindsight, however, larger patterns of change can be discerned" (2005, 399–400).

14. This is because space, and in a period in history that is becoming inexorably urbanized (Lefebvre 2003; Davis 2006b), urban space, mediates the most basic levels of human experience. Postmodernism, argues Jameson, is a period in capitalism in which the processes of rationalization and differentiation have reached near culmination. Hence, we have the self-referential quality of postmodern culture. "The self-reflective idiom of postmodernism merely show(s) that specialization and the division of labor had seized the arts just as much as anything else; if culture increasingly talked about itself, this was because it talked increasingly *to* itself" (Kunkel, 13, emphasis in the original). This is reflected in the spatial and the urban domains, which more and more resemble life in a wholly man-made world. Jameson writes in his recent *Valences of the Dialectic* (2009), for example, that "we have indeed secreted a human age out of ourselves as spiders secrete their webs— an immense all-encompassing ceiling . . . which shuts down visibility on all sides

even as it absorbs all the formerly natural elements in its habitat, transmuting them into its own man-made substance" (Kunkel, 16). For an excellent summary of the work of Judith Butler, and in particular the notion of subjectivation, see Salih.

15. At least insofar as Lefebvre is translated into English. I have not attempted to grapple with his publications in the original French.

16. See Erdreich and Rapoport; Holston 2009; and Premat. Holston writes that while Lefebvre was correct in predicting that the question of the "right to the city," a shift of struggles from "production to reproduction," would define urban life in late capitalism, he did not foresee that this struggle would occur primarily in the Global South (2009, 247).

17. The others being Abu Dhabi, Ajman, Fujeira, Ras al-Khaimah, Sharjah, and Umm al-Qaiwain.

18. Naming the Gulf as either Persian or Arabian will, no doubt, offend someone. I have no stakes in this debate. For purposes of simplicity, I henceforth refer to the Gulf as Arabian or Arab, a choice determined by the tendency in local usage in Dubai and other countries of the officially Arabic-speaking side of the Gulf.

19. What seems to be going on is something like a segmentary logic—"I against my brothers, my brothers and I against my cousins, my brothers, cousins, and I against the world." In other words, the Persian immigrants were considered Arab when in Persia but tended to be regarded as Persian when on the Arab side of the Gulf. Onley 2005 gives some figures in the context of a fascinating case study that he conducted on a Bahraini-Persian trading family. Whether one can extrapolate from this case study to other Gulf societies is, in spite of Onley's suggestion that we do, not clear.

20. Most locals to whom I spoke, however, maintained that today *'Ajami* or *Khodomoni* Emiratis (who are of Persian extraction) account for about 80 percent of the UAE citizens of Dubai. Numbers, however, are unavailable. Nadeya Sayed Ali Mohammed's recent book on the demographics of the Gulf states is one of the more serious attempts to grapple with the demographics of these societies, but, as the reviewer Jamil Jreisat has acknowledged, she is dealing with figures that, in the case of every Gulf state, are incomplete, irregular, and full of gaps (634).

21. While it would probably be an exaggeration to regard the Dubai reformers of the 1930s–1950s as mass movements in the same way as were the Iranian National Front led by Mossadegh, the Iraqi Communist Party, or the Nasserists of the 1950s (the last of which being a great inspiration to Dubai's own National Front of the 1950s), these reformers did represent a strong, popular, and intellectually lively critique of absolutist dynastic governance in Dubai. Reformist discourses can even be seen well into the 1970s, long after the Al Maktoum had consolidated its absolute rule (Abdulla 1980). A fair comparison can be made between the Dubai reformers and the reformers of Kuwait, whose roots like those of

their Dubai counterparts lie in the efforts of merchants to check the ruler's claims on rent incomes in times of economic depression (Casey, 57–58). Ultimately, unlike in Dubai and the UAE more generally, the 1938 Majlis Movement of Kuwait led to a parliamentary system with substantive powers in relation to the ruling Al Sabah, making Kuwait one of the more democratic countries in the Arab region.

22. As Yasser Elsheshtawy has pointed out. Personal communication, June 17, 2009.

23. See note 6 and Gardner 2008; Leonard; Longva; Vora 2008.

24. Longva, for example, applies to all foreigners in Kuwait the abstract category of expatriate, arguing that the main conflict between foreigners and Gulf nationals is one of political rights.

25. Here is Rem Koolhaas, for example, discussing the fate of one of OMA's Dubai projects and the role of local agents of the family-state: "There are always expats and consultants willing to do what is necessary to make the changes that are seemingly inevitable. And that was the case here. So, in October 2008, we discovered at the fair of real estate that actually our site had been radically razed to make space for . . . a weird three-part skyscraper, incredibly tall" (2009).

26. This paragraph is based upon Parker 2005, 136.

27. See note 5.

1. State, Citizen, and Foreigner in Dubai

1. Nor, it seems, even after that time and the more recent financial crisis. See *Sky News*.

2. As the report points out, the Migrant Workers' Convention states that all workers who are engaged in remunerated activity in a state of which they are not nationals are "migrant workers" (Human Rights Watch 2006, 20).

3. For the historical details in much of the remainder of this section, I am indebted to the work of Christopher Davidson and Fatma Al-Sayegh. On the reform movements, see Davidson 2008, 31–54; on the diversity and shifting role of Dubai's merchant community, see Al-Sayegh. The interpretation I give these facts, however, is different in some important ways from that of Davidson and Al-Sayegh. For Davidson and, to some extent, Al Sayegh and others (Fenelon; Heard-Bey), the modernization of twentieth century Dubai was primarily the result of the rulers' liberalism, wisdom, and foresight. For me, the rulers have been in a structurally conservative position and have tended to interfere with, rather than further, modernization. This difference in interpretation is partly owing to a difference in how "modernization" is defined. Unlike many other studies, my reading of modernization is as much, if not more so, social and political as it is infrastructural. Substantive modernization, pertaining to education, social welfare, and citizens' participation, would not have occurred if not for pressure by reformers. My argument

has therefore been inspired not so much by the standard works on the UAE, but by dissident and left-critical scholarship, for example Abdulla 1984; Halliday; and, at a more global, third world level, Prashad.

4. Readers interested in Dubai's post-oil relations with its Emirati neighbors and the larger Arab world should consult Davidson's solid, detailed account of this (2008, 167–76, 219–34). Dubai's approach to these questions has both converged with and diverged from those of Abu Dhabi and other UAE emirates. According to Davidson, like their counterparts in Abu Dhabi, Dubai's ruling family has striven to emphasize its loyalty to Arab causes (e.g., in the conflict with Israel) and its Islamic piety. For example, in his capacity as defense minister, Dubai's Sheikh Rashid put the UAE's resources at the disposal of Egypt's Sadat and Syria's Assad during the 1973 Yom Kippur War; donated millions of dollars to the PLO after its revival in 1974; and helped with the reopening of Palestine's Birzeit University after it went bankrupt in 1985. Both Dubai and the UAE provided aid to Lebanon when war broke out in 1975, and again after the Israeli invasion of 2006. Dubai has also funded and hosted Islamic conferences attracting top Muslim clerics and scholars from the wider Muslim world (e.g., the 2004 "Prophet's Way of Da'wa and Guidance" symposium, attended by Arab ministers and Muhammad Said Tantawi, head of the Azhar Mosque in Egypt). Along with this has gone Dubai's support of Shari'a-based banking. For example, Dubai now hosts the International Islamic Finance Forum and has acquired 40 percent stake in the Bank of Islam, based in Malaysia. This is all in addition to the project of heritage revival connecting the Dubai ruling family to a mythical Bedouin past, as discussed by Khalaf (1999, 2000). On the other hand, since independence in 1971, there has been a continuous divergence, albeit less profound today than before the mid-1990s, between Abu Dhabi's centralizing agenda and those of Dubai, which have tended to be more autonomist. While Rashid of Dubai was more assertive in lobbying for Dubai's autonomy, his sons Maktoum and Muhammad have come to accept Dubai's secondary status in relation to Abu Dhabi. They have more easily acquiesced to this, according to Davidson, because of Dubai's success as a postmodern city-state, however. In other words, while acquiescing to symbolic demands from the centralizers, such as folding the symbolic Dubai military into the central, UAE force, Dubai had finally secured a practical autonomy for a little over a decade between the mid-1990s and 2008 because of its success in tourism, real estate development, etc., (Davidson 2008, 229–30). The still ongoing financial crisis of 2008–9, however, has again raised the specter of centralization, with Dubai seeking bailouts of catastrophic investments from Abu Dhabi petrodollars.

5. This paragraph is largely drawn from Kanna 2010a.

6. It is important to mention another attempt to infuse greater popular participation, which occurred in April 1979, when a formation of nationalists under the aegis of the quasi-legislative National Council demonstrated for political modernization of the UAE. The recent revolution in Iran and referendum on establishing an

Islamic republic were the proximate causes, according to Abdulla (1980). The demonstrators were about 300 people, most prominently university students, representing a wide social and geographic spectrum of the UAE (Abdulla 1980, 20). Among the demands made by these "federalists" (Davidson 2008, 23) were "a shift of emphasis from big economic projects to ones that will facilitate the development of the productivity of individual citizens . . . more equal distribution of wealth, guarantees for freedom of political thought and the press," (Abdulla 1980, 19), and a stronger legislature. Dubai's Sheikh Rashid was among those most vehemently opposed to these demands (20; Davidson 2008, 223). According to Abdulla, the members of the UAE's supreme governing body, the Supreme Council, "were shocked at the very idea of demands being made on them. This is why Rashid and the others totally rejected it. It was less a rejection of what the demands said than the idea of making such demands" (Abdulla 1980, 20). Rashid made a serious threat to withdraw Dubai from the UAE federation, prompting a compromise in which Dubai would exchange a slight increase in its federal budgetary contributions for a tacit agreement that it would never again concede to further integration into the UAE (Davidson 2008, 224).

7. I am indebted to Engseng Ho, who encouraged me to think about issues of protection and rent. Incorrect inferences are solely mine.

8. Evidence of a new wave of immigration, such as in Heard-Bey, is only anecdotal, quantitative data being, presumably, unavailable.

9. On the *ḥawāla* trade, see Campbell et al., and O'Brien. On the international arms trade, see Traynor et al.

10. On the trade in diamonds, see Burke et al.; on the trade in endangered species, see Brown 2002; on the trade in stolen cars, see Bowcott. Parker and Moore is an excellent analysis of one of the markets for Dubai smuggling.

11. See introduction, note 5.

12. Based on my estimates from reading Human Rights Watch 2006 and the related Human Rights Watch 2003.

13. Numbers, as is often the case with the UAE, are tricky. At the time of my longest period of fieldwork (September 2003–August 2004), the per capita income of the UAE was over $21,000. I base this figure on an estimate from the website of the United Nations Economic and Social Commission for Western Asia, www.escwa.org.lb, consulted May 11, 2005. In the meantime, I have seen figures for 2008 estimated at between $24,000 and a staggering figure of nearly $39,000 (findarticles.com/p/articles/mi_hb6465/is_200803/ai_n26241592, consulted February 18, 2009). HRW's "Building Towers, Cheating Workers," estimates annual per capita income to be a little over $25,000 for the year 2006 (2006, 7).

14. In 2004, it was estimated that approximately 450,000 domestics worked in the UAE (Hilotin). More recently, the number was estimated to be about 268,000, or five percent of the population of the UAE (Youssef). Hilotin recounts the results of a 2004 academic conference on migrant labor. Among the interesting statistics it

cites is that 60 percent of families in the UAE hire housemaids to demonstrate their status and 25 percent to enable women of the family to work outside the home. The writer also claims that Emirati families average 2.2 domestic workers. There is no source given for the statistics, but the points about status and enabling formal economic participation for employer women have also been demonstrated in the case of Western Europe (Anderson 2001).

15.　Waldman gives figures for one representative year, 2003, during which migrants generated over $100 billion in remittances worldwide. In the same year, Sri Lankan migrants sent home $1.37 billion, constituting about 8 percent of GDP. Of the 193,069 Sri Lankan workers sent abroad in
2003, 101,414 (52.5 percent) were domestics.

16.　Waldman gives vivid examples of some of the worst cases.

17.　As mentioned in the introduction, the population of Dubai increased four-fold between 1967 and 1981, from 59,000 to 250,000 people. Between 1981 and 2004, it increased nearly five-fold. See Heard-Bey, 263 and *Complete Guide to Dubai* 2003–2004, 106.

18.　My translation.

19.　A typical example is the non-attributed article "Website Offering Escort Services in UAE Blocked," *Gulf News,* May 9, 2004. The subtitle of the piece reads: "Site was found flouting rules and values, says Emirates Internet and Multimedia."

20.　"Hundreds of Infiltrators Seized at UAE Border," *Gulf News,* February 10, 2004.

21.　"Four-day Raids, Investigations Lead to Arrest of More than 700 Illegals," *Gulf News,* May 6, 2004.

22.　"Four-day Raids."

23.　"Municipality Wing Deports 360 Expats in Six Months," *Gulf News,* December 8, 2003.

24.　"Four-day Raids."

25.　The next three paragraphs are drawn from Kanna, 2007.

26.　*Bidoun* literally means "without," i.e., without national identity papers. This is a group of Dubai-born people who officially belong to no country because the Dubai and UAE states refuse to grant them citizenship papers. No good studies of the Bidoun, to my knowledge, exist and I collected mostly anecdotal information about them from my Emirati interlocutors.

27.　It should be mentioned that Satwa is a larger neighborhood than the section designated for urban renewal and described here. The destruction of this part of Satwa was brought to my attention by an Emirati interlocutor who told me about her memory of the community at Satwa. The interlocutor took me to see the place, which was abandoned, save for the few remaining shacks and two or three more substantial concrete houses. The interlocutor, who as a relatively wealthy local, seemed to have no personal stake in remembering the community, suggested that the city government was involved in razing the dwellings, but when I asked why, she claimed not to know. When we parted that evening, the interlocutor told me to be very careful when writing about this topic, and to avoid any reference to the government. More recently, the UAE English-language daily, *The National,* carried a short video about Satwa which mentioned that in 2008 the Dubai Land Department evicted thousands of residents to make way for a development called Jumeirah Garden City (See Istabsir). The CEO of Meraas Development, the developer of Jumeirah Garden City, has said that the project "addresses every element of urban living through comprehensive planning, adopts sustainable building practices, implements cutting-edge designs and engineering, and always focuses on people, to ensure Jumeirah Gardens is a community that enriches the lives of everyone living and working within its borders" (AME Info 2008). As I will discuss in chapter 2, discourses of sustainability and politically progressive urbanism in the UAE often mask an elitist politics of space.

28. This exoticization of foreign poverty also tends to characterize representations more sympathetic to foreigners and the working class in Dubai, as can be seen in *The National*'s videos of Satwa and South Asian life in Dubai (Istabsir).

29. According to Human Rights Watch, by the most conservative estimate, 73 workers died at Dubai construction sites in 2004 and 2005. Because so few companies comply with the law requiring reporting of worksite injuries and deaths, the report's authors suggest the number is probably around 800 deaths in 2004 alone (2006, 66)

30. From a reader whose name was withheld by request. *Gulf News,* May 6, 2004.

31. From a reader whose name was withheld by request. *Gulf News,* May 5, 2004.

32. Letter by Dr. R. Gupta. *Gulf News,* May 10, 2005.

2. "Going South" with the Starchitects

1. This chapter is based on my "Urbanist Ideology and the Production of Space in the United Arab Emirates: An Anthropological Critique," in Mc-Donogh and Peterson forthcoming. I am indebted to Gary McDonogh and Marina Peterson for close, critical readings of the earlier version. Thanks also to Hassan-Uddin Khan, Suha Özkan, and Marc Treib for engagement with and critique of a version of this chapter presented at the Roger Williams University International Fellows conference in July 2008. Yasser Elsheshtawy has been a longtime interlocutor on matters architectural in Dubai and the wider Arab world. His deep knowledge of Arab cities and his sharp engagement, especially with this chapter but also with the larger project of this book and various related papers, has been invaluable. Last but not least, I presented a version of this chapter in October 2010 at the University of the Pacific anthropology research colloquium. My thanks to Laura Bathurst,

Annlee Dolan, Bruce Labrack, Sarah Mathis, and Analiese Richard for their critical comments.

2. The recuperation of the tactile and bodily reconnection with space is a primary aim of what Frampton calls "critical regionalism."

3. There have been various approaches to grappling with this question. Exemplifying one approach, writers such as Frampton, Jameson, and Adorno have critiqued architecture's aesthetic assumptions and probed its experiential, subjective ramifications. They have asked questions such as what are the meaning, genealogy, and politics of the concept of the "aesthetic"? Others, such as David Harvey, Sharon Zukin, and Ghirardo take a more urban-sociological angle, asking questions such as how do "expenditures for museums, skyscrapers, concert halls, and other objects of bourgeois gratification come at the expense of important and necessary" projects? (Ghirardo, 15). Lefebvre's approach represents something of a middle ground, inquiring both into the structural conditions by which urbanization has come to be a dominant feature of modernity and into modernity's experiential domain. Yet another approach is that of the so-called Los Angeles School (Dear; Soja 1989; 1996), which has rightly emphasized the indeterminable, "indefinite and constantly shifting spaces of postmodernity" and the "peripheries rather than centers, alternative rather than dominant narratives and a multiplicity of ways of knowing" (Short, 49–50) characteristic of the city in late capitalism. This sensitivity to indeterminacy and diversity is something less in evidence in the work of Marxists such as Harvey and Lefebvre (see introduction).

4. The GCC countries are Bahrain, Kuwait, Oman, Qatar, Saudi Arabia, and the UAE. See the introduction and chapter 1 for a discussion of the effects of the 2008 financial meltdown.

5. Thanks to Yasser Elsheshtawy for pointing out the non-Emirati precursors. Personal communication, June 17, 2009.

6. The scholars to whom I spoke did not want to go on the record.

7. See http://www.oma.eu/index.php?option=com_projects& view=project&id=1021&Itemid=10.

8. Thanks to Gary McDonogh for pointing this out.

9. Or, following Zukin, the Pompidou effect.

10. The original 1960 plan, it seems, is in the private collection of John Harris's family. I was not aware of the earlier document when I came across the 1971 document. Thanks to Yasser Elsheshtawy for bringing the existence of the earlier document to my attention. Research based on Elsheshtawy's access to the 1960 plan and interviews with Harris's family appears in Elsheshtawy 2009.

11. The document is not originally paginated. The paginations here are my own and begin with the page preceding the table of contents.

12. Personal communication, June 17, 2009.

13. In 2010, I interviewed Gjørv, whose views on her experiences making the film turned out to be, unsurprisingly, far more nuanced than what she has

written about the same subject. She would not, however, go on the record with her comments.

14. The speed of the realization of projects and the extremely short time-frames that local developers demand of architects are often noted and positively evaluated in urbanist accounts of UAE architecture, but rarely is the social context mentioned—a deregulated labor market consisting of cheap foreign labor drawn from the immense surplus labor pools of the Middle East and South Asia (see Human Rights Watch 2006 and Kanna 2007).

15. Gehry's talk about the local society being a "clean slate" resonates in striking and unappealing ways with another project in which he was simultaneously involved—a Jerusalem project of the U.S.-based Simon Wiesenthal Center carrying the Orwellian name "Museum of Tolerance," for which Gehry was until recently the chief architect. The land on which the museum is planned is an ancient Muslim cemetery called Ma'man Allah. Construction has already begun, unearthing scores of bones, according to Saree Makdisi. Even the head archaeologist at the site, an Israeli, has sharply criticized the project. Gehry recently announced that he was withdrawing from the project, ostensibly to focus on other, more urgent commitments.

16. Advertisement for EMAAR, which appeared in *Gulf News,* March 28, 2004.

17. To be fair, the dean's theory is not uncontested by architects working in the UAE. Another colleague of his, to whom I spoke, gave an opposite theorization of UAE architecture— it is a triumph of impermanence and consumer space, said this architect. Like the *New York Times*'s Ouroussof, this architect argued that Dubai was an example of the Generic Cities theory (Koolhaas 1978). The architect, who saw Dubai as an example of successful urbanism within the frame of generic cities, attributed this success to the city's rejection of permanence, continuity, and vernacular and emphasis on what he called "spontaneity" and "the psychology of attraction and enjoyment."

18. All references to the Harvard workshop in this chapter are indicated by CMES.

19. See the following website for images and plans of the Intelligent Tower: http://ardalanassociates.com/projects/tower/

20. Those interested specifically in Masdar should consult Moser.

21. This is to say nothing about the fact that the majority foreign population of the UAE is excluded from the Arab–Tribal framing of the identity of the nation-state.

3. The Vanished Village

1. Because of their numerical insignificance, and because they tend to choose to live on plots of land owned either by their family, or given to them by

the state. The Emiratis who do buy properties from companies like Nakheel and EMAAR tend to do so for investment purposes, usually renting these properties to expatriates after buying them.

2. I borrow this formulation from Todd Gitlin. See http://www. youtube. com/watch?v=Zw1Aji8FzJc

3. In both the UAE and the wider Arab region, these two terms are often used interchangeably.

4. In other words, those of "pure" Arab, or "Bedouin," background. This category is opposed to khodmoni, or 'ajami, those of Persian descent, as well as to those who are of "mixed" parents. See chapter 4 for a more extended discussion.

5. In recent years, and especially before the advent of wireless mobile phone technologies, young people would go to places such as shopping malls and "paper" each other. The practice basically consists of writing one's mobile phone number on a piece of paper and surreptitiously dropping it next to a person with whom the "paperer" would like to get in touch for a conversation, a date, etc. Papering was a way for youth to circumvent the surveillance of authority figures perceived as bent on policing gender or sexuality boundaries.

6. Interview conducted in both Arabic and English. These quotations are verbatim, not translated.

7. Interview in Arabic; my translation.

8. Interview in Arabic; my translation.

9. Conversation was in English.

10. Interview conducted in English.

11. Interview conducted in Arabic; my translation.

12. It is interesting to note that while this comic appears in an Emirati paper, the women in it are not dressed in a typically Emirati way, but rather in a style more typical of Egypt and Palestine. The Arabic in the speech bubbles is not fuṣḥa, Modern Standard Arabic, nor Emirati Arabic, but seems to be either Egyptian or Palestinian Arabic. Egyptian media and popular culture have long been, and continue to be, influential outside Egypt, and images and editorials from Egyptian sources regularly appear in the wider Arab press. Moreover, the message of this comic resonates with what several Emiratis told me were local concerns over sum'a (family reputation) and secrecy. For example, one Emirati woman discussed with me the "hush hush" mentality (her words) that in her view was characteristic of "traditional" Arab family life, within the UAE and without.

13. My translation from the original Arabic.

4. The City-Corporation

1. This chapter is based on Kanna 2010a.

2. My translation.

3. The parallels between the Dubai city–corporation and the local family corporation, as described for example in Field, are striking. Many of the qualities

attributed to Muhammad are the same as those of the figure of the family corporation chief—paternalism, wisdom, vision, leadership of the corporation as a social and even moral calling.

4. For a similar view, from an Arab nationalist perspective, see Al-Naqeeb.

5. In spite of their removal from ICD, they remain at EMAAR, Dubai Holding, and Dubai World. As part of this reshuffling, Maktoum also sacked Omar bin Sulayman as head of the Dubai International Financial Centre (DIFC) (Hall and Salama).

6. Abdulla's essay is a more critical contribution to a genre that tends to be more optimistic about the corporatization of the city. See, for example, al-Bayan 2004; al-Beshr; al-Malifi; al-Qadi; *Emirates Today*; Kalsi; Al Khaleej 2004.

7. See chapter 1, note 4.

8. At the request of most of them, I have given Naila and the other interlocutors in this chapter pseudonyms.

9. See, for example, Heard-Bey, especially the chapter on the emirate of Dubai, as well as Lorimer. This is not to say, however, that these boundaries are best understood in Western terms of "ethnicity," as lacking in porosity. James Onley makes the case that, before the age of oil, the maritime coastal Gulf was characterized by a quite different phenomenon—whereas, markers of *aṣl* (ethnic origin or "pedigree") were still observed, members of Arab and Persian groups intermarried and often fashioned their *aṣl* relative to local context. So, for example, the Safar family of Bahrain and Bushehr considered themselves either Arabized-Persians or Persianized-Arabs, relative to their locality. For Onley, this is evidence of the Arab-Persian hybridity that has characterized the region for far longer than have more rigid distinctions of *aṣl* and nationality (Onley 2005, 65). Although he does note a few cases in which Indians have intermarried with Arab and Persian families, Onley does not say much about how Gulf inhabitants originally from the subcontinent relate to this hybridity.

10. Pseudonym.

11. There are yet other subgroups among Dubayyans, such as Bani Yas Arabs from outside the Al Bu Falasah section and naturalized South Asians, mainly from Baluchistan. For an excellent summary, see Davidson 2008, 153–58.

12. This should not be taken to mean that they are legally a second class. In a formal sense, they are full citizens of the UAE and tend to be as materially well off as many "pure" Emiratis.

13. Davidson notes a similar practice at insurance companies, trading companies, and banks, which are required to meet quotas of UAE citizen hires and do so officially, but outsource technical work off the books (2008, 207).

14. Note how bin Bayyat refers to the private sector outside the Tecom enclave as the "government sector." In relation to the exceptional enclave, both private and public sector are, for bin Bayyat, indistinguishable and characterized by the same bureaucratic inefficiency.

15. I take these figures from the Web site of the UAE embassy in Washington, D.C. http://www.uae-embassy.org/uae/women-in-the-uae, accessed June 1, 2009.

16. Others, however, have pointed to anecdotal evidence indicating that Emirati women are more ambivalent about Dubai's boom. The presence of a growing foreign population is sometimes used as an excuse by the women's families to keep them from moving about as freely in public. Mohamad Chakaki, personal communication, December 1, 2009.

17. For this formulation, I thank an anonymous referee of an article on which much of this chapter is based (Kanna 2010a).

18. This interview is cited verbatim. Rana, who is fluent in English, chose to answer my questions primarily in that language.

19. Originally in Arabic; my translation.

20. Supposedly a practice of the Prophet Muhammad and therefore a sound act of *sunna,* or imitation of the Prophet, according to one authoritative recent Muslim tradition.

21. Note how Rana anthropomorphizes the corporations in the free zone, calling them *people.* This is paralleled in the official Tecom parlance, where members of the enclave are *community members.*

5. Indian Ocean Dubai

1. Thanks to Beth Notar for highlighting this passage. See Notar.

2. For this insight, I am indebted to conversations with and to the work of Neha Vora (2008, 2009a, 2009b). See also chapter 1.

3. This is not to suggest that working-class migrants have no, or different, material and consumer expectations of the Dubai experience. Both middle-class and working-class South Asians, like other foreigners, usually come to Dubai ultimately because they feel that doing so will improve their material conditions.

4. See, for example, excellent recent contributions by Adelkhah, Al Rasheed, Diedrich, Fuccaro (2005), Leonard, Longva, Onley (2007), and Vora (2008).

5. Notions of shared blood and or descent (*aṣl*), for example, are significant elements in national identity. Since independence in 1971, older notions of *aṣl,* which were not historically connected to notions of national identity, were drawn upon by the state to furnish itself with national boundaries. Thus, *aṣl* was mapped onto the logic of the modern nation-state, with its inflexible boundaries, etc.

6. From 1616 to 1872, Britain conducted its affairs with the Gulf states through the British Government of Bombay; from 1872 to 1947 through the British Government of India; from 1947 to 1948 through the Commonwealth Relations Office in London; and between 1948 and independence in 1971 through the Foreign Office (later Foreign and Commonwealth Office) in London. The initial

headquarters of the Government of India were Calcutta (winter) and Simla (summer). The winter headquar-ters officially moved to New Delhi in 1911 and actually did so in 1931 upon completion of its buildings. These buildings continue to house the President of India and the Indian Parliament. My thanks to James Onley, personal communication, December 27, 2010.

7. From the website www.emaar.ae/International/Index.asp. Consulted on June 29, 2005.

8. From the website www.emaar.ae/International/Index.asp. Consulted on June 29, 2005.

9. www.emaar.ae/Developments/Downtown/Index.asp. Consulted on June 29, 2005.

10 Majid Al Futtaim has already made inroads into Egypt, developing large projects in Alexandria and near Cairo. See Adham and Elsheshtawy 2004, 2009, and forthcoming. More recently, EMAAR began similar initiatives. See Turan.

11. www.emaar.ae/Developments/Downtown/Index.asp. Consulted on June 29, 2005.

12. www.cmaar.ae/Developments/Downtown/Index.asp. Consulted on June 29, 2005.

13. My emphasis.

14. See also the recent work of Syed Ali.

15. Rachel, whom I have given a pseudonym, speaks very little English, but her command of Arabic is near fluency. All our conversations were conducted in Arabic.

16. Another explanation for my neighbors' unfriendliness, in the meantime, occurs to me. The building in which my wife and I lived during my fieldwork trip of September 2003 to August 2004 was located in an unofficial red light district in Bur Dubai. There seems, in retrospect, to have been a disproportionate number of somewhat luxuriously dressed women of diverse national backgrounds accompanied by well-to-do looking men about the place. If my suspicions are true, it would obviously not be surprising why my neighbors were not looking for friendly neighborly relations with my wife and me.

Conclusion

1. Fattah (2005) says the number was 800; Davidson (2008, 187) claims that over 1,000 workers from different labor camps participated in the work stoppage.

2. For example, Fattah 2005.

3. To be fair, it should be noted that the other English-language daily, *Khaleej Times,* did make a more concerted effort to get the workers' perspectives. Workers are quoted in at least five different pieces on labor-employer conflicts

between September 5, 2005, and October 25, 2005. None of these quotes, however, came from the protestors of September 19. Thanks to Ines Hofmann Kanna for the *Khaleej Times* research.

4. Cash-flow problems in the construction sector are endemic to Dubai, according to the vice-president of another construction company to whom I spoke during my fieldwork. Clients consistently break contracts, leaving the contractor in a difficult situation, especially considering the length, expense, and unreliability of legal action. Workers, already in the most vulnerable position, are the easiest target in this situation. Much easier to deprive them of their wages to recoup costs than to bring charges against the client, who in any case can usually invoke citizen status against the usually foreign contractor and expect inaction or even protection from the state.

5. This is a quote of Abdul Khaleq Abdulla. The article does not make it clear whether Abdulla is referring to the workers or to the company as tarnishing the image of the UAE. Based on the political commitments evidenced by his earlier writings and interviews (1980, 1984), and his critique of the conditions under which foreign laborers toil (1980, 22), one assumes that Abdulla is referring to the company in this quote. Also, to be fair to Dr. Abdulla, Dubai dailies have a tendency to take quotes out of context or to highlight the government-friendly parts of interviews that are otherwise critical, as happened to me after a 2003 Harvard Graduate School of Design conference on Dubai, in which a *Gulf News* correspondent reinterpreted my quite critical comments as celebratory of Maktoum and Dubai.

6. Because I was not present for the speech and only possess its text, this comment about Koolhaas and the ones that follow will be somewhat speculative. Thanks to Waleed Hazbun for alerting me to the lecture. The lecture text and the images that go along with it can be accessed from the Koolhaas–OMA website: http://www.oma.eu/index.php?option=com_content&task=view&id=149&Itemid =25. All remaining quotes from Koolhaas are taken from Koolhaas 2009, unless otherwise indicated.

7. This sentence is accompanied by a slide depicting Michael Jackson with Emirati officials gazing at an architectural projection of a "frond" of one of the Nakheel Palm Islands.

8. To this is attached a map of the projected Dubai of the future, with enormous artificial islands and peninsulas jutting off the Dubai coast. See the Koolhaas–OMA Web site, cited in note 6.

9. The reference to Anna Wintour is accompanied by a slide with the following quotation, from Wintour speaking to the *Wall Street Journal* in February 2009: "I don't think anyone is going to want to look overly flashy, overly glitzy, too Dubai, whatever you call it. I just don't think that's the moment. But I do feel an emphasis on quality and longevity and things that really last."

10. I draw this formulation from a discussion with Laura Bathurst, Annlee Dolan, Bruce La Brack, Sarah Mathis, and Annie Richard at the University of the Pacific Anthropology research colloquium. My thanks for their engagement.

11. Conversation was in English. In the aftermath of the financial crisis and Dubai's crash, Abdul Khaleq Abdulla has similarly reflected on the meaning of Emirati identity. In essays in the daily *Al-Khaleej,* for example, he has discussed both the political-institutional and cultural-discursive conditions for rethinking the path of the Emirati polity and Emirati identity (2009a, 2009b). While with regard to the political and institutional conditions, he returns to familiar themes of Emirati integration and centralization (1980, see chapter 1, note 6), with regard to the second theme, Emirati identity, he says some intriguing things. In an essay entitled "Who Is Emirati?" ("*Man huwa al-Imārāti?*" 2009b), he argues for a new sense of Emiratiness, beyond and indeed in rejection of ethnocracy. This he summarizes in the following way: "I am Emirati because I am proud to be Emirati (*ana Imārāti wa aftakhir*)." This formula, for Abdulla, is the only relevant criterion for determining who is a real Emirati: Emiratiness has nothing to do with one's passport or with allegiance to a particular state or juridical order, but with an active identification with the venture of Emirati sovereignty and self-determination. Most significantly, "there is no relationship between birth and identity . . . (*lā 'alāqa bayn al-wilāda wa-l-hawiyya.*)" That is, there is no relationship between ethnocracy and Emirati ness. Ethnicity is not connected with the project of Emirati sovereignty. This kind of thinking is potentially more interesting and serious, because more deeply connected to local struggles, in conceptualizing a so-called new Emirati society than the type represented by Koolhaas with its superficial gestures toward a "new Islamic society."

BIBLIOGRAPHY

Abdulla, Abdul Khaleq. 1980. "The Revolution in Iran Stimulated the Existing Contradictions in the United Arab Emirates." *MERIP Reports* 85 (February): 19–22, 25.

———. 1984. *Political Dependency: The Case of the United Arab Emirates.* PhD dissertation. Georgetown University Department of Politics.

———. 2006. *"Dubai: Riḥlat Madīna 'Arabīyya min al-Maḥalliyya ila l-'Ālamīyya"* [Dubai: The journey of an Arab City from localism to cosmopolitanism] *Al-Mustaqbal al-Arabi* 323: 1–28.

———. 2009a. *"Al-Imārāt mā ba'd al-Azma al-Māliyya al-'Ālamīyya"* [The UAE after the world financial crisis] *Al-Khaleej.* September 29. Electronic document, http://www.alkhaleej.ae/portal/feac9f810a50-49f2-a443-564b457c7a 43.aspx (accessed February 12, 2010).

———. 2009b. *"Man huwa al-Imārāti?"* [Who is Emirati?] *Al-Khaleej.* October 27. Electronic document, http://www.alkhaleej.ae/portal/bf15e4de-5772-4a ec-bc52 7uu60a1350a6.aspx (accessed February 12, 2010).

Abu-Lughod, Janet. 1987. "The Islamic City: Historic Myth, Islamic Essence, and Contemporary Relevance." *International Journal of Middle East Studies* 19: 155–76.

Ackley, Brian. n.d. "Permanent Vacation: Making Someplace out of Non-Place." *Bidoun* 4. Electronic document, www.bidoun.com/4_permenent.php (accessed January 14, 2009).

Adelkhah, Fariba. 2001. *"Dubaï : Capitale Économique de l'Iran?"* In *Dubaï,* ed. Roland Marchal, 39–65. Paris: CNRS Editions.

Adham, Khalid. 2004. "Globalization, Museumification, and Urban Dreams." Panel paper, 9th International Conference of the International Association for the Study of Traditional Environments. Sharjah, United Arab Emirates, December 17.

Adorno, Theodor W., 1979/1997. "Functionalism Today." In *Rethinking Architecture,* ed. Neil Leach, 6–19. New York: Routledge.

Adorno, Theodor. 2005. *In Search of Wagner.* Rodney Livingstone, trans. New York: Verso.

Afary, Janet, and Kevin B. Anderson. 2005. *Foucault and the Iranian Revolution: Gender and the Seductions of Islamism.* Chicago: University of Chicago Press.

Agamben, Giorgio. 2005. *State of Exception.* Kevin Attell, trans. Chicago: University of Chicago Press.

Ahmad, Aijaz. 1992. *In Theory: Classes, Nations, Literatures.* New York: Verso.

Ahmad, Eqbal. 2006. *The Selected Writings of Eqbal Ahmad,* eds. C. Bengelsdorf, M. Cerullo, and Y. Chandrani. New York: Columbia University Press.

Al-Ali, Nadje Sadig. 2008. *Iraqi Women: Untold Stories from 1948 to the Present.* New York: Zed Books.

Al-Bayan. 2004. "*I'mār Tarsum Malāmiḥ Mashrū' Qalb al-Madīna al-Jadīda*" [EMAAR sketches the new city center project] *Al-Bayan,* June 23: 7.

Al Beshr, Badriyya. 2008. *Waq' al-'Awlama fī Mujtama'āt al-Khalīj al-'Arabī* [The Impact of globalization on the societies of the Arab Gulf]. Beirut: Center for Arab Unity Studies.

Ali, Syed. 2010. *Dubai: Gilded Cage?* New Haven: Yale University Press.

Al Jandaly, Bassma. 2004a. "Containers Become Workers' Homes," *Gulf News,* May 31. Electronic document, http://gulfnews.com/news/gulf/uae/general/containers-become-workers-homes-1.323748 (accessed February 4, 2010).

———. 2004b. "Families in Karama Rue Spread of Labour Camps." *Gulf News,* February 10. Electronic document, http://gulfnews.com/news/gulf/uae/general/families-in-karama-rue-spread-of-labour-camps-1.313217 (accessed February 4, 2010).

———. 2004 c. "Firm Pays Fine over 'Container Homes.'" *Gulf News,* July 4. Electronic document, http://gulfnews.com/news/gulf/uae/general/firm-pays-fine-over-container-homes-1.326405 (accessed February 4, 2010).

Al-Khaleej. 2004. "*Dubai Tataḥawwal min Qaria 'ala Ḍafāf al-Khor ilā Madīna 'Ālamīyya*" [Dubai is transformed from a village on the banks of the creek into a world city]. *al-Khaleej,* July 3.

Al Khalil, Ali. 2009. "Crisis Leaves Dubai Migrant Workers out in the Cold." *Dawn,* February 16. Electronic document, www.dawn.com/2009/text/int6.htm (accessed October 20, 2009).

Al Kiwari, Suad. 2004. "*Mā bayn al-Ams wa-l-Yawm?*" [What connects the past to the present?]. *Al-Ittihad,* June 20.

Al Malifi, Ibrahim. 2002. "*Dubai: Iqtiṣād al-Ma'rifa wa Thawrat al-Mīdia wa-l-Ma'lūmātīyya.*" [Dubai: The knowledge economy and the media and information revolution]. *Al-Arabi* 524 (July): 100–109.

Al-Naqeeb, Khaldoun Hasan. 1990. *Society and State in the Gulf and Arab Peninsula: A Different Perspective.* Trans. L.M. Kenny. London: Routledge.

Al Qadi, Ahmed. 2003. *"Al-Qubba al-Kristālīyya bi-Dubai: Mashru' Dakhm Takallufathu Miliār Dulār"* [The Dubai Crystal Dome: an enormous U.S. $1 Billion Project]. *Al-Bayan,* October 16:4.

Al Qasimi, Nurah Muhammad. 2000. *Al-Wujūd al-Hindī fi-l Khalīj al-'Arabī 1820–1949* [The Indian presence in the Arab Gulf 1820–1949]. Sharjah: *Dā'irat al-Thaqāfah wa-l'Ilm.*

Al Qasimi, Sultan bin Muhammad. 1986. *The Myth of Arab Piracy in the Gulf.* London: Croom Helm.

Al Rasheed, Madawi, ed. 2005. *Transnational Connections and the Arab Gulf.* New York: Routledge.

Al Sayegh, Fatma. 1998. "Merchants' Role in a Changing Society: The Case of Dubai, 1900–90." *Middle Eastern Studies* 34, no. 1: 87–102.

Al-Zawja al Mithaliyya. 2004. *"Al-Zawja al-Mithālīyya."* [The ideal wife] *Al-Ittihad,* June 26.

AME Info. 2005. "Facing Up to Our Ecological Footprint." February 14.Electronic document, http://www.ameinfo.com/53883.html (accessed May 27, 2008).

———. 2008. "Meraas Development Launches Dhs 350bn Jumeira Gardens." October 6. Electronic document, http://www.ameinfo.com/170513.html (accessed June 6, 2010).

Anderson, Benedict. 1991. *Imagined Communities: Reflections on the Origin and Spread of Nationalism.* New York: Verso.

Anderson, Bridget. 2001. "Just Another Job? Paying for Domestic Work." *Gender and Development* 9, no. 1: 25–33.

Anscombe, Frederick. 2005. "An Anational Society: Eastern Arabia in the Ottoman Period." In *Transnational Connections and the Arab Gulf,* ed. M. Al Rasheed, 21–38. New York: Routledge.

Arbab, Abdullah. 2004. "Dhows Barred from Selling Bargain Goods." *Gulf News,* April 19.

Arcspace. 2007. "Ando, Gehry, Hadid, and Nouvel, Saadiyat Island." February 7. Electronic document, http://www.arcspace.com/architects/aghn/aghn.html (accessed May 25, 2008).

Augé, Marc. 2000. *Non-Places: Introduction to an Anthropology of Supermodernity.* Trans. John Howe. New York: Verso.

Bach, Jonathan. 2002. "The Taste Remains: Consumption, (N)ostalgia, and the Production of East Germany." *Public Culture* 14, no. 3: 545–56.

Bakhtin, M. M. 1998. *The Dialogic Imagination: Four Essays.* M. Holquist, trans. M. Holquist and C. Emerson, eds. Austin: University of Texas Press.

Barber, Lynn. 2008. "Zaha Hadid." *Observer,* March 9. Electronic document, http://arts.guardian.co.uk/art/architecture/story/0,,2263977,00.html. (accessed June 4, 2008).

Barth, Fredrik. 1983. *Sohar: Culture and Society in an Omani Town.* Baltimore: Johns Hopkins University Press.

Baudrillard, Jean. 1970/2001. "Consumer Society." In *Jean Baudrillard: Selected Writings,* ed. M. Poster, 32–59. Stanford: Stanford University Press.

———. 1981/2001. "Simulacra and Simulations." In *Jean Baudrillad: Selected Writings,* ed. M. Poster, 169–87. Stanford: Stanford University Press.

BBC Radio 3. 2004. "Architecture in Dubai." Narrated by Julia Wheeler. Archived CD. George Katodrytis, personal collection (consulted in November 2004).

Benjamin, Walter. 1968. "Theses on the Philosophy of History." In *Illuminations,* ed. H. Arendt, trans. H. Zohn, 253–64. New York: Schocken.

———. 2002. *The Arcades Project.* Trans. H. Eiland and K. McLaughlin. Cambridge, Mass.: Harvard University Press.

Bloch, Ernst. 1986. *The Principle of Hope.* 3 volumes. Trans. N. Plaice, S. Plaice, and P. Knight. Cambridge, Mass.: MIT Press.

Bonine, Michael E. 1989. "Cities of Oil and Migrants: Urbanization and Economic Change in the Arabian Peninsula." In *Urbanism in Islam,* ed. T. Yukawa, 339–54. Tokyo: Proceedings of the International Conference on Urbanism in Islam.

Bose, Sugata. 2006. *A Hundred Horizons: The Indian Ocean in the Age of Global Empire.* Cambridge, Mass.: Harvard University Press.

Bowcott, Owen. 2002. "Criminal Trail that Leads from Carjackings to Streets of Asia." *Guardian,* February 22. Electronic document, http://www.guardian .co.uk/uk/2002/feb/22/ukcrime.owenbowcott (accessed February 4, 2010).

Bowers, Simon. 2009. "Sober Ruler of Dubai Whose Vision Is Crumbling in the Face of the Storm." *Guardian,* November 27. Electronic document, http:// www.guardian.co.uk/world/2009/nov/27/sober-ruler-dubai-vision-crumbling (accessed November 28, 2009).

Bowlby, Rachel. 1997. "Supermarket Futures." In *The Shopping Experience,* eds. P. Falk and C. Campbell, 92–110. London: Sage.

Boym, Svetlana. 2001. *The Future of Nostalgia.* New York: Basic Books.

Braudel, Fernand. 1986. *The Perspective of the World: Civilization and Capitalism 15th–18th Century,* vol. 3. Sian Reynolds, trans. New York: Perennial.

British Foreign Office 371/82047. 1950. "A Note on the Wealth of Dubai." Amersham, U.K.: Demand Editions.

Broudehoux, Anne-Marie. 2007. "Spectacular Beijing: The Conspicuous Construction of an Olympic Metropolis." *Journal of Urban Affairs* 29, no. 4: 383–99.

Brown, Matthew. 2008. "Hadid Leading Architectural Rush to the Emirates." *International Herald Tribune,* April 3. Electronic document (consulted May 25, 2008).

Brown, Paul. 2002. "UK revealed as a Key Location in Wildlife Smuggling." *Guardian,* December 9.

Brown, Wendy. 2006. "Finding the Man in the State." In *The Anthropology of the*

State, eds. Aradhana Sharma and Akhil Gupta, 187–210. Malden, Mass.: Blackwell.

Burke, Jason, Chris McGreal, Ed Vulliamy, and Nick Parton Walsh. 2000. "Africa's Deadly Trade in Diamonds." *Observer,* May 14. Electronic document, http://www.guardian.co.uk/world/2000/may/14/ sierraleone (accessed February 4, 2010).

Cahn, Peter S. 2008. "Consuming Class: Multilevel Marketers in Neoliberal Mexico." *Cultural Anthropology* 23, no. 3: 429–52.

Campbell, Duncan, Alison Langley, David Pallister, and Khaled Daoud. 2001. "US Targets Bin Laden's Money Men." *Guardian,* November 8, 2001. Electronic document, http://www.guardian.co.uk/world/2001/nov/08/afghanistan terrorism3 (accessed February 4, 2010).

Casey, Michael S. 2007. *The History of Kuwait.* Westport, Conn.: Greenwood Press.

Chaudhuri, K. N. 1990. *Asia before Europe: Economy and Civilization of the Indian Ocean from the Rise of Islam to 1750.* New York: Cambridge University Press.

CMES. 2007. "Reconceiving the Built Environment in the Gulf." Workshop, Center for Middle East Studies, Harvard University, April 28–April 29.

Coles, Anne and Peter Jackson. 1975. *A Windtower House in Dubai: Art and Archaeology Research Papers.* Archived material, Juma al-Majid Library, Dubai.

Collini, Stefan. 2009. "From the Motorcoach." *London Review of Books* 31, no. 22: 18–20.

Complete Guide. 2003-2004. *Invest and Live in Dubai.* Dubai: Concept Media FZ LLC.

Collins, Rodney. 2009. *From Coffee to Manhood: Grounds for Exchange in the Tunisian Coffeehouse.* PhD dissertation. Columbia University Department of Anthropology.

Complete Guide UAE. 2004. *Invest and Live in Dubai.* Dubai: Concept Media.

Crawford, Margaret. 1991. "Can Architecture Be Socially Responsible?" In *Out of Site: A Social Criticism of Architecture,* ed. Diane Ghirardo, 27–45. Seattle: Bay Press.

Crehan, Kate. 2002. *Gramsci, Culture and Anthropology.* Berkeley: University of California Press.

Davidson, Christopher M. 2005. *The United Arab Emirates: A Study in Survival.* Boulder, Colo.: Lynne Rienner.

———. 2008. *Dubai: The Vulnerability of Success.* New York: Columbia University Press.

Davis, Mike. 2006a. "Fear and Money in Dubai." *New Left Review* 41 (Sept/Oct): 47–68.

———. 2006b. *Planet of Slums.* New York: Verso.

Davis, Mike, and Daniel Bertrand Monk. 2008. *Evil Paradises: Dreamworlds of Neoliberalism.* New York: New Press.

Dear, Michael. 2000. *The Postmodern Urban Condition*. Malden, Mass.: Blackwell.

Deeb, Lara. 2006. *An Enchanted Modern: Gender and Public Piety in Shi'i Lebanon*. Princeton: Princeton University Press.

Deutsche Bank Research. 2006. "Container Shipping: Overcapacity Inevitable Despite Increasing Demand." April 25. Electronic document, http://www.dbresearch.com/PROD/DBR_INTERNET_DE-PROD/PROD0000000000 198081.PDF. (accessed April 13, 2008)

Diedrich, Mathias. 2005. "Indonesians in Saudi Arabia: Religious and Economic Connections. In *Transnational Connections and the Arab Gulf*, ed. Madawi Al Rasheed, 128–46. New York: Routledge.

Dilworth, Dianna. 2008. "Koolhaas Unveils New Waterfront City in Dubai." *Architectural Record*, May 12. Electronic document, http://archrecord.construction.com/news/daily/archives/080312koolhaas.asp (accessed June 7, 2010).

Dubai Ports World. 2007. "Global Shipping Lines to Sustain 15-20% Annual Growth." *DP World*, February 6. Electronic document, http://www.dpa.co.ae/news.asp?catid=1&id=49&PageId=21 (accessed on April 13, 2008).

Economist, The. 2002. "Beyond Oil." A Survey of the Gulf. March 23: 26–28.

Eickelman, Dale F. 1974. "Is there an Islamic City? The Making of a Quarter in a Moroccan Town." *International Journal of Middle East Studies* 5: 274–94.

Elsheshtawy, Yasser. 2004. "From Dubai to Cairo: Shifting Centers of Influence?" Panel paper, 9th International Conference of the International Association for the Study of Traditional Environments. Sharjah, United Arab Emirates, December 16.

———. 2009. *Dubai: Behind an Urban Spectacle*. London: Routledge.

———. 2010. "Resituating the Dubai Spectacle." In *The Superlative City: Dubai and the Urban Condition in the Early 21st Century*, ed. Ahmed Kanna. Cambridge, Mass.: Harvard University Graduate School of Design.

Elyachar, Julia. 2005. *Markets of Dispossession: NGOs, Economic Development, and the State in Cairo*. Durham: Duke University Press.

Emirates Today. 2007. "Mohammad's Leadership and Vision Changes Work Culture." *Emirates Today*, January 4: 4.

Erdreich, Lauren, and Tamar Rapoport. 2006. "Reading the Power of Spaces: Palestinian Israeli Women at the Hebrew University." *City and Society* 18, no. 1: 116–50.

Fanon, Frantz. 1963/1991. *The Wretched of the Earth*. Constance Farrington, trans. New York: Grove Weidenfeld.

Fattah, Hassan M. 2005. "Workers in Arab Emirates Protest, and Win." *New York Times*, September 25. Electronic document, http://query.nytimes.com/gst/fullpage.html?res=9F03E0D71430F936A1575AC0A9639C8B63&sec=&spon=&pagewanted=all (accessed February 4, 2010).

———. 2007. "Celebrity Architects Reveal a Daring Cultural Xanadu for the Arab World." *New York Times*, February 1. Electronic document, http://www.ny

times.com/2007/02/01/arts/design/01isla.html?_r=1&oref=slogin (accessed May 28, 2008).

Fazili, Sameera. 2009. "Remittances and Development." *Middle East Report* 252: 16–17.

Fenelon, K. G. 1976. *The United Arab Emirates: An Economic and Social Survey.* New York: Longman.

Ferguson, James. 2005. "Seeing Like an Oil Company: Space, Security, and Global Capital in Neoliberal Africa." Theme Issue, "Moral Economies, State Spaces, and Categorical Violence," *American Anthropologist* 107, no. 3: 377–82.

Field, Michael. 1985. *The Merchants: The Big Business Families of Saudi Arabia and the Gulf States.* Woodstock N.Y.: Overlook Press.

Fishman, Robert. 1977. *Urban Utopias in the Twentieth Century: Ebenezer Howard, Frank Lloyd Wright, and Le Corbusier.* New York: Basic Books.

Frampton, Kenneth. 1991. "Reflections on the Autonomy of Architecture. A Critique of Contemporary Production." *In Out of Site: A Social Criticism of Architecture,* ed. Diane Ghirardo, 17–26. Seattle: Bay Press.

———. 1998. "Towards a Critical Regionalism: Six Points for an Architecture of Resistance." In *The Anti-Aesthetic: Essays on Postmodern Culture,* ed. Hal Foster, 17–34. New York: New Press.

Franklin, Robert Lee. 1989. *The Indian Community in Bahrain: Labor Immigration in a Plural Society.* PhD dissertation, Harvard University.

Freeman, Carla. 2007. "The 'Reputation' of Neoliberalism." *American Ethnologist* 34, no. 2:252–67.

Freund, Charles Paul. 2001. "Muerte a Las Vegas." *Reason Online,* January. Electronic document, http://www.reason.com/news/show/27902.html (accessed June 4, 2008).

Friedman, Thomas. 2005. *The World is Flat: A Brief History of the Twenty-First Century.* New York: Farrar, Straus & Giroux.

———. 2006. "Dubai and Dunces." *New York Times,* March 15. Electronic document, http://select.nytimes.com/2006/03/15/opinion/15friedman.html?_r=1 (accessed February 4, 2010).

Fuccaro, Nelida. 2001. "Visions of the City: Urban Studies of the Gulf." *MESA Bulletin* 35: 175–87.

———. 2005. "Mapping the Transnational Community: Persians and the Space of the City in Bahrain, c. 1869–1937." In *Transnational Connections and the Arab Gulf,* ed. Madawi Al Rasheed, 39–58. New York: Routledge.

———. 2009. *Histories of City and State in the Persian Gulf: Manama since 1800.* New York: Cambridge University Press.

———. 2010. "Pearl Towns and Early Oil States: Migration and Integration in the Arab Coast of the Persian Gulf." In *Migration and the Making of Urban Modernity: The City in the Ottoman Empire,* ed. Ulrike Freitag. London: Routledge.

Gardner, Andrew. 2008. "Strategic Transnationalism: The Indian Diasporic Elite in Contemporary Bahrain." *City and Society* 20, no. 1: 54–78.

———. Forthcoming. "Engulfed: Citizens, Guestworkers, and the Structural Violence of the Kafala System." Manuscript.

Ghannam, Farha. 2002. *Remaking the Modern: Space, Relocation, and the Politics of Identity in a Global Cairo.* Berkeley: University of California Press.

Ghirardo, Diane, ed. 1991. *Out of Site: A Social Criticism of Architecture.* Seattle: Bay Press.

Gjørv, Eirin. 2007. "The Sand Castle: The Director's Take." Electronic document, http://www.pbs.org/wnet/wideangle/episodes/the-sand-castle/the-directors-take-eirin-gjørv/1792/ (accessed November 13, 2009).

Glancey, Jonathan. 2006. "I Don't Do Nice." *Guardian,* October 9. Electronic document, http://arts.guardian.co.uk/features/story/0,,1890945,00.html (accessed June 4, 2008).

Gray, John. 2005. "The World Is Round." *New York Review of Books,* August 11: 13–15.

Gulf News. 2005. "A Victory for all Workers." *Gulf News,* September 20, 2005. Internet version (consulted October 24, 2005).

———. 2009. "Knowledge of UAE Culture Prerequisite for Residents Visa in the Future." July 7. Electronic document, http://gulfnews.com/news/gulf/uae/heritage-culture/knowledge-of-uae-culture-pre-requisite-for-residents-visa-in-the-future-1.500303 (accessed July 9, 2009).

Gupta, Akhil. 2006. "Blurred Boundaries: The Discourse of Corruption, the Culture of Politics, and the Imagined State." In *The Anthropology of the State,* eds. Aradhana Sharma and Akhil Gupta, 211–42. Malden, Mass.: Blackwell.

Gupta, Akhil and James Ferguson. 1997a. "Beyond Culture: Space, Identity, and the Politics of Difference." In *Culture, Power, Place: Explorations in Critical Anthropology,* eds. A. Gupta and J. Ferguson, 33–51. Durham: Duke University Press.

———. 1997b. "Culture, Power, Place: Ethnography at the End of an Era." In *Culture, Power, Place: Explorations in Critical Anthropology,* eds. A. Gupta and J. Ferguson, 1–29. Durham: Duke University Press.

Habboush, Mahmoud. 2009. "FNC Urges Action on Identity." *The National,* June 2. Electronic document, http://www.thenational.ae/article/20090603/NATIONAL/706029863/1010 (accessed June 3, 2009).

Hadid, Diaa. 2005. "Disgruntled Labourers Win the First Round." *Gulf News,* Internet version, September 21. Electronic document, http://gulfnews.com/news/gulf/uae/employment/disgruntled-labourers-win-the-first-round-1.301542 (accessed October 24, 2005).

Hall, Camilla, and Vivian Salama. 2009. "Shakeup in Dubai Deposes Principal Emirate Figures: Biographies." Bloomberg.com, November 24. Electronic

document, http://www.bloomberg.com,/apps/news?pid=20601104&sid=a0
E6_6cfEeqI (accessed November 30, 2009).

Halliday, Fred. 2002. *Arabia without Sultans*. London: Saqi Books.

Harris, John. 1971. "Dubai Development Plan, Review, May 1971." In *Development Plans of the GCC States, 1962–1995*. Amersham UK: Archive Editions.

Harvey, David. 1985. *Consciousness and the Urban Experience*. Oxford: Blackwell.

———. 1989. *The Condition of Postmodernity*. Oxford: Blackwell.

———. 2001. *Spaces of Capital: Towards a Critical Geography*. Edinburgh: Edinburgh University Press.

———. 2005. *A Brief History of Neoliberalism*. New York: Oxford University Press.

———. 2008. "The Right to the City." *New Left Review* 53 (September–October): 23–40.

———. 2009. *Social Justice and the City*. Athens: University of Georgia Press.

Hawthorne, Christopher. 2008. "Architect Rem Koolhaas Saw What Vegas Didn't Have, Not What it Needed." *Los Angeles Times,* May 13. Electronic document, http://www.latimes.com/entertainment/news/arts/la-et-vegas13-2008may13,0,4985463.story (accessed June 4, 2008).

Hazbun, Waleed. 2008. *Beaches, Ruins, Resorts: The Politics of Tourism in the Arab World*. Minneapolis: University of Minnesota Press.

Heard-Bey, Frauke. 1982. *From Trucial States to United Arab Emirates*. New York: Longman.

Herb, Michael. 1999. *All in the Family: Absolutism, Revolution, and Democracy in the Middle Eastern Monarchies*. Albany: SUNY Press.

Heron, Katrina. 1996. "From Bauhaus to Koolhaas." *Wired* 4, no. 7, July. Electronic document, http://www.wired.com/wired/archive/4.07/koolhaas.html. (accessed June 4, 2008).

Herzfeld, Michael. 1991. *A Place In History: Social and Monumental Time in a Cretan Town*. Princeton: Princeton University Press.

———. 1993. *The Social Production of Indifference: Exploring the Symbolic Roots of Western Bureaucracy*. Chicago: University of Chicago Press.

———. 2005. "Political Optics and the Occlusion of Intimate Knowledge." Theme Issue, "Moral Economies, State Spaces, and Categorical Violence," *American Anthropologist* 107, no. 3: 369–76.

Hilotin, Jay B. 2004. "Should Maids Come under Labour Law?" *Gulf News,* April 3. Electronic document, http://gulfnews.com/news/gulf/uae/visa/should-maids-come-under-labour-law-1.318260 (accessed February 4, 2010).

Hoath, Nissar. 2003. "Raids Continue to Arrest Illegal Residents." *Gulf News,* September 21. Electronic document, http://gulfnews.com/news/gulf/uae/general/raids-continue-to-arrest-illegal-residents-1.366324 (accessed February 4, 2010).

————. 2004. "980 Illegals Arrested in June along the Borders." *Gulf News,* July 4. Electronic document, http://gulfnews.com/news/gulf/uae/visa/980-illegals -arrested-in-june-along-the-borders-1.326417 (accessed February 4, 2010).

Hoffman, Lisa, Monica DeHart, and Stephen J. Collier. 2006. "Notes on the Anthropology of Neoliberalism." *Anthropology News* 47, no. 6: 9–10.

Holston, James. 1989. *The Modernist City: An Anthropological Critique of Brasilia.* Chicago: University of Chicago Press.

————. 2009. "Insurgent Citizenship in an Era of Global Urban Peripheries." *City and Society* 21, no. 2: 245–67.

Humaid, Abdullah. 2004. "*Al-Sūq al-Musaqqaf*" [The covered market]. *Al-Ittihad,* July 3.

Human Rights Watch. 2003. "Dubai: Migrant Workers at Risk." September 19. Electronic document, http://www.hrw.org/en/news/2003/09/18/dubai-migrant-workers-risk (accessed May 11, 2005).

————. 2006. *Building Towers, Cheating Workers: Exploitation of Migrant Construction Workers in the United Arab Emirates.* Report 18, no. 8 E. New York: Human Rights Watch.

Hussein, Abdul-Ghaffar. 2000. *Qirā'āt fī Kutub min al-Imārāt* [Readings of books from the UAE]. Sharjah UAE: UAE Literary Union.

Ismail, Salwa. 2006. *Political Life in Cairo's New Quarters: Encountering the Everyday State.* Minneapolis: University of Minnesota Press.

Issa, Wafa. 2009. "Proposal Moots Job Security for Emiratis." *Gulf News,* February 14. Electronic document, http://gulfnews.com/news/gulf/uae/employment/proposal-moots-job-security-for-emiratis-1.51715 (accessed July 9, 2009).

Istabsir. n. d. "Al Satwa in a Changed World." Electronic document, htty://multimedia.thenational.ae/istabsir/index.html (accessed February 12, 2010).

Jacoby, Russell. 2005. *Picture Imperfect: Utopian Thought for an Anti-Utopian Age.* New York: Columbia University Press.

Jameson, Fredric. 1974. *Marxism and Form: Twentieth-Century Dialectical Theories of Literature.* Princeton: Princeton University Press.

————. 1991. *Postmodernism, or The Cultural Logic of Late Capitalism.* Durham: Duke University Press.

————. 2003. "Future City." *New Left Review* 21 (May–June): 65–79.

————. 2007. *Late Marxism: Adorno, or, The Persistence of the Dialectic.* New York: Verso.

————. 2009. *Valences of the Dialectic.* New York: Verso.

Joseph, Suad. 1977. "Zaynab: An Urban Working Class Lebanese Woman." In *Middle Eastern Muslim Women Speak,* eds. Elizabeth W. Fernea and Basima Q. Bezirgan, 359–71. Austin: University of Texas Press.

————. 1978. "Women and the Neighborhood Street in Borj Hammoud, Lebanon." In *Women in the Muslim World,* eds. Lois Beck and Nikkie Keddie, 541–57. Cambridge: Harvard University Press.

Jreisat, Jamil. 2005. Review of *Population and Development of the Arab Gulf States* by N. Mohammed. *International Journal of Middle East Studies* 37, no. 4: 634–36.

Kalbani, Maryam. 2004. "*Ainahum min-al Ta'addud?*" [Where are the polygamists?]. *Al-Ittihad,* July 4.

Kanna, Ahmed. 2005. "The 'State Philosophical' in the 'Land without Philosophy': Shopping Malls, Interior Cities, and the Image of Utopia in Dubai." *Traditional Dwellings and Settlements Review* 16, no. 2: 59–73.

———. 2006. "*Not Their Fathers' Days*": Idioms of Space and Time in the Urban Arabian Gulf. Dissertation. Harvard University Department of Anthropology.

———. 2007. "Dubai in a Jagged World." *Middle East Report* 243: 22–29.

———. 2010a. "Flexible Citizenship in Dubai: Corporate Subjectivity in the Emerging City-Corporation." *Cultural Anthropology* 25: 100–29.

———. 2010c. Review of *Dubai: The Vulnerability of Success* by C. M. Davidson. *Review of Middle East Studies* 43, no. 1: 79–81.

——— Forthcoming. "Introduction." In *The Superlative City: Dubai and the Urban Condition in the Early Twenty-First Century,* ed. Ahmed Kanna, Cambridge, Mass.: Harvard University Graduate School of Design.

———. Forthcoming. "Urbanist Ideology and the Production of Space in the United Arab Emirates: An Anthropological Critique." In *Global Downtowns,* eds. Gary McDonogh and Marina Peterson. Philadelphia: University of Pennsylvania Press.

Kanna, Ahmed, and Arang Keshavarzian. 2008. "The UAE's Space Race: Sheikhs and Starchitects Envision the Future." *Middle East Report* 248: 34–39.

Kazmi, Aftab. 2004. "Shanty Town in Al Ain Demolished to Make Way for Development Project." *Gulf News,* April 15. Electronic document, http://gulfnews .com/news/gulf/uae/general/shanty-town-in-al-ain-demolished-to-make-way-for-development-project-1.319475 (accessed February 4, 2010).

Khalaf, Samir. 1973. *Hamra of Beirut: A Case of Rapid Urbanization.* Leiden: Brill.

Khalaf, Sulayman. 1999. "Camel Racing in the Gulf: Notes on the Evolution of a Traditional Cultural Sport." *Anthropos* 94, nos. 1–3: 85–106.

———. 2000. "Poetics and Politics of Newly Invented Traditions in the Gulf: Camel Racing in the United Arab Emirates." *Ethnology* 39, no. 3: 243–61.

Khaleej Times. 2005. "Unpaid Workers are the New Newsmakers." *Khaleej Times,* September 26. Electronic document (accessed October 25, 2005).

Khalifa, Aisha B. 2003. *Slaves and Musical Performances in Dubai: Socio-Cultural Relevance of African Traditions.* Dissertation. Exeter, UK: University of Exeter.

Koolhaas, Rem. 1978. *Delirious New York: A Retroactive Manifesto for Manhattan.* New York: Oxford University Press.

———. 2009. "Dubai: From Judgment to Analysis." Lecture, Sharjah UAE Biennial, March 17. Electronic document, http://www.oma.eu/index.php?

option=com_content&task=view&id=149&Itemid=25 (accessed January 28, 2010).

Koolhaas, Rem, Ole Bouman, and Mark Wigley, eds. 2007. *Al Manakh*. New York: Columbia University/Archis.

Kracauer, Siegfried. 1995. *The Mass Ornament: Weimar Essays*. Trans., ed. Thomas Y. Levin. Cambridge, Mass.: Harvard University Press.

Kubrick, Stanley. 1971. *A Clockwork Orange*. Los Angeles: Warner Brothers. 136 minutes.

Kunkel, Benjamin. 2010. "Into the Big Tent." *London Review of Books* 32, no. 8: 12–16.

Kuppinger, Petra. 2004. "Exclusive Greenery: New Gated Communities in Cairo." *City and Society* 16, no. 2: 35–62.

Lacayo, Richard. 2008. "Rem Koolhaas." *Time,* April 29. Electronic document, http://www.time.com/time/specials/2007/article/0,28804,1733748_173375 2_1735981,00.html (accessed June 4, 2008).

Lefebvre, Henri. 1947/1991. *Critique of Everyday Life, Vol. 1: Introduction*. John Moore, trans. New York: Verso.

———. 1974/1991. *The Production of Space*. Donald Nicholson-Smith, trans. Malden, Mass.: Blackwell.

———. 2003. *The Urban Revolution*. R. Bononno, trans. Minneapolis: University of Minnesota Press.

Leonard, Karen. 2005. "South Asians in the Indian Ocean World: Language, Policing, and Gender Practices in Kuwait and the UAE." *Comparative Studies of South Asia, Africa and the Middle East* 25, no. 3: 677–86.

Levin, Thomas Y. 1995 "Introduction." In *The Mass Ornament: Weimar Essays by Siegfried Kracauer,* trans., ed. Thomas Y. Levin, 1–30. Cambridge, Mass.: Harvard University Press.

Li, Tania Murray. 2005. "Beyond 'the State' and Failed Schemes." Theme Issue, "Moral Economies, State Spaces, and Categorical Violence," *American Anthropologist* 107, no. 3: 383–94.

Longva, Anh Nga. 2005. "Neither Autocracy nor Democracy but Ethnocracy: Citizens, Expatriates and the Socio-Political System in Kuwait." In *Monarchies and Nations: Globalization and Identity in the Arab States of the Gulf,* eds. Paul Dresch and James Piscatori, 114–35. London: I. B. Tauris.

Lorimer, J. G. 1915/1984. *Gazetteer of the Persian Gulf, Oman, and Central Arabia*. Vol. 2. Amersham U.K.: Demand Editions.

Lubow, Arthur. 2000. "Rem Koolhaas Builds." *New York Times,* July 9. Electronic document, http://www.nytimes.com/library/magazine/home /20000709mag -koolhaas.html (accessed June 4, 2008).

Lukács, Georg. 1920/1996. *Theory of the Novel*. A. Bostock, trans. Cambridge, Mass.: MIT Press.

Makdisi, Saree. 2010. "A Museum of Tolerance We Don't Need." *Los Angeles*

Times, February 12. Electronic document, http://articles.latimes.com/2010/ feb/12/opinion/la-oe-makdisi12-2010feb12 (accessed February 18, 2010).

Malkki, Liisa. 1997. "National Geographic: The Rooting of Peoples and the Territorialization of National Identity among Scholars and Refugees." In *Culture, Power, Place,* eds. Akhil Gupta and James Ferguson, 52–74. Durham: Duke University Press.

Mamdani, Mahmood. 2004. *Good Muslim, Bad Muslim: America, the Cold War, and the Roots of Terror.* New York: Three Leaves.

Marchal, Roland, ed. 2001. *Dubaï: Cité globale.* Paris: CNRS Editions.

———. 2005. "Dubai: Global City and Transnational Hub." In *Transnational Connections and the Arab Gulf,* ed. Madawi Al Rasheed, 93–110. New York: Routledge.

McDonogh, Gary, and Marina Peterson, eds. Forthcoming. *Global Downtowns.* Philadelphia: University of Pennsylvania Press.

McNeill, Donald. 2009. *The Global Architect: Firms, Fame and Urban Form.* New York: Routledge.

Menon, Sunita. 2004. "Time was, and Time is . . ." *Gulf News,* February 5.

Michaels, Walter Benn. 2009. "What Matters." *London Review of Books* 31, no. 16. Electronic document, http://www.lrb.co.uk/v31/n16/walter-benn-michaels/ what-matters (accessed, January 17, 2010).

Middle East Council of Shopping Centres. 2003. *Directory.* Dubai: Marrakesh Media Consultants.

Mitchell, Kevin. Forthcoming. "The Future Promise of Architecture in Dubai." In *The Superlative City: Dubai and the Urban Condition in the Early Twenty-First Century,* ed. Ahmed Kanna. Cambridge, Mass.: Harvard University Graduate School of Design.

Mitchell, Timothy. 2006. "Society, Economy, and the State Effect." In *The Anthropology of the State,* eds. Aradhana Sharma and Akhil Gupta, 169–86. Malden, Mass.: Blackwell.

Mohammed, Nadeya Sayed Ali. 2003. *Population and Development of the Arab Gulf States: The Case of Bahrain, Oman and Kuwait.* Hampshire: Ashgate.

Monroe, Kristen. 2008. *Mobile Citizens: Space, Power, and the Remaking of Beirut.* PhD dissertation. Stanford University Department of Anthropology.

Moser, Sarah. Forthcoming. "Masdar: A 'Green' City in the Gulf." In *New Cities in the Muslim World,* ed. Sarah Moser. Cambridge, Mass.: M.I.T. Aga Khan Program for Islamic Architecture.

Moussly, Mona. 2009. "Dubai's Laborers Bear the Brunt of Financial Crisis." Alarabiya.net, March 1. Electronic document, http://www.alarabiya.net/ articles/2009/03/01/67503.html(accessed October 20, 2009).

Mustafa, Amr. 2004. "Make No Little Plans: Dubai's Transformation into a Global City." Panel Paper, Seventh Annual Sharjah Urban Planning Symposium, April 4–6. UAE: University of Sharjah.

Nagy, Sharon. 2000. "Dressing Up Downtown: Urban Development and Government Public Image in Qatar." *City & Society* 12, no. 1: 125–147.

Nakheel Real Estate Developers. 2004. Presentation on new projects at the American University of Sharjah Department of Architecture and Design, May 4.

Nepal News. 2009. "Nepali Workers Fired, Deported from Dubai." September 9. Electronic document, http://www.nepalnews.com/main/index.php/news-archive/1-top-story/1348-nepali-workers-fired-deported-from-dubai.pdf (accessed October 20, 2009).

Nordstrom, Carolyn. 2007. *Global Outlaws: Crime, Money, and Power in the Contemporary World.* Berkeley: University of California Press.

Notar, Beth E. 2010. "Off Limits and out of Bounds: Taxi Driver Perceptions of Dangerous People and Places in Kunming, China." Unpublished manuscript.

Nowais, Shireena. 2004. "Housemaid Contracts to Get Legal Teeth," *Gulf News,* April 28. Electronic document, http://gulfnews.com/news/gulf/uae/visa/housemaid-contracts-to-get-legal-teeth-1.320794 (accessed February 4, 2010).

O'Brien, Tim L. 2003. "U.S. Focusing on Dubai as a Terrorist Financial Center." *New York Times,* October 5. Electronic document, http://www.nytimes.com/2003/10/05/world/us-focusing-on-dubai-as-a-terrorist-financial-center.html?pagewanted=1 (accessed February 4, 2010).

Ong, Aihwa. 1999. *Flexible Citizenship: The Cultural Logics of Transnationality.* Durham: Duke University Press.

———. 2000. "Graduated Sovereignty in South-East Asia." *Theory, Culture and Society* 17, no. 4: 55–75.

———. 2007. *Neoliberalism as Exception: Mutations of Citizenship and Sovereignty.* Durham: Duke University Press.

Onley, James. 2005. "Transnational Merchants in the Nineteenth-Century Gulf: The Case of the Safar Family." In *Transnational Connections and the Arab Gulf,* ed. Madawi Al Rasheed, 59–89. New York: Routledge.

———. 2007. *The Arabian Frontier of the British Raj: Merchants, Rulers, and the British in the Nineteenth Century Gulf.* Oxford: Oxford University Press.

Ouroussof, Nicolai. 2008. "City on the Gulf: Koolhaas Lays out a Grand Urban Experiment in Dubai." *New York Times,* March 3. Electronic document, http://architecturelab.net/2008/03/04/city-on-the-gulf-koolhaas-lays-out-a -grand-urban-experiment-in-dubai/ (accessed February 4, 2010).

Parker, Christopher, and Pete W. Moore. 2007. "The War Economy of Iraq." *Middle East Report* 243 (Summer): 6–15.

Parker, Ian. 2005. "The Mirage: The Architectural Insanity of Dubai." *New Yorker,* October 17:128–43.

Prashad, Vijay. 2007. *The Darker Nations: A Peoples' History of the Third World.* New York: New Press.

Premat, Adriana. 2009. "State Power, Private Plots and the Greening of Havana's Urban Agriculture Movement." *City and Society* 21, no.1: 28–57.

Rahman, Anisur. 2001. *Indian Labour Migration to the Gulf: A Socio-Economic Analysis*. New Delhi: Rajat Publications.

Rosaldo, Renato. 1989. *Culture and Truth: The Remaking of Social Analysis*. Boston: Beacon Press.

Rugh, Andrea B. 2007. *The Political Culture of Leadership in the United Arab Emirates*. New York: Palgrave Macmillan.

Said, Edward W. 1978. *Orientalism*. New York: Vintage.

Salama, Samir. 2004. "Presidential Court Studies New Labour Rights Package," *Gulf News,* May 3. Electronic document, http://gulfnews.com/news/gulf/uae/general/presidential-court-studies-new-labour-rights-package-1.321265 (accessed February 4, 2010).

———. 2005. "Workers Must Enjoy Their Full Rights." *Gulf News,* September 21. Electronic document, http://gulfnews.com/news/gulf/uae/employment/workers-must-enjoy-their full-rights-1.301544 (accessed October 24, 2005).

Salamandra, Christa. 2004. *A New Old Damascus: Authenticity and Distinction in Urban Syria.* Bloomington: Indiana University Press.

Salih, Sara. 2002. *Judith Butler*. New York: Routledge.

Sawalha, Aseel. 1998. "The Reconstruction of Beirut: Local Responses to Globalization." *City and Society* 10, no. 1: 133–47.

Scott, James C. 1998. *Seeing like a State: How Certain Schemes to Improve the Human Condition Have Failed*. New Haven: Yale University Press.

———. 2005. "Afterword." Theme Issue, "Moral Economies, State Spaces, and Categorical Violence," *American Anthropologist* 107, no. 3: 395–402.

Seccombe, Ian J. 1987. *Work Camps and Company Towns: Settlement Patterns and the Gulf Oil Industry.* Durham, U.K.: Centre for Middle Eastern and Islamic Studies, University of Durham.

Sekher, T. V. 1997. *Migration and Social Change.* Jaipur and New Delhi: Rawat Publications.

Sharma, Aradhana, and Akhil Gupta. 2006. "Ethnographic Mappings: Bureaucracy and Governmentality." In *The Anthropology of the State,* eds. Aradhana Sharma and Akhil Gupta, 163–68. Malden, Mass.: Blackwell.

Shehab. 2009. "Brand Dubai (Wolff Olins)." *MBAs, Media, and the Middle East,* July 10. Electronic document, http://shehabhamad.com/blog/2009/07/10/brand-dubai-wolff-olins/ (accessed July 13, 2009).

Short, John Rennie. 2006. *Urban Theory: A Critical Assessment*. New York: Palgrave Macmillan.

Sigler, Jennifer. 2000. "Rem Koolhaas." *Index Magazine*. Electronic document, http://www.indexmagazine.com/interviews/rem_koolhaas.shtml (accessed June 4, 2008).

Singerman, Diane. 1995. *Avenues of Participation: Family, Politics, and Networks in Urban Quarters of Cairo*. Princeton: Princeton University Press.

Singerman, Diane, and Paul Amar, eds. 2006. *Cairo Cosmopolitan: Politics, Culture, and Urban Space in the New Globalized Middle East*. New York: American University in Cairo Press.

Sky News. 2008. "Dubai: Crisis, What Crisis?" November 25. Electronic document, http://news.sky.com/skynews/Home/Business/Mohammad-Al-Abbar-Tells -Sky-News-Dubai-Is-Not-In-Crisis/Article/200811415161490. November 25 (accessed February 10, 2009).

Smith, Andrea. 2003. "Place Replaced: Colonial Nostalgia and Pied-Noir Pilgrimages to Malta." *Cultural Anthropology* 18, no. 3: 329–64.

Soja, Edward. 1989. *Postmodern Geographies: The Reassertion of Space in Critical Social Theory*. New York: Verso.

———. 1996. *Thirdspace: Journeys to Los Angeles and Other Real-and-Imagined Places*. Malden, Mass.: Blackwell.

Thesiger, Wilfred. 1991. *Arabian Sands*. London: Penguin.

Thompson, E. P. 1963. *The Making of the English Working Class*. Harmondsworth, U.K.: Penguin.

Totah, Faedah M. 2009. "Return to the Origin: Negotiating the Modern and Unmodern in the Old City of Damascus." *City and Society* 21, no. 1: 58–81.

Traynor, Ian, Owen Bowcott, and John Aglionby. 2004. "Customs Examine British Link in Nuclear Parts Trade." *Guardian*, March 5. Electronic document, http://www.guardian.co.uk/uk/2004/mar/05/iran.libya (accessed February 4, 2010).

Turan, Neyran. Forthcoming "The Dubai Effect." In *The Superlative City: Dubai and the Urban Condition in the Early Twenty-First Century*, ed. Ahmed Kanna. Cambridge, Mass.: Harvard University Graduate School of Design.

Turner, Victor. 1969. *The Ritual Process: Structure and Anti-Structure*. Ithaca, N.Y.: Cornell University Press.

Tusa, John. 2004. "Interview with Frank Gehry." Electronic document, bbc.co.uk/ radio3/johntusainterview/gehry_transcripts.html (accessed June 4, 2008).

Vidal, John. 2008. "Desert State Channels Oil Wealth into World's First Sustainable City." *Guardian*, Janurary 21. Electronic document, http://www .guardian. co.uk/environment/2008/jan/21/climatechange.energy (accessed May 27, 2008).

Vitalis, Robert. 2007. *America's Kingdom: Mythmaking on the Saudi Oil Frontier*. Palo Alto: Stanford University Press.

Vora, Neha. 2008. "Producing Diasporas and Globalization: Indian Middle-Class Migrants in Dubai." *Anthropological Quarterly* 81, no. 2: 377–406.

———. 2009a. "National Identity in Future Perfect Tense: Reconstructions of History, Projects of Heritage, and Cosmopolitan Subjectivities in the UAE."

Panel paper, Annual Meeting of the American Anthropological Association, Philadelphia.

———. 2009b. "The Precarious Existence of Dubai's Indian Middle Class." *Middle East Report* 252, no. 39, 3: 18–21.

Waldman, Amy. 2005. "Sri Lankan Maids' High Price for Foreign Jobs." *New York Times,* May 8. Electronic document, http://query.nytimes.com/gst/fullpage .html?res=9501E6D71530F93BA35756C0A9639C8B63. (accessed February 4, 2010).

Wide Angle. 2007. *The Sand Castle.* Electronic document. http://www.pbs.org/ wnet/wideangle/episodes/the-sand-castle/introduction/975/ (accessed May 24, 2008).

Wide Angle Transcript. 2007. "Transcript for *The Sand Castle.*" Electronic document, http://www-tc.pbs.org/wnet/wideangle/shows/uae/transcript.pdf (accessed May 24, 2008).

Wilson, Ara. 2004. *The Intimate Economies of Bangkok: Tomboys, Tycoons, and Avon Ladies in the Global City.* Berkeley: University of California Press.

Winckler, Onn. 2000. "Gulf Monarchies as Rentier States: The Nationalization Policies of the Labor Force." In *Middle East Monarchies: The Challenge of Modernity,* ed. J. Kostiner, 237–56. Boulder, Colo.: Lynne Rienner.

Youssef, Marten. 2007. "Domestic Workers Form 5% of UAE's Population." *Gulf News,* November 11. Electronic document, http://gulfnews.com/news/gulf/ uae/employment/domestic-workers-form-5-of-uae-s-population-1.131364 (accessed June 5, 2010).

Zahlan, Rosemarie Said. 1978. *The Origins of the United Arab Emirates: A Political and Social History of the Trucial States.* New York: Macmillan.

Zaza, Bassam. 2004a. "Drug Dealers Sentenced to Life in Prison." *Gulf News,* April 23. Electronic document, http://gulfnews.com/news/gulf/uae/general/ drug-dealers-sentenced-to-life-in-prison-1.320302. (accessed February 4, 2010).

———. 2004b. "Drug Peddlers Caught with Narcotics, Face Life in Prison." *Gulf News,* May 18. Electronic document, http://gulfnews.com/news/gulf/uae/ general/drug-peddlers-caught-with-narcotics-face-life-in-prison-1.322641 (accessed February 4, 2010).

Zukin, Sharon. 2008. "Destination Culture: How Globalization Makes All Cities Look the Same." Trinity College Center for Urban and Global Studies Inaugural Working Papers Series. Electronic document, http://www.trincoll. edu/NR/rdonlyres/8FE6BF06-7F6E-4B7A-823C-CA42D688E054/0/ ZUKINATLAST.pdf (accessed January 24, 2010).

INDEX

Ahmed Kanna is assistant professor of anthropology and international studies at the University of the Pacific.